Third World Minerals and Global Pricing

for
BARBARA JEAN, OBI-IKE & UCHENNA
and
in memory of
CHIDI

Third World Minerals and Global Pricing
A New Theory

Chibuzo Nwoke

Zed Books Ltd.
London and New Jersey

Third World Minerals and Global Pricing: A New Theory was first published by Zed Books Ltd, 57 Caledonian Road, London N1 9BU in 1987.

Cover designed by Ian Hawkins
Printed and bound in Great Britain by
Biddles Ltd., Guildford and King's Lynn

Library of Congress Cataloging-in-Publication Data

Nwoke, Chibuzo.
  Third World minerals and global pricing.

  Bibliography: p.
  Includes index.
  1. Mineral industries—Developing countries.
I. Title.
HD9506.D452N86   1987   338.2'3   87-12621
ISBN 0-86232-441-6
ISBN 0-86232-442-4 (pbk.)

British Library Cataloguing in Publication Data

Nwoke, Chibuzo
  Third World minerals and global pricing:
  a new theory.
  1. Minerals industries—Developing countries
  I. Title
  333.8'5 091724   HD9506.D452

  ISBN 0-86232-441-6
  ISBN 0-86232-442-4 Pbk

Table 8 is reprinted from *Natural Resources and National Welfare: The Case of Copper* edited by Ann Seidman. Copyright © 1975 Praeger Publishers, Inc. Reprinted by permission of Praeger Publishers.

Table 5 is reprinted from *The Future of Nonfuel Minerals* by John Tiltan, by permission of The Brookings Institute. Copyright © Brookings Institute 1987.

Table 15 is reprinted from *The Race for Resources*. Copyright © 1980 by Michael Tanzer. Reprinted by permission of Monthly Review Foundation.

Contents

Preface

This book focuses on Third World minerals, and explores, both theoretically and analytically, the issue of the conflictual relationship between foreign mining firms and Third World governments in the sharing of the huge benefits derivable from mining the latter's rich resources.

My interest in the global struggle in the mining sphere was first aroused in the early 1970s. The quadrupling of the oil price by OPEC members had brought the question of the potential 'bargaining power' of other Third World minerals exporters into the limelight both in the world press, and in government and academic circles. Notions like 'resource diplomacy', 'interdependence', and 'the new international economic order' were increasingly being used to describe the supposedly 'new threat' of the Third World's 'bargaining power' in the international political economy.

However, as the years went by, it became apparent that both the threat and the real power of Third World governments were declining rather than gathering momentum. Nevertheless, even today, especially within academic circles, the relationship between the industrialized and the underdeveloped countries is still being described primarily in the context of an overall cumulative bargaining power of Third World host governments to garner increasing shares of the benefits from mining. At least from the standpoint of the Third World, one serious problem arising from this mode of analysis is that it has caused an increase in the supply price of the international firms' investment projects in the Third World in order to compensate for so-called risk and uncertainty. Available data, however, indicate that, contrary to the claim that the bargaining power of Third World governments is increasing cumulatively, the balance of power between Third World host governments and foreign mining firms has not shifted far, nor has it shifted quickly enough in favour of the Third World. Foreign mining firms have not remained idle while host governments have eroded their profitability in mining projects; rather, they have been constantly developing alternative defensive strategies with which to neutralize host governments' anticipated actions, that is, even before they have been thought of and introduced as policies.

Above all, in the bargaining model the relative benefits accruable to either host government or foreign investor are left undefined and are, therefore, indeterminate in their so-called bargain. In other words, the model does not recognize the important notions of average profits and, therefore, of superprofits. Because there has not hitherto been any conceptual limit on the fair levels of profits that the foreign investor should expropriate from the host country, the exploitation of the Third World host government has proceeded unconscionably and with legal sanction.

One important objective of this book is thus to provide a more meaningful methodological approach to the study of the relationship between Third World governments and foreign mining firms than that provided by the mainstream bargaining model. The alternative approach is based on a critical extension of Marx's rent theory.

I owe a word of appreciation, for his intellectual stimulation, to the late Professor Satish Raichur, head of the Economics Department at the University of Denver, Colorado. I deeply regret that he died even before the project had taken off.

I also want to thank Professor John McCamant for his kindness in reading drafts of the manuscript quickly. He provided useful comments in a friendly environment.

I must also acknowledge the various forms of financial assistance and the travel grant I received from the Graduate School of International Studies at the University of Denver. The travel grant enabled me to visit the Library of Congress in Washington, D.C., and CIPEC headquarters in Paris for preliminary research. Also, I want to thank Mr Peter Parkinson of CIPEC for arranging for me to use CIPEC's library.

I want finally to thank my wife, Barbara Jean, who provided the appropriate environment that enabled me to devote my time to the research and the writing of this book. She typed all the drafts, and was always available as a 'sounding board' for my ideas. Barbara's help and encouragement came while she pursued her own two full-time careers as wife and librarian.

I, alone, am responsible for any errors of omission or commission in this book.

CNN
Hershey, Pennsylvania

Introduction

The Problem

In the history of world mining, metropolitan firms have always dominated Third World minerals production and marketing. This situation persists today, despite the fact that formal sovereignty over natural resources now rests with the governments of minerals-exporting countries.

While the political and economic circumstances of minerals-supplying Third World countries vary greatly, what they do have in common is that paradoxically, their economies, once richly endowed with natural resources, are now poor. Today, especially in progressive quarters, the problems of poverty and underdevelopment in Third World minerals-exporting countries are understood to be the result of metropolitan mining firms' historical dominance over these countries' vast raw materials projects. Notice how Nkrumah, in the early 1960s, expressed Africa's resources problem:

> Africa is a paradox which illustrates and highlights neo-colonialism. Her earth is rich, yet the products that come from above and below her soil continue to enrich, not Africans predominantly, but groups and individuals who operate to Africa's impoverishment.
>
> If Africa's multiple resources were used in her own development, they would place her among the modernized continents of the world. But her resources have been, and still are being used, for the greater development of overseas interests.[1]

This situation exists in African and other Third World countries because of the prevailing ideologies that guided government–investor relations in those countries before and after the Second World War. There was a widespread belief that natural resources belonged to these multi-national corporations (MNCs) that had found them. Governments were entitled to levy limited royalties in ways that effectively precluded the collection of more than a small proportion of their legitimate and often huge gains, known as 'rents'. The terms were laid out within concession agreements, which were 'negotiated' at the beginning of investments, and typically extended over periods sometimes as long as one century. Ideologically, this attitude was supported by the corporations' profession of belief in the sanctity of contracts between investors and governments. Moreover, the metropolitan controllers of colonial states, that is, the home governments of these corporations, perpetuated this ideology.

The governments of independent countries in the Third World were also constrained in their relations with foreign minerals investors by the possibility of diplomatic, economic, and military intervention by the investors' home governments. Although military and diplomatic intervention by governments of advanced countries may seem less likely today, the possibility of strong, direct, diplomatic or military intervention probably still exists, especially where mineral resources are considered of great strategic importance to the major world powers, for example, Middle East oil to the United States.

This study concerns the issue of the equitable distribution of the enormous wealth inherent in the production of the Third World's internationalized mineral resources. It emphasizes that, while the peripheral minerals-exporting governments and the metropolitan consuming countries are inextricably tied together in the capitalist world economy (because of the strategic nature of minerals in the advanced minerals-consuming countries, the uneven development of minerals across the globe, and their preponderance among the exports of Third World countries), it appears that the distribution of gains from the Third World's minerals largely favours metropolitan countries and their mining firms.

This study seeks to contribute to the field of international political economy, which aims at rethinking many of the Western-oriented ideas and misconceptions that predominate in the literature concerning the problem of Third World development. Such ideas have been circulating for more than 25 years in mainstream academic circles; but they are now being found wanting in progressive scholarship both as an explanation of the persistent poverty and underdevelopment in the Third World, and as a basis for constructing meaningful development policies. More explicitly, in the minerals area, the misconceptions that need rethinking arise from the writings of bargaining 'theorists', which predominate in the literature on the relationship between host Third World governments and foreign mining investors.

A Critical Review of the Bargaining Model

The bargaining approach had its origin in attempts to explain concession agreements in the post-war period, particularly those concluded in Latin America in the 1960s.[2] In the bargaining model, mining rent, quasi-rent, monopoly profits and normal returns to investments are not distinguished, but are lumped together as 'gains', distributed between host governments and foreign investors through a highly political 'bargaining process'. Thus, while the presence of mining rent is not denied in the model, the government's rent receipts, like its other incomes, are indeterminate in this bargaining process.

According to the model, a wide range of influences affect the bargain that is struck, and agreements are frequently renegotiated in line with changes in the determinants of bargaining power. While, analytically, this shift in bargaining power would exist only when there is an effective host government monopoly of resources, *vis-à-vis* foreign investors, bargaining theorists generally do not make this requirement explicit.

The bargaining model was introduced by Vernon; it was developed and refined in North America at Harvard University, and by Mikesell in Oregon.[3] Vernon was concerned with the conditions of mineral concessions in Third World countries. As he saw it, a Third World country was distinguished from an advanced country only by the absence of general laws and policies, including those of taxation, within which the exploration of minerals could operate. Thus, according to him, a system of laws developed in the process of negotiating a concession agreement.

In Vernon's model, the bargaining position of the foreign investor in negotiating the first concession agreements in the Third World country was strong, since the host government was typically ignorant of the value of its own natural resources. In his view, this environment changed considerably with the success of investments under the early concession agreements. The host government then began to develop general laws, policies, and administrative approaches for the minerals sector, reducing the risk of new investment for foreign investors.

New concession agreements were also, according to Vernon, fiscally much more favourable to the government. These new agreements contributed to suspicions that the earlier concessions had been unfair to the host countries, and additional pressures were applied to renegotiate existing concession agreements. A 'bilateral monopoly' thus existed, Vernon maintained, between the government and the established concessionnaires, and agreements were revised, usually in a series of steps, in favour of host governments. As he saw it, the renegotiation of concession agreements was occasionally blocked by pressures from the home governments of the investing companies. While he believed that the basis of this resistance was weak in international law, he recognized also that it was occasionally supported by diplomatic pressures of considerable importance. On the whole, however, in his view, these pressures became progressively less effective over the post-war period, and by the late 1960s governments' 'rights' to 'renegotiate' had been well established. According to Vernon, it was this verbal establishment of the host government's rights over resources that was important in the so-called bilateral monopoly, and not the presence of monopoly in the foreign firm's supply of new investment. On the whole, Vernon's analysis generated a substantial literature on the general bargaining model of government–investor relations and this model came to be applied to new, as well as to established, concessions, without taking into account the real lack of competition in the supply of mineral investments.

Following Vernon, in the versions of the bargaining model articulated by Mikesell in 1971, by Moran in 1974, and by Smith and Wells in 1975, the concession agreements upon which minerals projects were launched in the Third World were simply a matter of market-place bargaining between host governments and metropolitan mining MNCs. According to Moran, the relative bargaining strength of host governments and MNCs is a function of a number of factors, including the characteristics of the project under negotiation (such as its size or technological choice), the characteristics of the host country (such as its local market size, or rate of growth), and exogenous factors (such as the extent of competition in the international market).[4] While the relative bargaining position of the MNCs and host governments varies from case to case, MNCs will, according to Moran, be able to constrain the exercise of state power when their investment in the host country is small, when the host country has a very limited domestic market to offer, or when the MNC is not threatened by serious international competition. On the whole, Moran sees a trend whereby the balance of bargaining power is beginning to shift from the MNCs. This change, according to him, has occurred partly because competition between MNCs of diverse nationalities has increased, a development that 'strengthens rather than weakens, the position of the Third World countries because it gives them more alternatives to choose from'.[5]

Moran also stressed the significance of the learning process and the increased sophistication that, he maintains, has developed among Third World bureaucrats in recent years, citing the 'continued growth in host-country skill in monitoring and analysing multinational corporate activities'.[6] The increased interest observed among host governments in pooling information, co-ordinating foreign investment policies, or presenting a unified position in North–South negotiations prompted Smith to also suggest that their new power 'will not easily be eroded'.[7] Hence, according to Moran, although there are still a large number of cases where the balance of bargaining power is heavily tilted towards the mining MNC, 'one would expect the benefits from foreign investment in the aggregate to be rising and the cost of securing those benefits to be falling, over time'[8] for the host government.

In summary, according to the bargaining model, the initial terms of the agreement were unfavourable to the host government because of the investors' aversion to 'risk' and because of the host government's ignorance about the minerals industries. After the initial investments had proved successful, however, the terms of the original agreements began to appear unfair to the host government which then sought to renegotiate them.

At issue was the distribution of the surplus income between the host government and the foreign investor, which the model vaguely referred to as 'profits', 'benefits', or 'gains', but also included mining rent proper and average profits. According to the model, the company, in resisting renegotiation, asserted the sanctity of contract and perhaps sought support from international law; but the most important constraints upon the host government's appropriation of its 'gains' were its supposed effect on the perceptions of future foreign investors, the government's ignorance of how far it could push the bargain without jeopardizing current or future gains, and, for short periods, the foreign corporation's use of its wealth to manipulate domestic politics. Nevertheless, in the model, such constraints and political interferences were not considered to have secured the investors' interests for long.

In the bargaining model, the domestic political process is considered important to the allocation of the gains, in the sense that the government's share will be larger if it can mobilize popular support around the issue, or if domestic radical nationalist or socialist pressure groups challenge it. Also, the government's bargaining power will tend to be strengthened over time as political interest is mobilized, knowledge increases, and negotiating and administrative skills improve, so that successive renegotiations increase the government's share of the 'benefits'. The government is more likely to demand renegotiations — and to make severe demands in renegotiating the terms — when the realized profitability of mineral investment is high.

Summarily described, advocates of the bargaining model emphasize shares of 'profits', rather than the extraction of mining rent; promulgate the notion that the fiscal terms of minerals concessions are fixed only for brief periods between the successive renegotiation of agreements; and maintain that a government's bargaining power, and so the share of profits obtainable by it, are determined by the practice in other parts of the geographic region of the mineral-owning country.

While the predominantly North American bargaining model appeared reasonably to describe the historical experience of Third World governments in minerals concession agreements, particularly from the 1950s to the early 1970s, its assistance to a government's efforts to develop minerals-related development policies was limited. Rather, the model emphasized the indeterminacy of the concession agreements process. On the whole, it seemed to establish that investors' fears of instability in concession terms were fully justified and based on an inevitable, but unpredictable, historical process. The bargaining model is based on half truths. And while foreign investors might yet decide that the commitment of funds to a minerals project was worthwhile, such a commitment should, according to the model, be made only after granting them generous allowances for risk.

In effect, the expectation created by the bargaining model — that concession terms might easily be changed by the government — has contributed to increasing the supply price of investment and to reducing host government revenue, whether or not the changes were implemented. While the model did not deny the existence of monopoly, according to it, the monopoly relationship has its origins in host government law rather than, as is actually the case, in the foreign investors' exclusive possession of the technology, managerial capability and marketing networks essential for the international exploitation of the Third World's mineral deposits.

While the bargaining model does, to some extent, address the issue of distribution of gains from the Third World's internationalized mineral resources, it fails to identify the relationship between metropolitan MNCs and Third World governments within the context of the changing relations between the metropole and the periphery of the world capitalist system as a whole. From the bargaining perspective, the objectives and interests of foreign investors (MNCs) appear unrelated to those of the larger system of which they are a part, or to the national objectives and interests of their individual metropolitan home governments.[9]

Another important weakness of the bargaining model is its apparent suggestion that the trend towards increased bargaining power of Third World host governments is cumulative and irreversible. Having observed the superficial changes of the neo-colonial period, bargaining theorists quickly heralded a 'new international economic order' and the increased role of the peripheral state. But the assumption of progression and irreversibility has been challenged by trends that emerged in the late 1970s, that is, the recapturing of total control over the periphery's raw materials by metropolitan mining MNCs.

In other words, the balance of bargaining power between host governments and foreign mining firms has not shifted in favour of the governments either as far, or as quickly as those maintain who talk of the increased bargaining power of Third World host governments. It is important to understand that metropolitan mining MNCs have developed a whole range of defensive strategies with which they have effectively neutralized the nationalist, or anti-imperialist, policies of peripheralized host governments, thus preserving the original function of the latter's economies, that is, that of providing the industrialized world with mineral resources.

The fallacy propagated by the bargaining model with regard to the progression and irreversibility of the new bargaining power of Third World governments can be further exposed by pointing to the structural limits to the reforms attempted at international organizations in the on-going North–South 'negotiations'. Upon receiving political independence, Third World governments began to present a united front in international organizations to indicate an interest in redressing the exploitation that their economies had commonly experienced in the world economy. An important illusion subsequently disseminated by the bargaining model is that the diplomatic negotiations that go on within such organizations have led to a new international economic order, that is, to a new and equitable division of income between the advanced and the underdeveloped nations in the world capitalist economy. However, it has become increasingly apparent that meaningful reforms have been limited, despite the united front exhibited by Third World governments in these organizations.[10] In fact, at best, their powers have been confined to 'bargaining' for what amounts to a pittance, or concessions. Moreover, the future prospects of their success are dim, to the extent that even the limited concessions they receive in North–South negotiations are seen as impinging on the profits, that is, prosperity, of the advanced countries. Furthermore, Third World governments are subordinated by imperialist forces in the capitalist world division of labour. Therefore, contrary to the bargaining model, whatever new power Third World governments can be said to have gained in the world economy cannot be irreversible.

Finally, the bargaining model is very imprecise in its definition of the relevant gains, the distribution of which is conflictual in the 'bargain' between host governments and metropolitan MNCs. Above all, the model is rarely theoretical, generally leading to pure description.

The Marxian Rent Approach

There is obviously a need for a new methodological approach to the analysis of government–foreign investor relations in the world mining business, one based on the concept of Third World producer power, that is, the power of Third World governments arising from their proprietorial rights over their rich mineral resources. This producer power can be properly appreciated only in the context of the historical roles of the individual governments of minerals-exporting countries in the international capitalist system, into which these countries were forcibly integrated as colonies, specifically in order to provide the industrialized world's supply of mineral resources.

It is against the background of the shortcomings of the bargaining model in appreciating the implications of the systematic workings of the international capitalist economy that this study proposes to refocus current thought on the relationship between metropolitan MNCs and Third World host governments, with respect to the distribution of the wealth from contemporary world mining. The alternative approach presented in this study is based on Marx's theory of ground-rent. It provides the most soundly based theoretical foundation of the classical world division of labour, as well as the most appropriate starting point for investigating the relationship between Third World minerals-exporting governments and metropolitan mining MNCs.

Marx's rent theory recognizes two kinds of surplus profits: differential rents and absolute rents. In world mining, differential rent is a surplus profit stemming from the comparative advantages of the Third World's mines, which offer higher ore grades, lower labour costs, and higher average profits than those in advanced countries. Operating cost differences in favour of the Third World are so enormous that, even discounting marketing costs, Third World minerals-exporting governments could be receiving differential rents greatly exceeding the present amounts of royalties and profit-shares they receive. The problem today is that these governments are so dependent on metropolitan mining MNCs that some of the differential rents are indirectly appropriated by the MNCs.

Marxian absolute rent is, by its nature, monopolistic. It can be defined as the surplus profit from the monopoly price of raw materials. Absolute rent can be distinguished from other monopolistic incomes and monopoly prices in terms of who determines its magnitude and who enjoys it as income, as well as on the basis of how it relates to the value actually created in mining. The question is whether, as in the case of monopoly prices and incomes in general, a monopoly based on the scarcity of a natural resource prevents other supposedly non-monopolistic producers that is (those in the advanced countries) from sharing the higher surplus value created in this sphere of production. What is different today is that Third World minerals-exporting governments cannot be said to have an effective monopoly over natural resources, neither can the advanced countries' mining MNCs be accurately described as non-monopolistic producers of natural resources.

Mining rents are relevant to capital accumulation both in the metropolis and in the periphery of the world capitalist economy. Third World governments of minerals-exporting countries largely depend on these surplus profits to carry out their own capitalist, albeit peripheral, development. If all the surplus profits are indeed captured by these governments, however, capital accumulation may not take place at a 'suitable' rate in metropolitan countries because their mining MNCs would be receiving only average — instead of excess or super — profits. Hence, in this study today's so-called minerals crisis is presented in terms of the struggle — between metropolitan mining MNCs (backed by their home governments) and Third World 'landlord' governments of minerals-exporting countries — to appropriate surplus profits from mining.

In this study, the terms 'Third World landlord governments', 'host governments', and 'governments of minerals-exporting countries' are used interchangeably to refer to the coalition of class forces representing the ruling classes of peripheralized and mono-cultural economies. Briefly defined, 'mono-culture' is the shaping, by imperialist powers, of portions of the periphery to specialize only in the supply of a few industrial raw materials to the industrialized world, leading to the underdevelopment of other productive (capitalist) forces in the particular peripheral area. In other words, unlike the situation in industrialized economies, in mono-cultural economies it is the interest of 'landed property', not of 'capital',[11] that prevails, on balance, as the decisive interest of the nation-state in the capitalist world market. Mono-culture is thus not a natural phenomenon, but a colonial invention that structures the role of those areas falling under imperialist domination. Above all, it entails the creation and nurturing of dependent ruling classes in the periphery which, in the neo-colonial period, organize metropolitan mining MNCs' unrestricted access to the Third World's rich raw materials at low cost.

In this study, 'Third World landlord governments' thus refers to the ruling classes of peripheralized economies that perform a specific role in the global capitalist division of labour, that is, primarily providing the industrialized world with cheap raw materials. In the world mining business and in the struggle over surplus profits, these governments are confronted by the enormous power of large mining MNCs (backed by their industrialized home governments).

While the relationship between these two principal actors in world mining is superficially contradictory, it is not necessarily antagonistic, because peripheralized economies of landlord governments are organic components of the world capitalist economy ruled by metropolitan capital.[12] In other words, despite the local political independence of mono-cultural economies, they still constitute an underdeveloped part of the world capitalist economy. Because of this, the producer power of Third World landlord governments is limited, especially *vis-à-vis* the enormous power of metropolitan mining MNCs. However, precisely because of their structural linkages and mutual interests, mining MNCs are compelled to make periodic concessions to landlord governments. An underlying issue in this study is that such concessions are exploitative because they do not maximize Third World producer power.

The extension of the Marxian rent concept in this study has the practical significance of identifying the origin of the so-called conflict in the world mining sphere today. It also allows us to appreciate the pattern that the distribution of the enormous surplus profits from the sphere would assume today if the exploitation of the landowner by the capitalist did not exist. Simply described, this pattern would be as follows: average profits would go to the capitalist mining entrepreneur, while differential and absolute mining rents would go to Third World landlord governments.

As extended in this study, the rent approach presents the new field of international political economy with a much needed and measurable concept of the producer — that is, the rent-maximizing — power of Third World minerals-exporting governments. Without this concept, it has been impossible meaningfully to analyse whether or not existing Third World governments are realizing their full potential in the world economy as owners of important mines. Again, it is my contention that they are not so doing, the implications of the bargaining model to the contrary.

Very few attempts have been made to extend Marx's rent theory to contemporary world mining. Those works that do exist are merely uncritical applications of the theory's 19th-Century tenets. From the standpoint of Marxian scholarship, a major contribution of this study is, therefore, perhaps its critical perspective. Briefly summarized, it argues that in today's world mining business, unlike the 19th-Century agriculture on which Marx based his rent theory, there are no bases for (1) the creation or exaction of absolute rent, (2) the full appropriation of differential rent I, or (3) the formation and appropriation of differential rent II[13] by Third World landlord governments, owners of the world's richest mines (see Chapter 2). This is so, the study maintains, because of the unique circumstances which apply to the present, and which had not, therefore, influenced Marx's theory. First, with respect to the mechanism of absolute rent, which is of a monopoly nature, while Marx conceived of landowners with absolute monopoly over land or natural resources, today's landowners, that is, Third World governments of minerals-exporting economies, do not have such an absolute monopoly over minerals and are not even organized in systematic and concerted action *vis-à-vis* capitalist mining entrepreneurs. Second, with respect to differential rent I, while the basis for the formation of this form of surplus profits exists in today's world mining sector, the competition among capitalist entrepreneurs envisaged by Marx does not apply in today's monopoly capitalism. Third, with respect to differential rent II, Marx's notion of the 'greater power' of landlords, which would allow them to impose short and frequently changed leases on capitalist entrepreneurs, is inapplicable in today's world mining sphere where Third World governments have been known to offer exploitation rights for up to 105 years.

The major thesis of this study is, then, that whereas Third World governments and metropolitan mining MNCs are inextricably linked in the world mining business, the distribution of gains from international mining has favoured the latter, primarily because of the limits imposed on the former by the prevailing power structure in the global capitalist economy. From the standpoint of Third World governments, their relationship with metropolitan mining MNCs is exploitative because of the governments' limited abilities to maximize their individual potential producer power as owners of the world's richest mines. This allows the MNCs to receive super profits, that is including rents, instead of only normal profits.

One objective of this study is to provide a theoretical foundation for analysing the distribution of the gains from world mining more meaningful than that provided by the largely descriptive bargaining model now predominant in the natural resources literature. Because of the virtual neglect of Marx's rent theory, and its uncritical application in existing works, this study also seeks critically to extend Marx's rent theory to world capitalist mining. Another objective is to underline the limited ability of Third World governments to capture rents in full, by employing a political economy analysis which exposes the concrete processes of exploitation involved in the relationship between Third World landlord governments and metropolitan mining MNCs.

The Scope of this Study

This book is organized in seven chapters, of which the first provides a brief critical review of the prevalent bargaining model, *vis-à-vis* the Marxian rent approach adopted. Chapter 2, 'Rent Theory and the Distribution of Wealth from Contemporary World Mining', constitutes the theoretical foundation of the study. After presenting classical rent theory in historical perspective, this chapter critically analyses the application of Marx's rent theory to the contemporary world mining business. Chapter 3, 'The Struggle Over Surplus Profits', discusses the limited policy options open to Third World minerals-exporting governments *vis-à-vis* metropolitan mining MNCs' defensive strategies, based on capitalist expansion and the manipulation of technological innovation.

The study then goes on to analyse empirical evidence regarding the central argument that Third World governments are failing to maximize their potential producer power. First, with respect to absolute rent, it is argued that the pre-condition for Third World governments to exact this form of surplus profits, which is of a monopolistic nature, is that they operate effective minerals cartels. Chapters 4 and 5 deal with the limited prospects of Third World governments exacting absolute rents in today's world through their producers' associations. With respect to capturing differential rent I, the best pre-condition is for a government to own and work the mine. Chapter 6, 'Differential Rent in the World Copper Industry', analyses the limited ability of the governments of Third World copper-exporting countries to capture this second form of surplus profits because they lack authentic control over their rich mines. Chapter 7, 'Conclusion', summarizes the major points covered in the study and highlights its central thesis that Third World governments are limited in their ability to maximize their producer power because their peripheralized states are subordinated in the world capitalist division of labour, and specifically assigned to be the industrialized world's providers of industrial raw materials at low cost. Chapter 7 also suggests a number of future research tasks.

Notes

1. Kwame Nkrumah, *Neo-colonialism: The Last Stage of Imperialism* (International Publishers, New York, 1965) pp. 1–2. On the pillage of Latin America, see Eduardo Galeano, *Open Veins of Latin America: Five Centuries of the Pillage of a Continent* (Monthly Review Press, New York, 1973).

2. See Ross Garnaut and Anthony Clunies Ross, 'Relationships Between Governments and Mining Investors', *Materials and Society* 5, no. 4, 1981, pp. 438–41, for a useful summary of the essence of the bargaining model of government–investor relations in the world mining business. The discussion in this section draws largely from their insights.

3. See Raymond Vernon, 'Longrun Trends in Concession Contracts', *Proceedings of the American Society of International Law,* April 1967, pp. 81–90; Raymond Mikesell (ed.), *Foreign Investment in the Petroleum and Mineral Industries: Case Studies of Investor–Host Country Relations* (The Johns Hopkins Press. Baltimore, 1971); David N. Smith and Louis Wells, *Negotiating Third World Concession Agreements: Promises as Prologue* (Ballinger Press, Cambridge, Mass., 1975); and Theodore H. Moran, *Multinational Corporations and the Politics of Dependence: Copper in Chile* (Princeton University Press, Princeton, N.J., 1974).

4. See Theodore Moran, 'Multinational Corporations and Dependency: A Dialogue for Dependentistas and Non-Dependentistas', *International Organization* 32, no. 1, Winter 1978, pp. 82–4.

5. *Ibid.*, p. 84.

6. See Moran, *Multinational Corporations and the Politics of Dependence,* pp. 166–7.

7. See Tony Smith, 'Changing Configurations of Power in North–South Relations Since 1945', *International Organization* 31, no. 1, Winter 1977, p. 13.

8. Moran, 'Multinational Corporations and Dependency', p. 84.

9. See Carlos Fortin, 'The State, Multinational Corporations and Natural Resources in Latin America', in Jose J. Villamil (ed.), *Transnational Capitalism and National Development* (Humanities Press, Atlantic City, N.J., 1979) pp. 205–22.

10. See, for example, Harry Magdoff, 'Limits of International Reform', *Monthly Review* 30, no. 1, May 1978, pp. 1–11.

11. Mohssen Massarrat, 'The Energy Crisis: The Struggle for the Redistribution of Surplus Profit from Oil', in Petter Nore and Terisa Turner (eds.), *Oil and Class Struggle* (Zed Press, London, 1980) p. 45.

12. *Ibid.*

13. According to Marx, absolute rent stemmed from the monopoly ownership of land. His *differential rent I* was caused by natural differences between lands, while *differential rent II* was caused by variations in the amount of investment in different lands.

1. Rent Theory and the Distribution of Wealth from Contemporary World Mining

Introduction

The concept of rent in the mineral industries can be traced from late 17th-Century mercantilists whose writings first presented land rent as an object of serious theoretical concern.[1] The rent concept was virtually neglected for about a century when it was restored to an important position, not only as an object of serious theoretical concern but also as a vital political issue. By the beginning of the 20th Century, interest in land rent had subsided; today, most textbooks mention the rent concept only briefly. Nevertheless, this dramatic decline in interest in the subject should not be interpreted as the impending demise of the concept, for it remains important in contemporary capitalism.

In particular, Marx's treatment of rent theory in capitalist society provides the most useful and relevant theoretical framework for analysing today's problem of the distribution of the wealth from the Third World's internationalized mineral resources. More specifically, the theory helps place the problem in its proper context within the operations of the capitalist world division of labour between Third World minerals-exporting governments and metropolitan mining firms. The primary objective of this chapter is thus to extend Marx's theory of ground-rent in capitalist society to contemporary world mining.

Rent Theory in Historical Perspective

The roots of rent reach far into the past. Ground-rent, a toll exacted by the owners of the land from those who use it, is almost as old as private land ownership. It appears whenever a particular social class controls access to the soil. It has assumed a variety of forms at different stages in the development of human society. In the mercantilist period, capital from the cities began to invade agricultural areas, where it gave rise to new relationships in agricultural production and to the new character of rent: ground-rent within a capitalist mode of production.

Mercantilism is the first phase in the history of capitalism's relations with agriculture in the central capitalist formations. It is characterized by the beginning of the commercialization of agriculture and by the disintegration of feudal production relations. In England, for example, where the development of capitalism could be most clearly observed, the growth of commerce destroyed subsistence farming and caused agriculture to rely increasingly on the market.

Under feudal conditions, land was not originally saleable; the peasant was guaranteed access to land and no member of the community could be driven off the land, or proletarianized. The serf worked his own land for part of each week; the rest of the week he worked for the landlord, without wages. In extracting this unpaid labour of the serf, the landlord received 'labour-rent', that is, rent in the form of labour. From this mode, a new form of rent developed in which the producer/peasant was made to divide his product, rather than his labour, between the landlord and himself. The landlord thus received 'rent-in-kind'; while a serf no longer worked under the watchful eyes of his lord, he was still compelled, by legislation, to surrender a part of his produce.

During the mercantilist era, however, the growth of trade created a greater concern for wealth in money form and a need for a quickening of economic activity. In place of rent-in-kind, the money equivalent of the serf's product was now paid over to the lord as 'money-rent'. Money-rent — rent-in-kind converted into its money equivalent — is thus the last form of what can be called 'feudal-rent', that is, payment in the form of the unpaid labour a serf was forced to surrender to his lord. Money-rent is fixed, and is, therefore, independent of fluctuating agricultural prices and of the total money income of the peasant. It is this fact that situates it at the end of the epoch of feudal-rent.

The introduction of money-rent clearly indicated that the old feudal forms of exploitation were being superseded by new forms. The replacement of labour-rent and rent-in-kind by money-rent showed that feudal-rent was ceasing to be the prevailing and normal form of the appropriation of surplus value. Moreover, unlike capitalist society, it was only as an exception that access to land was regarded at that time as an 'investment', that is, one expected to bring in a profit proportional to the money-capital invested in the land.

Under typically capitalist conditions, rent is paid in money form and is retained from surplus value produced by wage labour; it is quite different from rent in feudal society. Capitalist rent appears whenever a society considers the land itself and its products as commodities. In the capitalist extractive sphere, rent results from the investment of capital that must bring in at least an average profit. Like capitalist industry, and unlike rent in feudalism, capitalist rent presupposes a separation of the producers from their means of production. In particular, rent in capitalist agriculture further implies a separation between the basic means of production and the farmer-entrepreneur, that is, between the owner of the land and the owner of capital. It is in this circumstance that rent in capitalism is distinguished, and separated, from capitalist profit.

Under capitalism, all land commands rent. However, the more fertile and accessible land will command the higher rents. The less fertile and less accessible will command absolute rent, that is, the minimum rent that must be paid for even the worst land. The former will command differential rent, an extra rent paid for the advantages of choice soil fertility or location. Even though the mercantilists and the physiocrats did not themselves clearly expound the inherent ideas, these concepts had their origins in the pre-classical period; the ideas were only to be refined and sustained later by the classical economists, including Marx who, in particular, criticized the classicists.

Important economic changes had taken place in the classical era which influenced the concepts of value and of rent.[2] First, prior to the fairly widespread development of capitalist methods of organization in agriculture, no clear distinction between rent-earning land and profit-earning capital invested in the actual farming of the land could have been made. Second, attention in economics was being diverted from the sphere of exchange to that of production, and the idea that labour was the 'source' or 'cause' of wealth and value grew. In the agricultural sphere, this kind of differentiation could be made only with the emergence of a separate class of agricultural capitalists. Logically following this, the emergence of profit on capital as a new category of class-income sharply differentiated from other types of income cleared the way for the full development of classical political economy. Profit, the new general category of class-income, became recognized as qualitatively different from the interest on money, the rent of land, and the wages of labour.

The first major theoretical product of these changes was the classical concept of the 'natural price' of labour.[3] Along with this development grew the idea that, in the final analysis, it was the expenditure of social effort, with labour time as its appropriate measure, that conferred value upon a commodity.[4] In other words, according to the classical economists, nature's contribution in production was free, that is, without cost to man. The only true production cost was, therefore, expenditure of human labour. Hence, they argued, even though in the creation of wealth labour used land, the creation of value remained the prerogative of labour alone.

The classical labour theory of value had proved useful in illuminating the problem of the origin and persistence of the value-difference between output and input stressed by the classical school of political economy. The fundamental economic problem then centred on the best methods to increase the nation's wealth. And, given the emerging force of industrialism, the availability of a surplus from which capital could be accumulated became vital. One of the most important themes of classical analysis then became the further probing into the character of this surplus and into the factors influencing its magnitude.

To the classicists, agriculture was no longer the only productive activity; manufacturing could also generate a surplus. In particular, the classicists, profoundly influenced by the Industrial Revolution, had ideas about production and the role of natural resources that went well beyond those of the pre-classicists. Land, as a natural resource, had become vital to them to provide raw materials inputs for the industrial process. Unlike the pre-classicists, the classicists appreciated the importance of cheap minerals to keep down the cost of labour, a phenomenon which later received important political and theoretical considerations.

Although Adam Smith has correctly been credited as founder of the classical school of political economy, it was Ricardo who further developed the ideas of that school. In particular, it was Ricardo's analytical groundwork on the concept of rent that elevated the classical interpretation of the subject to an unprecedented high point.

With Ricardo, the emphasis of political economy shifted from production to distribution. He considered political economy 'an inquiry into the laws which determine the division of the produce of industry amongst the classes who concur in its formation' and not, as Smith and Malthus had defined it, 'an inquiry into the nature and causes of wealth'.[5] This new stress on distribution seemed consistent with the changing circumstances of the time. The transition from agriculture to manufacturing in Ricardo's time brought with it questions about the relative shares of landlords and capitalists; the rudimentary factory system of Smith's day was nearly in full bloom in Ricardo's time, forcing the labour problem to the forefront of economic analysis.

Ricardo's doctrine concerned determining the laws that regulate the distribution of industry's produce, less the landlord's rent, among capitalists and labourers. In distribution, the share given to land, from Ricardo's point of view, determines the proportions that labour and capital, the other factors of production, will receive.[6] Ricardo did not include rent among the costs of production because he considered land to be costless. To him, therefore, rent figured only as a transfer payment quite unrelated to any countervailing flow of services required in the production process. Rent, in Ricardo's conception, was paid primarily because land differed in fertility and location; according to him, payment of rent, unlike the payment of profit to the capitalist and of wages to the labourer, was not in the nature of an incentive to call forth desired services. Instead, rent was payment 'for the original and indestructible powers of the soil';[7] he viewed the soil as fixed in quantity and available for utilization even in the absence of rent payments.

The phenomenon of rent, viewed as the third income of distribution had, however, occupied the attention of thinkers prior to Ricardo. The physiocrats had called rent the 'net-product', and considered it a liberality of nature and a gift of God, rightly appropriated by the landowner. And Adam Smith, while he withheld the title of creator from nature and bestowed it upon labour, had nevertheless asserted that up to a third of land was due to the collaboration of nature. The size of rent, according to Smith and the earlier economists, was determined both by the demand for agricultural produce and, on the supply side, by the costs of production, which could be affected by differential fertility or locational advantages.

By Ricardo's time, some 40 years after the appearance of Smith's *Wealth of Nations*, land rent remained an 'unearned surplus', but its value had become attributed largely to differences in soil fertility and location. Emphasis was then beginning to be placed on the cost or supply determinants of land rent. Rent had become the result of increasing costs in agricultural produce due to diminishing returns, that is, crop yields increasing less than proportionately as labour and capital were applied to the cultivation of land. Historians of economic thought, however, unanimously point out that observations about the important phenomenon of the law of diminishing returns predate Ricardo's application of that law.

Ricardo's theory of rent was a response to the pressing social and economic problems of his time. Tenant farming was widespread in England. Early in the 19th Century, as the country shifted from net exports of grain to net imports, the theory of rent assumed added significance because of the important issue of protection for domestic agriculture. In particular, his theory of rent was sparked by the then impending parliamentary debate, in 1815, on the Corn Laws.[8] Generally, the trend of wheat prices[9] and the unique political developments in England during the post-Napoleonic years seemed to sustain the triumph of Ricardo's concept of rent.[10] Ricardo entered the debate on rent from an entirely new tack, brushing aside as 'mere fancy' earlier suggestions of cooperation on the part of nature,[11] and suggesting that rent implied avarice, not liberality, of nature. 'The labour of nature is paid,' wrote Ricardo, 'not because she does much, but because she does little. In proportion as she becomes niggardly in her gifts she exacts a greater price for her work. Where she is munificently beneficent she always works gratis.'[12]

The essence of Ricardo's theory of rent was thus that, far from being an indication of nature's generosity, rent was the result of man's grievous necessity, caused by the pressure of population and want, of having to resort to relatively poor land. The theory reflects both the differential and marginal principles. The differential principle holds that production costs differ for outputs produced on different plots of land, as well as for outputs produced with the help of varying doses of inputs of capital and labour on the same plot of land. According to the marginal principle, the exchange value of output is always regulated by the cost of production incurred under the most favourable circumstances. The price of corn will thus, according to Ricardo, cover the cost of production incurred at the extensive margin of cultivation, that is, cost-of-production incurred on the least fertile and least favourably located land, whose output is nevertheless needed to fill existing demand. Alternatively, the price will cover the cost of production incurred at the intensive margin of cultivation, that is, cost of the output produced with the last dose of input of labour and capital required to satisfy demand. Thus, rent was a surplus that accrued to the owner of land cultivated under conditions of cost more favourable than those prevailing at the margins. To Ricardo, 'rent is always the difference between the produce obtained by the employment of two equal quantities of capital and labour'.[13]

In attempting then to demonstrate the process of rent formation, and so to prove that the earth's fertility alone could never be the cause of rent, Ricardo pointed, as a model, to the situation in a newly settled country where land would be a free good and where only the best land would be utilized.[14] According to him, land would yield no rent if its supply was in excess of the people's demand for it: 'For no one would pay for the use of land when there was an abundant quantity not yet appropriated, and therefore at the disposal of whosoever might choose to cultivate it.'[15] In this first approximation of Ricardo's model, therefore, no rent is paid.[16] But when, according to him, second-grade land was subsequently taken into cultivation, rent would appear on the first-grade land, this rent being the difference in the costs of production on the two grades of land:

> When, in the progress of society, land of the second degree of fertility is taken into cultivation, rent immediately commences on that of the first quality, and the amount of that rent will depend on the difference in the quality of these two portions of land.[17]

With the utilization of third-grade land, second-grade land would begin to earn rent and the rent on first-grade land would rise, etc. The produce of marginal land will, from Ricardo's perspective, bring in enough revenue to cover production expenses plus the average rate of profit on the investment in labour and capital. Because the value of farm produce depended on the labour required per unit of output on the least productive land in use,[18] the worst land offered no rent while the better land produced a surplus that was kept by the landowner as rent. This was Ricardo's explanation of rent as measured from the extensive margin of cultivation.

Ricardo realized, however, that while it may have been possible to avoid cultivating less fertile lands by, for example, resorting to intensive cultivation of first-grade land, intensive cultivation would increase the returns on older lands only to a certain point. The practical limit was determined by the law of diminishing returns because, according to him, it would be absurd to expect that a limited area of land could produce an unlimited quantity of subsistence. Because of the law of diminishing returns, Ricardo believed that rent also arose from the intensive cultivation of land,[19] for, in cases where recourse to new lands was impossible, the decreasing returns yielded to capital successively applied to the same land were bound to increase its rent. If labour and capital were successively added to a piece of land while technology was held constant, each additional unit of investment would add successively less to the output than previous units. The last unit of labour and capital required to fill the existing demand must pay for itself and provide an average rate of profit as well; according to Ricardo, earlier units will yield a surplus return, which is rent.

Ricardo himself witnessed the operation of the law of diminishing returns first hand. Earlier writers had identified two factors that tended to increase the cost of agricultural production, that is, intensive cultivation of land and the use of less fertile land. In 1815, Ricardo added a third — land more remote from the market — a factor involving transportation costs of foodstuffs from farm to market. To him, transportation costs depended upon the distance of the producing land from the market-place; cultivation would spread from the nearer to the more distant lands as demand increased, while the increased costs of transportation raised the price of food to consumers.

Ricardo was also aware that rent could originate through differences in location. For example, he maintained that another way to avoid cultivating less fertile lands was for English colonists to cultivate the best lands of foreign countries, that is, lands equal in fertility to first-grade land in the home country. Presumably, the products of the foreign countries would be exchanged for the home country's manufactured goods, to which the law of diminishing returns would not apply. However, when, according to Ricardo, transportation costs, which increase production costs, are taken into account, the exercise would lead to the same result, namely a rent for those nearest the market. If lands of equal fertility are situated at varying distances from the market, the farthest land worked must pay the normal returns to labour and capital, while the more favourably located land will yield extra returns because of cheaper transport costs; these extra returns, according to Ricardo, constituted rent.[20]

Ricardo applied the same reasoning to mining rents as he did to land rent.[21] The rent of mines was, to him, a function of differences in quality. And, granting ordinary profits on stock necessary to carry on the enterprise, the returns to capital from the poorest mines (which paid no rent), would, according to Ricardo, regulate the rent of other productive mines:

> Mines, as well as land, generally pay a rent to their owners; and this rent, as well as the rent of land, is the effect and never the cause of the high value of their produce. The metal produced from the poorest mine that is worked must at least have an exchangeable value, not only sufficient to procure all the clothes, food, and other necessaries consumed by those employed in working it, and bringing the produce to market, but also to afford the common and ordinary profits to him who advances the stock necessary to carry on the undertaking . . . . This mine is supposed to yield the usual profits of stock. All that the other mines produce more than this will necessarily be paid to the owners for rent.[22]

In other words, from Ricardo's perspective, the marginal mine, like the marginal land, paid no rent but simply returned the cost of production, including normal returns on capital. Mines of superior quality returned all these, and more; the extra amount constituted rent.

Ricardo's doctrine revealed that the interests of landlords were opposed to the general interests of all classes of society. His doctrine thus led to the overthrow of that same majesty of the 'natural order' his predecessors had used to rationalize the unequal workings of the system. He had reasoned that landed proprietors were interested in rapidly increasing population, which increased demand for food and forced the cultivation of new lands. He also thought that landed proprietors preferred that these new lands be as sterile as possible, requiring much toil and thus causing increases in rents.[23]

It was Ricardo's study of rent that convinced him to advocate free trade. However, unlike the physiocrats and Smith, whose notions of free trade were based upon a general harmony of interests, Ricardo's free trade was based upon the clearly demonstrated fact of high grain prices with their concomitant high rents. Ricardo's free trade propositions seemed to be the means of checking the disastrous movement towards high rent. To him, free trade, that is, the free importation of corn into Britain (implying that distant lands were richer than any in Britain), would help avoid the need to cultivate Britain's inferior lands and thus reduce the high price of corn, which was the cause of high rents. Even though he recognized that the landlord class would lose revenue, Ricardo believed that, in the long run, such a policy was in their interest.

Ricardo's rent theory can also be said to have endangered the reputation and livelihood of landlords because it suggested that their income, not being a product of labour, was anti-social. Ricardo seemed indifferent to this implication because he thought his theory actually absolved landlords of any complicity in the matter. From his point of view, the landed proprietors played a purely passive role and did not figure in the cost of production; the price of corn was not high because high rent was paid, but a high rent was paid because the price of corn was high.[24] And even if the landlords were made to forego all of their rent, he reasoned that a fall in the price of corn would not follow as a result. Such a measure, according to him,

> would only enable some farmers to live like gentlemen [i.e., landlords], but would not diminish the quantity of labour necessary to raise raw produce on the least productive land [which is what figures in the cost of production] in cultivation.[25]

On the whole, Ricardo's contribution to classical political economy significantly affected political thought and action. In particular, the Ricardian rent doctrine was more than just an important theoretical weapon of the capitalist class in its campaign against the Corn Laws; Ricardo's emphasis on distribution had raised the question of class relations and had begun to direct attention to social and historical factors in economic analysis. And, after he had admitted the possibility of a conflict between individual and common interest, and of exploitation arising from one form of property, it opened the way for post-Ricardians similarly to criticize other forms of exploitation.

Post-Ricardian socialists and populist radicals alike drew their intellectual ammunition from Ricardo and built on his theories. Karl Marx was the most famous post-Ricardian socialist to develop his own rent theory from the perspective of what he thought to be in labour's strategic interests.

Even though Marx inherited the core of his system from the classicists, his sharpest polemical writings were directed against the analytical procedure and conclusions of the classical tradition of economic thought. Marx re-opened familiar classical problems such as the laws governing the distribution of income and how they affect the economy's long-term prospects. Like the classicists, Marx approached the problem of value in terms of labour and regarded only physical objects as embodiments of value. His scheme of income distribution was organized around a set of social class categories and his theory of accumulation was linked to the behaviour of profits.

However, where the classicists believed that the important social groupings involved three classes — capitalists, landowners, and wage-labourers — Marx compressed this scheme into a twofold division, based on legally recognized rights to property. In his analysis of income distribution, the essential groupings in capitalism separated those who owned the means of production from those who did not. As owners, capitalists and landowners were thus, to Marx, a common genus whose interests were directly pitted against those of the working men who were obliged to sell their labour-power in order to sustain even the minimum standard of living for themselves.[26]

Marx devoted over 600 pages of his *Capital* and *Theories of Surplus Value* to a critique of the classical rent theory, on the basis of which he built his own theory of rent.[27] Two inseparable objectives — form analysis and critique — shaped his work on rent for, in developing a theoretical understanding of rent, he also wished to provide a critique of classical theories of its form. His rent analysis was related to the more general debate on value;[28] he discussed rent as a secondary issue, in order to explain an important problem he identified in the classical labour theory of value.

Marx's rent analysis in value theory shows early, in his *A Contribution to the Critique of Political Economy*. After considering some 'historical notes on the analysis of commodities', he concludes by noting four possible objections that, he thought, Ricardo's labour theory of value provoked.[29] His efforts eventually to solve these problems appear in each of the three volumes of both *Capital* and *Theories of Surplus Value*. According to him, the fourth, and 'apparently the decisive', objection to the labour theory of value was this:

> if exchange-value is nothing but the labour-time contained in a commodity, how does it come about that commodities which contain no labour possess exchange-value; in other words, how does the exchange-value of natural forces arise?[30]

This problem, Marx maintained, was solved in his theory of rent. His primary objective was to show how the ownership of a specific factor of production — land — gave rise to an apparently independent category of distribution, in spite of the fact that land, a material use value, could not itself be productive of value.

From Marx's perspective, economic value in capitalist society is produced by human labour alone; in this sense, land has no value. The production system is organized by capitalists and manned by workers who are paid wages, which are less than the total value they produce. The resulting 'total social surplus value' is divided between the capitalist and the landowner as profit and rent, respectively. Profits are derived from the power of private ownership by the capitalist over the produced means of production, while land rents are derived from the power afforded by private ownership of land. Together, the capitalists' and the landowners' control of production exploits the labourer, for he could not carry on independent production. However, while the capitalist at least assumes some risks, that is, advances capital and organizes the process of production, the landowner is a purely passive agent, idly enjoying his juridical right to impose a private tax on the economy at large.

In view of the above perspective, Marx thus defined rent, within the context of his value theory, as a revenue received by landowners who are able to wrest this revenue from those who would use their land.[31] To him, rent was both a result of the private ownership of a natural resource and a deduction from total social surplus value;[32] the amount of rent was limited, in all cases, by the total value produced by labour.[33]

In feudal society, the rent that a feudal lord exacted from his dependants, both in the form of direct labour and in the form of tribute-in-kind, emerged directly from the political power relations between them. In capitalist society, rents are equally coerced; but here the mechanism of coercion is hidden by the economic freedom assumed in the system.

In Marx's analysis, two specific forms of rent were identified — differential rent and absolute rent — each of which he considered to be a historically contingent form of revenue, taken from surplus value, and representing the outcome of a particular class struggle.[34] However, to him each form of rent was different in its origins and effects.

Recall that Ricardian differential rent stemmed from the application of equal amounts of investment of capital and labour to equal amounts of land with varying fertility or location. While noting two minor qualifications,[35] Marx labelled this conception, applied to agriculture, differential rent I (DR I).[36] In view of his estimate of the productive powers of capital, he also identified and studied differential rent II (DR II),[37] which stemmed from the intensive margin, that is, the differences in additional output obtained by applying successive investments to the same plot of land or side by side in different plots of land.[38]

In other words, from Marx's perspective, differential rent can arise equally as a result of movements to increasingly more fertile lands as with movements to increasingly less fertile ones. His argument on this is clear:

> Fertility, although an objective property of the soil, always implies an economic relation, a relation to the existing chemical and mechanical level of development in agriculture, and therefore, changes with this level of development. Whether by chemical means (such as the use of certain liquid fertiliser on stiff clay soil and calcination of heavy clayey soils) or mechanical means (such as special ploughs for heavy soils), the obstacles which made a soil of equal fertility actually less fertile can be eliminated (drainage also belongs under this head). Or even the sequence in types of soils taken under cultivation may be changed thereby, as was the case, for instance, with light sandy soil and heavy clayey soil at a certain period of development in English agriculture. This shows . . . that historically, in the sequence of soils taken under cultivation, one may pass over from more fertile to less fertile soils as well as vice versa.[39]

Thus, whereas Ricardo considered fertility to be merely a natural phenomenon, Marx thought of it as social.[40] In his analysis of differential rent, Marx was then able to free himself from Ricardo's dependence on the assumption of historically diminishing returns; and, in so doing, he did away with 'the primitive misconception of differential rent [he] found among men like West, Malthus and Ricardo'.[41]

In summary, Ricardo's and Marx's theories of differential rent in the agricultural context produced the same results when it was assumed that equal quantities of capital and labour were applied on lands of different fertility; their theories diverged, however, as soon as Marx showed that different quantities of capital and labour could be applied on lands of different quality. Marx's DR I, like Ricardo's differential rent, was due to purely natural variations in soil fertility, geographical location, climatic conditions, etc. His DR II was due to variations in the conditions of production resulting from differences in intensity of capital investment; farming enterprises that were relatively highly capitalized, and hence relatively efficient, produced DR II.[42]

Marx had observed that after the abolition of the Corn Laws in England, cultivation became even more intensive. A great deal of wheat land was converted to other purposes, particularly cattle pastures, while fertile wheat land was drained and improved. Capital for wheat cultivation was thus concentrated in a more limited area. 'Economically speaking,' wrote Marx, 'we mean nothing more by intensive cultivation than the concentration of capital upon the same plot rather than its distribution among several adjoining pieces of land.'[43] From his point of view, the better land, rather than the worst, was selected for intensive cultivation because it was very likely that capital invested in it would be profitable, 'since it contains the most natural elements of fertility which need but be utilised'.[44] With improvements on the better soil, its artificially increased differential fertility would, according to Marx, then coincide with its natural differential fertility as soon as the lease expires, 'for rent is fixed when land is leased'.[45] And as long as the lease lasts, the surplus profit arising from successive investments of capital will, according to Marx, flow into the pockets of the farmer-entrepreneur.

To Marx, the issue was not whether or not rents might tend to rise with the development of capitalism; rather he was concerned with the way rents rose and how this affected the investment, and therefore accumulation, of capital in agriculture. Under a short-term lease, the owner of land may, after the farmer-entrepreneur has improved the land (by applying more fertilizer, selecting better seed, or using machinery) siphon off a part of the resulting extra yield (surplus profit) as DR II, which presupposes DR I. The landowner may also claim a part of any additional surplus profit derived from a general increase in the amount of capital invested. The landowners' appropriation, in these ways, of the fruits of improvements acted as a check to investment, and helped retard the development of agriculture. Referring to 19th-Century agriculture in England, Marx observed: 'This is why the tenants [farmer-entrepreneurs] have fought for long leases and on the other hand, due to *the greater power of the landlords,* an increase in the number of tenancies at will has taken place, i.e., *leases which can be cancelled annually.*'[46] It was, therefore, contrary to Ricardo, not only the limitedness of land but the conditions of land tenure and ownership that militated against new investment of capital in farming.

Marx did not stop at simply refining Ricardo's theory of differential rent (especially with respect to its extension to the intensive margin) but identified and discussed a second form of rent — absolute rent — with its greater implications for class struggle. To Marx, Ricardo's proposition that marginal land earned no rent was unnecessarily restrictive and contravened common sense since no landowner will let out even marginal land for no rent.[47] According to Marx, absolute rent will appear when owners hold even the poorest land from cultivation unless some payment is made. Rent could then be paid even on the worst land because of the absolute monopoly of private property:

> Landed property is here the barrier which does not permit any new investment of capital in hitherto uncultivated or unrented land without levying a tax, or in other words, without demanding a rent, although the land to be newly brought under cultivation may belong to a category which does not yield any differential rent and which, were it not for landed property, could have been cultivated even at a small increase in market-price, so that the regulating market-price would have netted to the cultivator of this worst soil solely his price of production. But owing to the barrier raised by landed property, the market price must rise to a level at which the land can yield a surplus over the price of production, i.e., yield a rent.[48]

Marxian absolute rent differed from Ricardian differential rent in that the former may affect prices:

> differential rent has the peculiarity that landed property here merely intercepts the surplus-profit which would otherwise flow into the pocket of the farmer . . . On the other hand, if the worst soil cannot be cultivated — although its cultivation would yield the price of production — until it produces something in excess of the price of production, rent, then landed property is the creative cause of this rise in price. *Landed property itself has created rent.*[49]

With differential rent, the price of a commodity is determined by the labour time of its production at the margin; this will not have any systematic relation to the value of the commodity based on its average time of production on all lands. Landlords or capitalist farmers will appropriate this part of the surplus value either as DR I or super profits, respectively, according to the superiority of the land in question over the margin. With absolute rent, on the other hand, the price of a commodity will bear no relation to the labour time of production at the margin; commodities that are land- (or natural resource-) intensive in production will be more expensive according to the magnitude of absolute rent, which depends on the comparative power of landowners *vis-à-vis* capitalist-farmers.

To Marx, absolute rent was surplus value created alone by exclusive ownership of natural resources. This form was distinct from Ricardo's differential rent, which depended only on quality differences between plots of land. From Marx's perspective, both differential rent and absolute rent nevertheless constituted a deduction from surplus value, produced from surplus labour, which would have gone to the capitalist as super profit. To the individual capitalist, the rent of land was simply another production cost. The capitalist's concern, then, is how to reduce, or pre-empt, the landlord's rent.

According to Marx, all rent — feudalistic, slave, Asiatic, or capitalistic — was the economic realization of landed property, 'the legal fiction by grace of which certain individuals have an exclusive right to certain parts of our planet'.[50] His theoretical task was not limited to identifying common elements of all forms of rent; rather, to underline the class struggle, he wished to show that rent took a specific form in each mode of production and that forms of property holding differed with different modes of production. As he saw it, rent in capitalism took the form of surplus over average profits on capital; and

23

'modern landed property' was the form of property holding in capitalism.[51] Marx's notion of modern landed property was that rent, being inseparable from this form of social ownership, could not, as Ricardo believed, be conceived as deriving from nature; modern landownership was, to Marx, a form specific to capitalism, whose characteristics could be derived from capital's requirements. More specifically, modern landed property resulted from capital's transformation of traditional relations in agriculture to serve two important requirements: ensuring a supply of wage labour for capital,[52] and ensuring a supply of food to feed the wage labour in the new towns.[53]

From Marx's perspective, despite the apparently intimate connection between capital and modern landed property[54] in the exploitation of wage labour, modern landed property was actually contradictory to capital. The basis of that contradiction was the landlord's rent. The same landowner's power that enabled him to exclude wage labour from the land was also a potential fetter against capital. In other words, after capital and landed property had together established the industrial reserve army in capitalist society, the negative aspect of their relationship became dominant: first, landed property was a negation of capital in that it had no direct bearing on production, and second, the landowner's income was deducted from capital's, thus limiting his super profit.[55]

Unlike Ricardo, Marx did not particularly concern himself with the distributional implications of his analysis.[56] He did consider his analysis of rent in the agricultural context to be applicable to all natural means of production. This is how he began the concluding chapter of his rent analysis:

> Whenever rent exists at all, differential rent appears at all times, and is governed by the same laws, as agricultural differential rent. Whenever natural forces can be monopolised and guarantee a surplus-profit to the industrial capitalist using them, be it waterfalls, rich mines, waters teeming with fish, or a favourably located building site, there the person who by virtue of title to a portion of the globe has become the proprietor of the natural objects will wrest this surplus-profit from functioning capital in the form of rent.[57]

Understand that in his *Capital*, Marx used the concept of ground-rent in relation to both the feudal and capitalist modes of production. In the feudal mode of production, ground-rent was based on a direct relation between the ruling feudal nobility and the peasantry. Because the relationship was between landlord and the actual tiller of the soil, the normal form of surplus value was the peasant's surplus labour (labour-rent) which was only 'transformed' into money-rent in late feudalism, that is, as capital moved into agriculture in 16th-Century Britain. The development of money-rent necessarily stimulated more fundamental transformations in agriculture.

> With the coming of money rent the traditional and customary relation between the landlord and the subject tillers of the soil . . . [was] turned into a pure money relation fixed by the rules of positive law. The cultivating possessor thus [became] virtually a mere tenant. This transformation [served] on the one hand . . . to expropriate gradually the old possessors and to put in their place

capitalist tenants. On the other hand it [led] to a release of the old possessors from their tributary relation by buying themselves free from their landlord so that they [became] independent farmers and free owners of the land tilled by them.[58]

This dispossession of the smaller peasant-farmers and the creation of a landless, propertyless class, who had to hire themselves for wages to live, was an important symptom, and also an important cause, of the dissolution of feudal relations in the countryside. Capital from the cities had moved into agriculture. New relationships in agricultural production now arose, and rent acquired a new character called ground-rent. Describing this new stage, Marx wrote:

> When the capitalist tenant farmer steps between the landlord and the actual tiller of the soil, all relations which arose from the old rural mode of production are torn asunder. The farmer becomes the actual commander of these agricultural labourers and the actual exploiter of their surplus labour, whereas the landlord maintains a direct relationship, and indeed simply a money and contractual relationship only with this capitalist tenant. Thus, the nature of rent is also transformed . . . *From the normal form of surplus value and surplus labour, it becomes a mere excess of this surplus labour over that portion of it which is appropriated by the exploiting capitalist in the form of profit.*[59]

In capitalist society it is capital, not land, that brings agricultural labour under its sway and productiveness. With the appearance of the capitalist who must receive payment for his employed capital, rent takes the form of a surplus over this payment to capital. From a 'normal' form of surplus value and surplus labour of feudal society, rent in capitalism has

> become transformed into an excess over the portion of the surplus-labour claimed in advance by capital as its legitimate and normal share, and characteristic of this particular sphere, the agricultural sphere of production. *Profit, instead of rent, has now become the normal form of surplus-value and rent still exists solely as a form, not a surplus-value in general, but of one of its offshoots, surplus-profit.*[60]

In other words, in capitalism the magnitude of rent depends on the limits set by the average profit claimed in advance by capital.[61] The average rate of profit determines how the total surplus value produced is divided out among the several capitalists, that is, the division of 'unpaid labour'. It is important to understand where and how rent comes into this dividing out of the surplus value in capitalist society.

Rent is not part of the average rate of profit as, for example, is interest. It is part of surplus value that can be extracted by the landowner: unearned income. The landowner is not a recipient of wages because he does not work; therefore, what he receives as rent can only come from the product of unpaid labour. Rent is something over and above the average profit that entrepreneurs expect to get on the capital they employ.

A crucial question is, then, how the landowner is able to get something over and above the average profit on the capital actually employed. With respect to differential rent, according to Marx, the landowner in 19th-Century agriculture was able to get this extra profit simply because of his private ownership of land. Private ownership of land also functioned as an obstacle to the equalization of the rate of profit in such a way that the surplus profit produced in 19th-Century capitalist agriculture (an enterprise of comparatively low organic composition of capital) was prevented from entering the general stream of capitalist profits. This extra profit went, according to Marx, from the capitalist-farmer's pockets into those of the landowners. Thus, instead of the distribution of surplus value being normally equalized, as in capitalist manufacturing industry, we may illustrate how it would not be equalized in the case of Marx's extractive sphere, as follows:

Surplus Value

C	V	S	(C+V+S)	Capitalist Profit	Rent
50	50	50	150	30	20

where C stands for 'constant capital'
    V for 'variable capital'
    S for 'surplus value'
    C+V+S for the 'value' of the commodity.

The landowner is able to appropriate 20 as rent because it is over and above the 30 that the capitalist has already pre-empted as his average profit. The landlords, according to Marx, could appropriate a part of the surplus value produced on the land simply because they owned it. From his perspective, landowners exploited their 'monopoly' by appropriating, in the form of rent, a part of the surplus value that capitalists would have received as super profit.

In general, the larger the size of the surplus value appropriated by the landowner as both differential and absolute rent, the smaller the size of the capitalist-farmer's super profits. It is then easy to see how the landowner's power, that is, rent in general terms, can represent a fetter to the investment of capital and, therefore, to capital accumulation.

Before concluding this section, it is important to underline that central to Marx's theory of rent is the idea that production based on land constitutes a twofold monopoly in capitalism. In the first place, he perceived the capitalist's monopoly of the land economy. This monopoly originates in the limitedness of land, and is, therefore, inevitable in capitalist society. This monopoly enables the capitalist to fix the price of food or raw materials according to production rates on the worst land so as to cover his production costs plus average profit. It is the surplus profit obtained by the investment of capital on better land (or by a more productive investment of capital) that forms differential rent.

The only consequence of the limitedness of land in capitalist society is thus the formation of differential rent. This rent comes into being quite independently of private property in land, which simply enables the landowner to take it from the farmer-entrepreneur. Differential rent will be collected by the landowner, from the capitalist-farmer, on the basis of his right of private ownership. Assuming that free competition among entrepreneurs exists, the landowner would always find a capitalist who would be satisfied with the average profit and who would give him the surplus profit (differential rent).

Private property in land does not create differential rent; it merely transfers it from the capitalist-farmer to the landowner. However, the influence of private landownership is not, from Marx's perspectives, restricted to appropriating differential rent alone; the landowner cannot be assumed to permit the capitalist farmer to exploit, gratis, even the worst and most disadvantageously located land, which only produces the average profit on capital. On the contrary, landownership is, to Marx, a monopoly in capitalism; the landowner can demand payment from the capitalist-farmer for this land also. That payment — absolute rent — has no connection whatever with the differences in productivity of various investments of capital — differential rent — but has its genesis in the private ownership of land. Marx therefore recognized a second form of 'monopoly', that of private property in land. It is important to understand that this monopoly is neither historically nor logically linked with the previous one. It is also necessary to recognize that his absolute rent exists side by side with his differential rent.

This section has presented Marx's rent theory in historical perspective. While his analysis of rent has received limited recognition (its application usually confined to the relationship of capital and landed property in the sphere of national agriculture), the theory extends far beyond this realm, as Marx himself suggested. In order further to appreciate the nuances of his rent theory, the next section will attempt uncritically to extend his treatment of rent theory to the international mining sphere today.

Marx's Rent Theory in Today's World Mining Sphere

Overview

In contemporary world mining, as was the case in 19th-Century British agriculture that influenced Marx, a basic material element of production (mineral land) is of limited quantity. The limited mineral deposits at issue today are the low-cost, high-grade mines located mostly in the Third World. Because of the more rapid industrialization of advanced countries, their own high-ore grades have been more rapidly exhausted, compared to those located in Third World areas, that is, those in the periphery of the world capitalist system. For the advanced countries, the era of cheap minerals discoveries has ended; most of their new mines, apart from those in Third World areas, are in remote and difficult areas like Alaska, the North Sea, Siberia, and other off-shore areas.

Today's world mining appears to exhibit another feature similar to that which informed Marx's treatment of rent theory in 16th-Century agriculture: the dominance of capitalists in the production of the world's mineral deposits. And, even though all land today is occupied by separate private enterprises, as in Marx's time, landed property does exist. In other words, while metropolitan mining firms dominate the international mining business today, property rights over the world's most productive minerals deposits rest exclusively and legitimately with Third World governments. This fact of ownership can, theoretically, represent a *potential fetter* to international mining capitalists, similar to that posed by Marx's landlords to the English capitalist farmers.

In the context of today's capitalist world market, Third World governments that own these mines are the class-representatives of landlord states; mining MNCs that dominate the organization of the capitalist world's limited supply of productive mineral bases are the class-representatives of metropolitan capital. Since the minerals in question are exploited by capitalist operators, the conditions of their exploitation, which will make possible an average profit for the metropolitan mining MNC and a rent for the Third World landlord government, will be determined by their confrontation at the world level. Conceptually, we must, therefore, distinguish between the power of the landlord government's 'monopoly' and that of the metropolitan mining MNC.

Differential and Absolute Rents Today

Compared with the more favourable conditions characteristic of mining in Third World areas, the high costs characteristic of mining in the advanced countries today represent the marginal condition of minerals production. The costs of producing minerals in the advanced countries are, generally, increasing. In the case of oil, for example, in 1977 the cost of production in the Middle East amounted to 15 cents per barrel; in the North Sea they varied between £2.00 and £6.00 per barrel that same year.[62] This situation is worsened by public policies pertaining to pollution control requirements and public land management in the metropolitan countries (see Chapter 6, in the case of copper). With respect to oil, in 1976, the estimated cost of the Alaskan pipeline was, for example, four times the original estimate.[63]

Because of the increasing social need for minerals and the limitedness of rich mines in the world, the high cost conditions in places like Alaska and the North Sea, along with the low cost conditions in the Third World, must be developed, and their outputs made profitable. Also, the market price for minerals must be based on the cost of production in the marginal conditions like Alaska and the North Sea. In other words, world minerals prices must be fixed high enough to allow the average creation of surplus value even in these marginal conditions. This way, multinational mining corporations operating in the advanced countries, that is, under marginal conditions that Alaska and the North Sea provide, would be able to obtain the average rate of profit, while others producing under more favourable cost conditions in the Third World (for example, the Middle East and Africa) would obtain relatively large surplus profits.

In today's world mining business, the surplus profit that arises from the difference between the individual price of production (of an individual mining MNC able to monopolize access to the more favourable conditions of production in the Third World) and the general or average price of production (based on conditions in the advanced countries) is similar to what Marx had labelled differential rent in 19th-Century capitalist agriculture in Britain. This kind of rent, according to him, 'does not enter as a determining factor into the general production price of commodities, but rather is based on it'.[64]

To reiterate, in capitalism, according to Marx, differential rent arises in any situation where there is an unequal product from two equal applications of capital. In today's world mining business, DR I (differential rent I) would arise through the comparative advantages of the Third World countries' higher ore grades, lower labour costs, and more attractive tax laws (and, therefore, higher average rates of profit). DR II (differential rent II) would arise through MNCs' application of heavy technology in mining today, that is, through the intensification of investment.

As was the case with differential rent in 19th-Century agriculture, differential rent in today's world mining business arises from capitalist monopoly in the working of the world's available mines. And, *the only consequence of the limitedness of the world's mineral bases is the formation of differential rent.*

Because of state ownership of the rich mines in the world's minerals sphere, Third World landlord governments would be able, following Marx's rent theory, to appropriate the differential rent from international mining today. This would be possible because in capitalism differential rent is an extra surplus over and above the average profit on capital invested in the extractive sphere. Assuming free competition among metropolitan MNCs in the international mining business, an individual Third World landlord government would, theoretically, be in a good position to find an MNC that would be satisfied with receiving only the average profit and that would be willing to surrender the surplus profit to the government as differential rent.

It must, however, be emphasized that it is not the Third World governments' ownership of rich mines that would create differential rent in world mining. Rather, this ownership would simply make it possible to transfer the differential rent from the coffers of the mining MNC to those of the Third World government.

In summary, in today's world mining, differential rent is thus, conceptually, the surplus profit from mines where (because of better quality or additional investment of capital) the cost of production is lower than on the less profitable mines (so long as the cost of production on the less profitable mine determines the price at which minerals are sold). But the question arises: in capitalism, what happens to this less profitable, that is, marginal mine? There would be no problem where the capitalist operator and the owner of the mine are the same person, since the capitalist would be content, in principle, with the (average) profit alone. The situation would not be the same, however, where the owner of the mine does not work it himself. In this case, obviously the payment of a rent to the landlord will be a precondition for this mine to be open for production. As long as the selling price of minerals in the world market is less than, or equal to, the cost of production of minerals in the marginal mines, they will remain unworked, because capitalist operators would not be able to pay this rent without encroaching on their own average profit; by transferring their capital to the manufacturing industry they can just as easily realize this average profit. But, as soon as the selling price of minerals rises sufficiently to bring in a rent, the exploitation of the marginal mine could be undertaken.

The source of this payment is explained by the fact that minerals produced under the marginal conditions in the advanced countries, like those produced under Third World conditions, are sold, not at their price of production $(C + V + average\ profit)$ but at their value $(C + V + S)$, with S consisting of average and surplus profits. In other words, in addition to the surplus profit that arises through the differential qualities of the world's mines, a second form of surplus profit would arise over and above differential rent. Under conditions of capitalist competition, this second form of surplus profit, generated in the mining sphere, should be wiped out or 'equalized' among other spheres. However, the international mining business is characterized by landownership; and, according to Marx's theory of rent, the private ownership of land is a monopoly in capitalism, which would act as an obstacle to the equalization of this second form of surplus profit, an obstacle which would prevent the value of raw materials from being reduced to their price of production. This would then give rise to the formation of absolute rent, a surplus profit which the landowner retains.

Marx's absolute rent exists in capitalism so long as there exists the monopoly of private ownership over natural resources. In mining today, absolute rent would depend on the limitedness of rich minerals deposits and on the increasing demand for minerals. The 'monopoly ownership' of Third World landlord governments would be stronger, and the magnitude of absolute rent exacted by them would be greater, as the demand for minerals expands and the supply of rich mineral deposits becomes more limited. For example, and to put this explanation in historical perspective, when, in the second half of the 18th Century, the industrialization of Britain had greatly increased demand for food to feed the growing numbers of workers in the cities, the monopoly position of British landowners could be said to have been strengthened, and absolute rent therefore increased, as land became very densely populated and little if any virgin, fertile, or uncultivated land remained. This monopoly was, however, weakened by the development of virgin land in America. The British landlords' fight to maintain import duties on corn, such as those imposed by the Corn Laws, was a last desperate attempt by the landed gentry to maintain their 'monopoly'. As we shall observe in Chapters 4 and 5, Third World landlord governments also have problems with the 'monopoly' of their landownership in today's global mining business.

Marx's theory of rent presents a useful insight into two aspects of the potential power of Third World landlord governments *vis-à-vis* metropolitan mining MNCs (and their home-states). Being landlord governments, they are, theoretically, in a position to appropriate differential rent and to impose absolute rent. This is how to define the potential producer power of the governments of Third World minerals-exporting countries today in their relationships with metropolitan mining firms, backed by their home governments. If what has been euphemistically called the bargaining power of

Third World host governments is to be correctly evaluated, that is, in the context of the contemporary global capitalist division of labour, it must be based on their ability, or inability, to maximize this potential producer power.

The negative relationship between rent and excess profits in capitalism implies that if Third World landlord governments were able to maximize their producer power in the above sense, the metropolitan mining MNCs, and their minerals-consuming home governments would then, indeed, find themselves in a crisis. A crisis situation would exist because the MNCs' increasing profitability from super profits, including capital accumulation in the metropolis, would be jeopardized.

To illustrate further, hypothetically, how both differential and absolute rents are formed and how the landlord government can appropriate these rents, suppose there are three grades of mines in the mining sphere — the worst, the medium, and the best — all of equal size. Suppose also that the average rate of profit earned generally by mining capital is 30 percent and that the mining firm in question obtains this average rate. And, suppose the following: (1) that the total capital outlay of the firm working the worst mine is $1,000, consisting of $500 in constant capital and $500 in variable capital; (2) that this firm, working the worst mine, pays $100 in absolute rent; and (3) that it produces 140 pounds of minerals. Assume that the firm would not work the worst mine if it did not receive the 30 percent average rate of profit ($300) on its total capital outlay of $1,000 and that the landlord government's monopoly of landownership is strong. Then, if the worst mine is to be worked at all, the 140 pounds of minerals must yield $1,400. In other words, the price per pound of the mineral from that particular mine must be $10. Minerals mined from the better quality mines will, of course, command the same price in the world market as those produced from the worst mine. But, with respect to the differing qualities of the three mines, the picture will be as portrayed by figures in Table 1.

As the table shows, in the worst mine, after the capitalist-oriented mining firm has collected its 30 percent profit on its total capital outlay and the government has received its absolute rent, there is no surplus value left for the government to garner as differential rent or for the firm to appropriate as super profit. On the other hand, in the medium-quality mine, there appears a surplus value of $200, over and above the basic absolute rent of $100 and the average profit of $300. This surplus profit would then accrue to the landowner government as DR I, arising from the relative quality of the medium mine *vis-à-vis* the worst. Similarly, on the best mine, in addition to the $100 in absolute rent applicable to all mines, the magnitude of DR I which appears, and can be appropriated by the landowner government over and above the average profits, is larger ($400) as compared with the $200 applicable to the medium mine.

For Marx, the division of rent essentially involved a power relation between the landowner and the capitalist. In order to illustrate that it was the landowner's monopoly ownership of natural advantages that enabled him to appropriate differential rent, he had used the example of land on which a waterfall happens to be located:

The possession of this natural force constitutes a monopoly in the hands of its owner; it is a condition for an increase in the productiveness of the invested capital that cannot be established by the production process of the capital itself; this natural force, which can be monopolised in this manner, is always bound to the land.[65]

Table 1

The Differential and Absolute Forms of Mining Rent

	Worst Mine	*Medium Mine*	*Best Mine*
a) Volume of Production (in pounds)	140	160	180
b) Value of mineral (at $10.00 per pound)	$1,400	$1,600	$1,800
c) Constant capital	$500	$500	$500
d) Variable capital	$500	$500	$500
e) Total capital outlay	$1,000	$1,000	$1,000
f) 30 percent profit on capital outlay	$300	$300	$300
g) Price of production (e + f)	$1,300	$1,300	$1,300
h) Absolute rent	$100	$100	$100
i) Surplus profit received by landowner as DR I [b – (g + h)]	0	$200	$400
j) Total surplus value (f + h + i)	$400	$600	$800
k) Profit as percentage of total surplus value (f/j × 100)	75%	50%	37.5%
l) Rent as percentage of total surplus value $\frac{(h + i \times 100)}{j}$	25%	50%	62.5%

The landowner has the option of either preventing or permitting the exploitation of his waterfall by the capitalist. And, if the landowner permits the exploitation of his waterfall, according to Marx, the surplus profit which arises from the employment of this waterfall is not due to capital, but to the utilisation of a natural force which can be monopolised, and has been monopolised, by capital. Under these circumstances, the surplus-profit is transformed into groundrent, that is, it falls into [the] possession of the owner of a waterfall . . . and precisely because this surplus does not stem from [the capitalist's] capital as such, but rather from [his] control of a limited natural force distinct from his capital which can be monopolised, is it transformed into groundrent.[66]

To continue with my hypothetical illustration, suppose that an extra investment of $500 (250C + 250V) on the best mine results in an increase in production, from 180 pounds to 280 pounds, as shown in Table 2. On the total of $1,500 ($1,000 + $500), the mining firm still has to realize an average rate of profit of 30 percent ($450). The 280 pounds of minerals will be sold for $2,800 since the selling price will continue to be determined by the price of production at the worst mine, that is, $10 per pound. After the firm has received its average profit of $450, there is $850 left of the new total surplus value of $1,300. The $850 will then accrue to the landlord government as total rent. Of this amount, $100 is absolute rent and $400 is DR I; the remaining $350 is, therefore, the surplus value derived from the additional increase in the amount of capital invested. It is DR II, which the mining firm will endeavour to keep as super profits but which the landlord government will want to get included as rent as soon as its minerals contract with the MNC expires. Without the landowner's claim to DR II, that amount would certainly go to the mining firm as super profit. Theoretically, it is the landowners' appropriation of such 'fruits' (DR II) either of more intensive mining or of improvements in mining technology, that can today act as a check to the future investment of capital in the Third World and retard the metropolitan mining firms' accumulation in the sphere.

The point I am leading up to is that, in capitalism, the landlord's rent has an inverse relation to the capitalist's increasing profitability. This situation is clearly demonstrated in Tables 1 and 2. Table 1 shows that as the total surplus value in the sphere increased from $400 on the worst mine to $800 on the best, the landlord government's share of this surplus progressively increased from 25 percent in the worst mine to 62.5 percent in the best mine, obviously at the expense of the super profits of the firm whose share fell from 75 percent in the worst mine to 37.5 percent in the best. Moreover, as Table 2 shows, the mining firm's profit, as a percentage of total surplus value on the best mine, fell even further, from 37.5 percent to 34.6 percent after the additional investment of $500 had increased the total surplus value in the best mine from $800 to $1,300.

These illustrations suggest that even under ideal conditions, where the mining capitalist can receive the average rate of profit in the mining sphere, his overall potential for increasing his profitability (and therefore, his chances to accumulate capital) can still be adversely affected by the landowner's full appropriation of rent. As we shall observe in later parts of this study, however, because of special features in today's mining sphere that did not inform Marx's rent theory, the profitability of metropolitan mining MNCs does not appear to be so adversely affected today by the landlord's rent.

Table 2

Form of Rent on Best Mine with Intensive Investment of Capital

	Best Mine
a) Volume of production (in pounds)	280
b) Value of mineral (at $10.00 per pound)	$2,800
c) Constant capital	$750
d) Variable capital	$750
e) Total capital outlay	£1,500
f) 30 percent profit on capital outlay	$450
g) Price of production (e + f)	$1,950
h) Absolute rent	$100
i) Surplus profit received by landowner as DR I	$400
j) Surplus profit received by landowner as DR II [b − (g + h + i)]	$350
k) Total surplus value (f + h + i + j)	$1,300
l) Profit as percentage of total surplus value (f/k × 100)	34.6%
m) Rent as percentage of total surplus value [(h + i + j)/k × 100]	65.4%

In the world mining sphere, minerals deposits are of differing qualities and are found in widely varying conditions; there is, therefore, a difference between costs and market prices for each type of mineral deposit. The fact of the differences between the qualities of the different mines in the world is a clear indication of the existence of DR I today; it also means that the magnitude of DR I accruing to landlord governments will vary from deposit to deposit. Consider, for example, Figure 1 (based on Table 1), which describes the relative advantages of landlord governments, with respect to the varying qualities of their mines and, therefore, the sizes of their potential rent. The figure shows that while the owner of the worst mine would receive only the basic absolute

Figure 1

Structure and Relative Sizes of Landlord's Rent in Mining Sphere, Reflecting Quality Differentials Between Mines

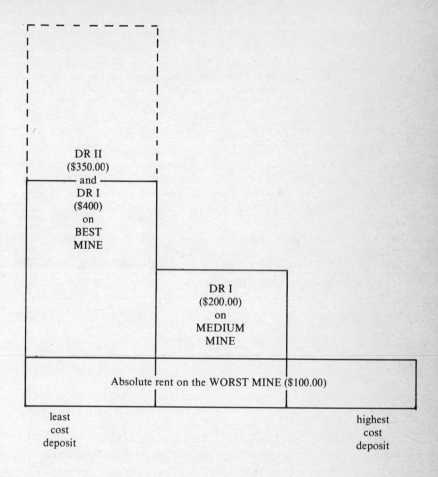

Differential Rent + Absolute Rent = Total Surplus from Minerals
Project Accruable as Mining Rent to Landowners

rent of $100, the owners of the medium and best mines would receive, in addition to absolute rent, $200 and $400, respectively, as DR I. Moreover, as the figure shows, the owner of the best mine could receive, in addition to absolute rent and DR I, a second type of differential rent (DR II) in the sum of $350, arising from the mining entrepreneur's added investment of capital in the best mine.

In international mining today, not only the quality of the minerals but also their geographical location and the ease or difficulty of extracting them can affect the individual costs of production and, therefore, the relative sizes of surplus value appropriable by individual landlord governments as DR I. With respect to quality, in the case of oil, the two main commercial characteristics are its gravity, measured in API degree, and its sulphur content. For example, while the gravity degree of Nigerian oil ranges between 34 and 35 and its sulphur content is 0.25, Libyan oil has a gravity degree of 40–41, with a sulphur content of 0.23.[67] In terms of quality, Libyan oil is thus superior to Nigerian which implies a higher DR I for Libyan crude oil because it will cost less to refine it.

With respect to geographical location, deposits closer to a given market will enjoy advantages for proximity that may be reflected in higher DR I to them. Because DR I can also be affected by transportation costs, a particular landowner's gains from the extra fertility of his mine may be neutralized by long distances for transporting his minerals to the market. The chronic bottlenecks created for Zambia by the closure of the Zambia–Rhodesian border (see Chapter 5) must have had this effect of neutralizing the potential DR I from the country's otherwise very rich copper ores.

More generally, however, since World War II, transportation costs have been greatly reduced through technological innovation and investment; the physical location of minerals deposits has become a relatively less important factor in determining the economic potential of mines. In the context of the world mining sphere, location would be important only in understanding the relative sizes of the differential rent going to landlord governments. In the case of oil, for example, North African deposits are closer to the present world market for oil (Western Europe and U.S.A.) than are deposits in the Middle East. Based on this proximity alone, oil from North African deposits, sold in the world market, would earn more DR I than that from the Middle East. For example, in 1973 Kuwaiti crude oil cost more (28 francs per ton) than Algerian crude (3.8 francs per ton) to transport to market.[68] On the basis of transportation costs alone, the DR I from Algerian crude oil can, therefore, be said to have been higher than that produced in Kuwait in 1973.

Finally, the size of DR I for a particular mineral deposit may be affected by the geological conditions of the deposit, that is, the ease or difficulty of extracting the minerals. Mines with more favourable geological conditions will tend to cost less to research and explore and will therefore provide more DR I.

Above all, it is important to understand clearly the differences between Marx's preconditions for the formation of the different types of rent and his preconditions for their appropriation by the owner of land. Table 3 provides a useful summary of these requirements with respect to 19th-Century capitalist agriculture in England. As the table shows, the formation of Marx's DR I required the limitedness of land, the differential fertility of land, and the capitalist monopoly of the land economy. In addition to these, the formation of his DR II required the intensive investment of capital, or improvements, on *the best* land under cultivation. The formation of his absolute rent required the

Table 3

Marx's Preconditions for Rent in 19th-Century Capitalist Agricultural Sphere

Type of Rent		Marx's Preconditions for Formation of Rent		Marx's Precondition for Landowner's Appropriation of Rent
DIFFERENTIAL RENT (I)	a)	limitedness of land		private property in land
	b)	capitalist monopoly of land economy		
	c)	differing fertilities of land		
DIFFERENTIAL RENT (II)	a)	intensive investment or improvements on best land under cultivation		greater power of landlord *vis-à-vis* capitalist
ABSOLUTE RENT	a)	monopoly of private property on land		monopoly of private property in land
	b)	low organic composition of capital in sphere		

monopoly of private property in land, a monopoly which prevented the equalization of the surplus profit from the agricultural sphere, which had a low organic composition of capital, with other spheres. In all three cases, Marx's only precondition for the appropriation of rent in capitalist society was private property in land, which he considered a monopoly, reflecting the greater power of landowners *vis-à-vis* capitalists.

This section has been concerned with extending, uncritically, Marx's treatment of rent theory in capitalist society to the contemporary world mining business. The primary objective was to grapple with the underlying tenets of Marx's theory. To summarize, Marx, unlike Ricardo whose work on rent he criticized, recognized two types of rents: differential and absolute. Moreover, his differential rent was of two varieties: DR I and DR II. However, only in the case of DR I are all of Marx's requirements (though only with respect to the formation, not appropriation, of rent) completely satisfied and therefore applicable in today's world.

Some Contemporary Difficulties with Extending Marx's Absolute Rent and DR II to Today's World Mining Sphere

Most works on Marx's theory of rent are typically uncritical and argue for the existence of absolute rent in contemporary capitalist society. Two such attempts are the works of Massarrat and Nore on oil.[69] While Nore at least mentions 'the shortcomings of Marx's treatment of the concept' of absolute rent, he himself is wrong in assuming that the total surplus profit in the oil industry is equivalent to differential rent, and that this differential rent 'takes the form of absolute rent when the state, as landowner, manages to extract rent for the marginal oil well in operation'.[70] Nore's observation erroneously implies that there is, indeed, a basis for Marxian absolute rent in the oil industry today. Thus, even though he talks about Marx's 'shortcomings' (which, by the way, he did not clearly define) Nore himself is guilty of an important shortcoming: assuming that the oil-producing state today has 'the historical strength of the landowning class . . . which forces capitalists using its land to pay a rent, even for the marginal land'.[71]

Marx's concept of absolute rent was sound for feudal society and even 19th-Century capitalist England. The difficulty with the concept arises precisely when it is generalized and applied to modern capitalism, a fact that contemporary Marxist scholarship does not yet appreciate.

In feudal society, landownership was indeed concentrated in the hands of the seigneur, and this enabled him to impose a levy, which may be called an absolute rent, on the individuals within his domain, either in the form of the corvee or of payment in kind. Even in capitalist England in the 19th Century, agricultural land was still very much concentrated in the hands of the semi-feudal titled aristocracy who wielded political power directly in the House of Lords and who, undoubtedly, imposed certain kinds of payment on their tenants. In particular, the agricultural land rent that emerged as a direct result of the Corn Laws could thus, for example, be viewed as an absolute rent. Such rent, however, represented a threat to the interests of capital but, in the transition from feudal to capitalist society, the power of landed property to impose private levies on economic expansion has waned as the power of capital has increased.[72]

In capitalist society, as agricultural production evolved from peasant small-holdings to large and highly capitalized farms, the power of capital can be said to have supplanted the power of landed property. The result has, most probably, been the elimination of the landowner's absolute rents by the capitalist. Marx's idea of absolute rent, therefore, deserves to be restricted to certain limited and historically specific circumstances. If absolute rent (based on the political and economic power of landlords) was central to feudal society, it seems, by contrast, largely external to the contemporary capitalist mode of production.[73]

Recall that, according to Marx, an absolute rent would form in spheres where land is a basic condition of production. The landowner's monopoly would then become a barrier to the capitalist process of the equalization of the rate of profit, preventing part of the surplus value from being transferred into other spheres of production, by diverting it into the pockets of the landowner in the form of absolute rent. The magnitude of this absolute rent will be, from Marx's perspective, equal to the value of each unit of output minus its production price. More specifically, his suggestion was that the monopoly power of the private ownership of land will enable landowners to add a levy (absolute rent) to the theoretical price of agricultural commodities, so that those commodities will sell precisely at their value. As a consequence, even marginal land will, according to him, always earn rent, contrary to the Ricardian theory. To Marx, landed property itself created absolute rent.

To begin with, while Marxian absolute rent was based on agricultural conditions with a low organic composition of capital, it is now generally accepted that minerals production today represents an activity with a high organic composition of capital. Moreover, as later chapters of this study will show, Third World landlord governments today cannot be said to have nearly as effective a 'monopoly' of private property over the world's minerals deposits as Marx had observed of the English landed gentry. These circumstances obviously confound the preconditions for the formation of Marxian absolute rent in the minerals industries today.

Also, Marx did not explain why landlords must restrict absolute rent to value minus production cost. If, according to Marx, landowners have the power to extract the difference between value and production price, there is no reason why they should not have the power to extract even more.[74]

Furthermore, while Marx explained rent without reference to any imperfections or monopolies in the market, it is clear that in the minerals industries today free-competition capitalism has been supplanted by monopoly capitalism; large, vertically and horizontally integrated oligopolies have emerged and become dominant over monocultural economies in the periphery of the global capitalist system. Even though the number of firms in international mining has certainly increased with the entrance of Japanese and

Western European firms, the situation today can still not be regarded as constituting 'free competition'. At best, what exists today is competition among a few large firms. The foundation of Marx's absolute rent had assumed the landlords' monopoly power *vis-à-vis* capitalists' monopoly power. However one may choose to describe the situation today, it does not constitute an effective monopoly power for Third World landlord governments *vis-à-vis* metropolitan mining MNCs.

Marx had proposed that the power of private property is based precisely on its ability (and interest) to withhold its land from productive use until those capitalists whose enterprises are characterized by an organic composition of capital that is less than the average will agree to pay an absolute rent. The formation of Marxian absolute rent thus presupposes the limitedness of land. For example, assume that mineral deposits are not a limited or scarce commodity but are superabundantly available. Under such a condition, competition in the minerals market would drive rent on the marginal mine to zero, that is, it would eliminate absolute rent. Now, assume that minerals deposits are no longer in superabundant supply but are rather limited, and that competition still exists in the commodity market. Rent at the marginal mine will then become a positive, non-zero quantity. This quantity will reflect the limited supply of, but increasing demand for, minerals; in other words, it will emerge as a function of the total productivity in relation to the total consumption of minerals. However, this rent will, therefore, really be a levy on the increasing demand for minerals, rather than an absolute rent in the strict Marxian sense.[75]

The pertinent question today is whether the advanced countries' demand for the Third World's minerals is increasing, and if so, whether Third World landlord governments today can levy a rent on this demand. To restate the question, can landlord governments raise the world price of their minerals by withholding production?

The question is pertinent because Marxian absolute rent depended on the monopoly power of landowners. While the chances of Third World landlord governments thus to impose an absolute rent in the minerals sphere today will depend on their ability to operate producers' cartels, Third World minerals producers' associations (the most symbolic international institutions of modern landed property today) are not, and cannot operate as, cartels. In other words, the assumption that Third World landlord governments have a systematic, concerted and generalized minerals monopoly *vis-à-vis* metropolitan mining MNCs and their minerals-consuming governments cannot be said to apply today. Third World landlord governments as a group, as modern landed property, cannot be regarded as a monopoly in any meaningful sense of the term. Excluding the 'monopoly' each landlord government has over its own particular resource bases, in general, the real economic and political power of Third World landlord governments in the global capitalist economy is fairly minute, especially in comparison with the power of metropolitan mining MNCs.

Furthermore, minerals cannot now be considered a scarce commodity. This is because technology has made possible the development of substitute and scrap materials, and even the mining of the sea. It is quite conceivable, then, that Third World landlord governments would even compete among themselves to attract and maintain the investments of metropolitan mining MNCs. This scenario again confounds the foundation of Marx's landlord's absolute rent in today's world mining sphere, because Marx had not assumed competition between landowners. On the contrary, today's Third World landlord governments do compete with each other to attract foreign mining MNCs to exploit their minerals resources precisely in order to obtain the wherewithal to advance their own capitalist, though peripheral, economies. As peripheral, capitalist, minerals-exporting governments, their immediate priority is definitely not to withhold their minerals bases from 'productive use' for any significant length of time.

In conclusion, Third World landlord governments do not have a monopoly in the fixing of the world price of minerals because they do not constitute an effective cartel in any meaningful sense of the term in the sphere. Hence, as Chapter 4 will show in the case of oil, whatever 'levy' arises from the increasing global demand for oil, that is, absolute rent, is not today the absolute prerogative of Third World landlord governments. This rent is rather shared with the governments of the advanced minerals-importing countries, and metropolitan mining MNCs. The first two capture parts of absolute rent in the form of taxes, while the latter's share is in the form of excess profits.[76]

A second important difficulty with uncritically extending Marx's rent theory to the contemporary world mining business arises with respect to his notion of DR II. Recall that Marx's DR II was informed by his observation of the intensive cultivation of the best wheat land in England, even after the abolition of the Corn Laws. His DR II is a surplus profit arising over and above absolute rent and DR I; it is formed through more intensive investments of capital, or improvements, on the better land under cultivation.

From his perspective, the natural fertility of the soil can be increased artificially by the farmer-entrepreneur's intensive investment of capital, or by improvements such as the application of drainage or fertilizers on the better land. Rent, according to him, is fixed when land is leased. The extra surplus profit arising from the farmer-entrepreneur's artificially-induced increase in differential fertility of the soil will, therefore, accrue to him, according to Marx, so long as the lease lasts.

As soon as the lease expires, however, because of what Marx saw as the greater power of the English landowners *vis-à-vis* the capitalist farmers, the extra surplus profit arising from the capitalist's artificially induced increased differential fertility may be taken into account in determining the current level of the landlord's rent, that is, increasing the level of rent by the magnitude of this new (extra) surplus profit. As Marx observed it, the greater power of the landlords *vis-à-vis* capitalist-farmers allowed them to impose typically short-term leases, despite the capitalist-farmers' demands for more certain conditions of tenure. With a short-term lease, he argued, a capitalist-farmer may, after improving the land, lose part of the resulting surplus profit to an increase in the landowner's rent; in other words, part of the surplus profit arising from the capitalist-farmer's extra investments in land may, instead of accruing to the capitalist as super profit, be appropriated by the landowner as DR II when the terms of the lease are renegotiated.

It is important to understand that, like Marx's concept of absolute rent, his concept of DR II was sound for 19th-Century capitalist agriculture in England. Again, the difficulty with the concept arises precisely when one tries to extend it to the contemporary world mining sphere.

Recall that Marx's first precondition for the formation of DR II is that the intensive investment, or improvement, be applied to the *best*, not the worst, land. DR II is, understandably, based on the best land, because its fertility will afford the best possibility of extra profitable investment. His second precondition for the landowner's appropriation of DR II is the landowner's greater power *vis-à-vis* the capitalist's. This greater power, stemming from the 'monopoly' of landownership, will allow the landowner to bargain for short-term contractual arrangements to work the land, arrangements which, in turn, will facilitate the landlord's chances to claim DR II. The difficulty, however, is that none of these requirements seems to be satisfied in the contemporary world mining sphere.

In the first place, the heavy technology characteristic of mining today is not *primarily* applied for the intensification of investment on the '*best land*', in this case, the Third World's minerals deposits, but on the *worst*, the mines of the advanced countries. Conceptually, this situation confounds Marx's basic precondition for the formation of DR II.

The function of heavy technology connected with the intensification of investment in mining today is not directly related to the formation of DR II as Marx described it. The opèn-pit technique is a good example of heavy technology that today is connected with the intensification of investment and the improvement of the productivity of mines. A description of its present use in copper mining will suggest that its effects do not contribute to the formation of a surplus profit that Marx labelled 'potential rent'.

The open-pit mining technique, as opposed to traditional underground mining, permits metropolitan mining MNCs profitably to work the low-grade deposits, most of which are located in advanced countries such as the U.S. and Canada, that is, outside the traditional copper-exporting countries in the Third World. As a rule, the copper content of ore tends to be lower in open-pit mining than in traditional underground mining. In 1962, some 47 percent of the total copper production of the advanced countries came from open-pit mining; by the end of the 1960s, this figure had increased to almost 60 percent.[77]

With the open-pit mining technique, the cost of mining low-grade ores, as well as the grade of ore itself, in the advanced countries can be substantially reduced. In the case of Canada, for example, costs range from $3.50 to $10.00 per ton of ore using the traditional underground method, to between $1.00 and $1.50 per ton, by the open-pit method; the difference stems largely from reduced labour costs, since relatively fewer and less-skilled workers are required in the open-pit method. Labour costs here range from 30 to 50 percent of operating costs, whereas in underground mining they account for 50 to 65 percent.[78]

As an example of intensive investment in mining today, the open-pit technique, therefore, fails to satisfy Marx's precondition for the formation of DR II because the primary objective of the technique is to facilitate the profitable mining of the comparatively lower ore grades characteristic of mines in the advanced countries. In other words, the open-pit technique is not employed today in such a way as to increase further artificially the existing natural quality advantages that the Third World's copper ores enjoy *vis-à-vis* those of the advanced countries. Conceptually, there is thus no basis for the formation of Marx's DR II, an extra surplus value that appears over and above DR I, which arises through the original differences in natural qualities between mines. Moreover, whereas Marx had assumed that the extra investment, or improvement, involved in the formation of DR II was available only to the entrepreneur working the best land, the open-pit technique is, today, on the contrary, highly standardized and can be acquired by most large metropolitan mining MNCs.

The open-pit operations that predominate in the advanced countries require enormous expenditures in fixed equipment such as trucks, bulldozers, and giant shovels. The enormous amount of fixed equipment required must, however, be put in motion by labour in order for its expenditure to be a 'viable investment'. A stable work force in the advanced countries where open-pit operations predominate is, therefore, essential for these open-pit projects to be profitable. Strikes by open-pit workers in the advanced countries can thus be extremely dangerous to the mining companies employing the technique. It can then be argued that while the *primary* function of the open-pit technique in today's mining is to reduce labour-input in the advanced countries, the technique also tends to increase the power of their workers to affect the mining MNCs' profitability.

Under these circumstances, it is not surprising that metropolitan mining MNCs remain eager to produce in Third World regions where not only are ore grades higher, but labour cost is cheaper and tax laws more attractive. Metropolitan MNCs controlling such areas can still gain surplus profits and also use their open-pit technique profitably.

It is only in the above indirect sense that the open-pit technology, like any other example of intensive investment in today's mining, is applied to the Third World's (best) mines. Marx's precondition for the formation of DR II cannot, therefore, be said to exist in mining today. Moreover, since the technology in question is fairly generalized anyway, the MNCs' search for Third World regimes favourable to them then becomes the key to their super-profitable minerals investment there. In other words, it is the extra expenditure typically put out by metropolitan mining MNCs to bribe corrupt government officials and to nurture brutal right-wing governments that is the key to the MNCs' super-profitable investment in the Third World. As Tanzer has put it:

> . . . each of these governments has given the mining firms a free hand to exploit its country's rich mineral resources, and they have also proved effective at

suppressing all movements, including the discontent of miners themselves, which would threaten the multinationals' prerogatives. Even more important, these regimes have shown themselves to be 'stable' —which for the companies means that the same favourable terms under which they begin a project will be in force when the project starts to pay off several years later.[79]

The long-term favourable investment climate typically provided by today's landlord governments is in direct opposition to the typically short-term leases imposed by Marx's landlords on the English capitalist-farmers. The favourable investment climate typically offered by Third World landlord governments to metropolitan mining MNCs has included, in the history of the mining industry, long tenure concessions sometimes of up to 105 years! As I argue in Chapter 3, this granting of exclusive rights to metropolitan mining firms constitutes an effective monopoly in favour of the firms. Obviously, minerals concessions today are typically less frequently broken prematurely and renegotiated; even if DR II existed today, this situation would not allow Third World host governments to appropriate any part of this surplus profit, whether it arises from open-pit mining or from other intensive investments.

In summary, it is not only Marx's precondition for the existence of DR II that is lacking today; the precondition for its appropriation by Third World landlord governments is also absent. His notion of the greater power of landlords *vis-à-vis* capitalists, which would enable the former to impose short and frequently changed leases on the latter, is clearly inapplicable with respect to today's world mining sphere where Third World landlord governments actually go out of their way to provide extra-favourable investment conditions for metropolitan mining MNCs.

This section has pointed out some difficulties with extending Marx's concepts of absolute rent and DR II to today's world mining sphere. But these difficulties do not suggest that his contribution was less than useful. On the contrary, though both his notions of absolute rent and DR II are problematic in today's world, they are still important, especially when understood as the definition of the typical power of landownership. By thus critically appreciating Marx's notions of absolute rent and DR II, we can conclude early in the analysis that Third World minerals-exporting governments, as landowners, are not able to apply, let alone maximize, two important aspects of their *potential* producer power: their potential ability to impose a levy on the increasing global demand for minerals (absolute rent), and their potential ability to impose short-term minerals leases in order to appropriate part of any extra surplus value that may arise from intensive investments in the sphere (DR II).

Marx's rent theory is still useful also because the preconditions for the formation of his DR I are completely satisfied today. There are a limited number of mines in the world today; qualitatively, few of these are very rich. Also, there is a capitalist monopoly, which means that the market value of minerals is based on conditions of production in the advanced countries' poorer mines. The mining MNCs controlling access to the richer, Third World's mines will, therefore, be in a position to receive a surplus profit over and above the average profit that the local firms in the advanced countries will receive. However, according to the classical Marxist rent mechanism, which assumed effective competition among capitalist-entrepreneurs, the landowner's right of property ownership would enable the governments of the Third World simply to appropriate this surplus profit from the operating mining MNC as DR I.

In sum, Marx's rent theory is important for it recognizes the *potential power* that landed property's ownership over land affords to the landowning class to extract surplus value, or rents, produced by labour. His theory of groundrent provides the most appropriate starting point for theoretical analysis of the distribution of wealth between the principal classes in the global extractive sphere.

In essence, Marx had ascribed a greater 'monopoly' power, stemming from landownership, to the landowning class, *vis-à-vis* the capitalist class which, according to him, enabled the landowners simply to appropriate differential rents I and II from the capitalist, and to levy an absolute rent on him even on marginal land. The situation today, however, is one where metropolitan mining MNCs, not Third World landlord governments, enjoy effective monopoly power in the natural resources sector.

In fact, the only influence that Third World landlord governments have today is their legal title to the world's richest mines. On the other hand, the comparatively enormous power of metropolitan mining MNCs is based on their symbiotic relations with their superpower home governments, their large size, and their control over important resources such as information, capital, technology, and sophisticated managerial capability.[80]

Finally, Marx had applied his rent theory mainly to 19th-Century capitalist agriculture where groundrent was received by the landed gentry, to whom, he thought, capitalism was practically alien and who would thus be interested in checking the progress of capitalism. Hence, from Marx's perspective, the landlord's rent was a potential fetter to capitalist accumulation.

However, even though Marx's analysis recognizes the inverse relationship between the capitalist's surplus profits and the landlord's rent, the essence of his theory was not, even implicitly, to advocate that capitalists, not landowners, should appropriate rent. In fact, as I noted earlier Marx, unlike Ricardo, was hardly concerned with the distributional implications of his rent analysis, even though Marx's landlord had deducted from the capitalist not just two kinds of differential rents (I and II) but also absolute rent.

Marx's rent theory is directly related to his law of value and the exploitation of labour in capitalist society. With this theory, he wanted to show that in the special case of the labour process, that is, capitalist production, which was dependent upon land or natural resources, the landowner was in a position to share with the capitalist some of the surplus value produced only by wage labour.

In attempting to extend Marx's rent theory to world mining today, the immediate and relevant issue in this study is, therefore, not who — Third World landlord governments or metropolitan mining MNCs — should appropriate the rents involved. Rather, the central issue is whether, in view of Marx's scheme of the distribution of wealth between landlords and capitalists in 19th-Century capitalist agriculture, the situation in today's relationship between Third World landlord governments and metropolitan mining MNCs is 'normal', in the sense that landowners receive all the rents and capitalist entrepreneurs receive only average profits. In that context, it is my contention that the situation today is not normal because Third World landlord governments are not able to capture all the rents involved, and metropolitan mining MNCs receive super, not average, profits.

Moreover, this unique situation is not exactly accidental, in view of the systematic workings of the capitalist world division of labour where the producer power of Third World landlord governments has clearly been peripheralized. It is precisely in this sense that the situation today is not normal, and that the relationship between metropolitan mining MNCs and Third World landlord governments can be said to be exploitative in favour of the former. The task for contemporary political economy is thus to expose the concrete processes of exploitation involved in the world mining sphere.

Summary and Conclusion

Marx's theory of rent in capitalist society provides a very useful theoretical framework for understanding today's minerals problem in its proper context of the struggle over the enormous surplus value produced from the Third World's internationalized mineral resources, between the primary actors involved in international mining today, that is, metropolitan mining MNCs and Third World landlord governments. The theory lays an important foundation for recognizing the opportunities offered by landownership and the potential power that this ownership can afford landowners to extract the surplus produced by labour in capitalist society.

Understand that, for Marx, capitalist production in the extractive sphere involved a twofold monopoly — the capitalists' monopoly of production on land and the landowners' monopoly of private property in land. The capitalists' monopoly of land-economy originates in the limitedness of land and is, therefore, inevitable in any capitalist society. It is this monopoly that leads to the fixing of the price of raw materials in such a way as to allow the capitalist producing on the worst land to receive the average profit, while the capitalist producing on the better land will receive the excess profit. This excess profit is potential rent, which, according to Marx, is appropriable by the landowner, even though it comes into being quite independently of private property in land. Assuming that free competition exists in the extractive sphere — and since differential rent is an excess profit arising over and above the normal (average) profit on capital — the landowner will, according to Marx, always find a capitalist who will let him appropriate this excess profit and be satisfied with receiving only the average profit.

But the influence of private landownership in capitalist society is, from

Marx's perspective, not limited simply to the landowner's ability to appropriate differential rent. No landowner will, according to him, allow a capitalist to exploit, without some payment, even the worst land that produces only the average profit on capital. To Marx, landownership is, therefore, a second kind of monopoly involved in capitalist production in the extractive sphere, on the basis of which the landowner demands payment from the capitalist for this worst land also. That payment, which has its genesis in the monopoly ownership of land, is Marxian absolute rent; it has no connection at all with the difference in productivity of various investments of capital in the extractive sphere, which is what forms differential rent. Marx's notion of the monopoly of private property in land is neither logically nor historically linked with his notion of the capitalist's monopoly of land-economy, which originates in the limitedness of land.

The critical extension of Marx's rent theory in this chapter clears up the question of the origin of the wealth from international mining today, and makes apparent the exploitative relations involved in the distribution of this surplus value between metropolitan mining MNCs and Third World landlord governments. As treated in this chapter, the rent approach is very useful for explaining what course the wealth of Third World landlord governments could be taking today if (1) competition among metropolitan mining MNCs were allowed absolute free play, and Third World landlord governments had authentic ownership and control of the facilities and expertise crucial in international mining today; and if (2) instead of the enormous power of metropolitan mining MNCs, there existed effective, systematic, and concerted minerals cartels organized by Third World producers' associations *vis-à-vis* these firms and their home governments. According to the classical rent mechanism, if the first condition existed today, the differential rent arising from the richer ores and lower wage levels in the Third World's mines would be fully appropriated by the owners of these mines, the Third World landlord host governments. And if the second condition existed, Third World landlord governments would be in a position to impose on the minerals-consuming countries an absolute rent on the global demand for minerals. With respect to Marx's rent theory in general, these conditions do not exist in contemporary international mining.

With respect to absolute rent, the question is whether the landlord monopoly of Third World governments prevents other non-monopolistic producers in the metropolitan countries from sharing the enormous surplus value created in international mining. What is different today is that the immense influence of metropolitan mining MNCs, in setting the so-called monopoly price of minerals, cannot exactly be described as that of non-monopolistic producers; and whatever influence Third World landlord governments have today does not constitute an effective monopoly over minerals. Today, most of the extra surplus value from the increasing global demand for minerals is, therefore, not appropriated by Third World landlord governments but by metropolitan countries and their MNCs. Marxian absolute rent arises from the private monopoly ownership of land; where this monopoly does not exist, neither, in the strict Marxian sense, does absolute rent.

With respect to differential rent, the best precondition for a landlord government to maximize this surplus profit is for it independently to operate its own mines. Third World host governments are, however, heavily dependent on metropolitan mining MNCs to operate the mines, process the minerals, and sell the products. Therefore, significant portions of the differential rent appropriable by such host governments can be concealed in, and drained away through, the artificial and false price mechanism of metropolitan mining firms.

In conclusion, to the extent that metropolitan mining MNCs can claim portions of the absolute rent on global minerals demand today and drain parts of the differential rent from the world's rich mines, the landlord, or producer power of Third World governments does not constitute an effective fetter to the metropolitan mining firms' increasing profitability and accumulation. One can say this because what these firms would, in effect, obtain by operating in the Third World would be not just average profits but two kinds of excess profits, including elements of both absolute and differential rent. Both kinds of excess profits are, according to Marx's rent theory, potentially the landowner's income. If Third World governments were able thus to appropriate these excess profits in full, the increasing profitability of the MNCs would obviously be jeopardized, including the continued supply of the mineral to their home governments. It is this scenario that would constitute a real minerals crisis situation for the metropolitan mining MNCs and their minerals-consuming home governments. On that score, however, metropolitan mining MNCs and their home governments are not in a real crisis today. As the rest of this study will show, not only do Third World landlord governments lack the monopoly power to levy an absolute charge on global minerals scarcity, but their technological and managerial dependence on metropolitan mining MNCs does not allow them to appropriate the full differential rent from mining their rich mines today. In other words, contrary to the classical Marxian rent mechanism, the full appropriation of the landowners' potential rent by Third World landlord governments in today's world is in no way automatic.

Notes

1. A current and comprehensive presentation of the evolution of rent theory, from the pre-classical to the neo-classical period, is provided in Chibuzo N. Nwoke, 'The Evolution of Rent Theory in the History of Economic Thought', Graduate School of International Studies, University of Denver, 1981 (mimeographed).

2. For an interesting insight into the social background, the intellectual environment, and the economic history of the classical age, see Ronald L. Meek, *Studies in the Labor Theory of Value* (Monthly Review Press, New York, 1956).

3. Although the concept originated from his predecessors, Adam Smith was the first to appreciate and emphasize its significance by reasoning that for each class of employment, there is an ordinary, or average, rate of remuneration prevailing in the market at any particular time. See Adam Smith, *The Wealth of Nations* (Ward, Lock, and Co., London, n.d.) chap. 7.

4. The classical assertion that it was the expenditure of labour that conferred value on a commodity followed the formulation of Ricardo's distinction between *wealth*, a sum of use values to the creation of which both land and labour contributed, and *value*, determined by labour time alone. Having thus eliminated land as a determinant of value, it was possible to clarify that labour contributed value to commodities via the expenditure of the labour itself. *not* via the reward paid to it. Meek, *Studies in the Labor Theory of Value*, p. 42.

5. The passage is from Ricardo's letter to Malthus in 1820, as quoted in H.W. Spiegel, *The Growth of Economic Thought* (Prentice-Hall, Inc., New Jersey, 1971) p. 319.

6. It is held that Ricardo began his formal analysis of land rents as early as he did, in the second chapter of his *Principles,* because, as he explained in a letter dated 13 June 1820 to J.R. McCulloch, 'by getting rid of rent, which we may do on the corn produced by labour in manufactures, the distribution between capitalist and labourer becomes a much more simple consideration'. See Piero Sraffa and M.H. Dobbs (eds.) *The Works and Correspondence of David Ricardo* (Cambridge University Press, Cambridge, 1962) Vol. 8, p. 194.

7. David Ricardo, *The Principles of Political Economy and Taxation* (Everyman's Library, London, 1969) p. 33.

8. The debate on the Corn Laws came at the period following the Napoleonic Wars; that period witnessed a growing conflict of interest between the manufacturing classes (who wished to compete in the international market by reducing the price of foodstuffs, thus lowering wages and the cost of production) and the landlords (who desired to maintain the high price of grain by preventing the importation of cheaper corn). See Jacob Oser, *The Evolution of Economic Thought* (Harcourt Brace and World, Inc., New York, 1970) p. 88.

9. Gide and Rist have pointed out that Ricardo, so often represented as a purely abstract thinker, was in reality a very practical man, and a close observer of those facts that were then occupying the attention of both public and Parliament.

> High rents following upon high prices contributed the most important phenomenon in the economic history of England towards the end of the eighteenth and the beginning of the nineteenth centuries . . . The exceptionally high price, due to extraordinary causes, chief among them being the Napoleonic wars and the Continental blockade, could not last long, although the average during the years 1810–13 remained as high as 106 shillings.

Further, Gide and Rist continued, in 1813, a commission appointed by the House of Commons to inquire into the price of corn concluded that new lands could not produce corn at a cost less than 80 shillings a quarter. See Charles Gide and Charles Rist, *A History of Economic Doctrines From the Times of the Physiocrats to the Present Day* (S.C. Heath and Co., Boston, 1948) pp. 160–1.

10. In the Corn Law controversy, Ricardo's theory had shown that economic progress would best be served by importing food supply and paying for imports with manufactured goods, i.e., by repealing the Corn Laws and establishing free trade. His theory therefore provided the supporters of free trade with an admirable rationale. The interests of landed classes were said to be in conflict with those of society; but by repealing tariffs and other restrictions on the import of grain, society's interests would, according to Ricardo, be promoted at the expense of landlords, even though this may not be so in the long run.

11. Ricardo was, however, unsuccessful in freeing himself from the influence of the old theory, which survived and even appeared under his very name. Note his definition of rent as payment for the use of the original and indestructible powers of the soil and that he continually described those powers of the soil as 'natural', 'primitive', 'indestructible', implying that they were independent of all labour.

12. Ricardo, *Principles of Political Economy and Taxation*, p. 39.

13. *Ibid.*, p. 36.

14. *Ibid.*, p. 34.

15. *Ibid.*

16. 'Rent is paid only because land is not unlimited in quantity and uniform in quality, and because, in the progress of population, land of an inferior quality, or less advantageously situated, is called into cultivation.' *Ibid.*, p. 35.

17. *Ibid.*

18. 'The exchangeable value of all commodities, whether they be manufactured, or the produce of mines, or the produce of land, is always regulated, not by the less quantity of labour that will suffice for their production under circumstances highly favourable, and exclusively enjoyed by those who have peculiar facilities of production; but by the greater quantity of labour necessarily bestowed on their production by those who have no such facilities; by those who continue to produce them under the most unfavourable circumstances; meaning — by the most unfavourable circumstances, the most unfavourable under which the quantity of produce required renders it necessary to carry on the production.' *Ibid.*, p. 37.

19. In other words, rent also arose from the intensive cultivation of land where the revenue received from the marginal output could be compared with the cost of producing that extra output, just as it was at the extensive margin.

20. Obviously, Ricardo could not have foreseen the incredible developments in transportation that were to take place in the next fifty years, which reversed the law of diminishing returns and confuted its prophets.

21. See Ricardo, *Principles of Political Economy and Taxation*, chap. 4.

22. *Ibid.*, p. 46.

23. Hence, while the community has an immediate interest in agricultural improvements, landlords merely have a 'remote interest'. 'The interest of the landlord is always opposed to that of the consumer and manufacturer. Corn can be permanently at an advanced price only because additional labour is necessary to produce it; because its cost of production is increased. The same cause invariably raises rent, it is therefore for the interest of the landlord that the cost attending the production of corn should be increased. This, however, is not the interest of the consumer; to him it is desirable that corn should be low relatively to money and commodities, but it is always with commodities or money that corn is purchased. Neither is it the interest of the manufacturer that corn should be at a high price, for the high price of corn will occasion high wages, but will not raise the price of his commodity.' *Ibid.*, p. 225.

24. 'Rent does not and cannot enter in the least degree as a component part of its price' Ricardo, *Principles of Political Economy and Taxation*, p. 41.

25. *Ibid.*

26. For a more detailed discussion of Marx's method see R. Meek, *Studies in the Labour Theory of Value*, pp. 146–56.

27. The present discussion of Karl Marx's rent theory will be based on his *Capital: Volume 3, A Critique of Political Economy* (International Publishers, New York, 1977) pp. 614–813. Marx's analysis of the development of the theory of land rent is

in volume 2 of his *Theories of Surplus Value* (Progress Publishers, Moscow, 1968) pp. 15–372.

For comments on, and discussions of, Marx's rent theory, see the following: Robin Murray, 'Value and Theory of Rent', *Capital and Class* 3, 1977, pp. 100–22; Ben Fine, 'On Marx's Theory of Agricultural Rent', *Economy and Society* 8, no. 3, August 1979, pp. 241–78; Michael Ball, 'Differential Rent and the Role of Landed Property', *International Journal of Urban and Regional Research* 1, no. 3, 1977, pp. 380–403; Keith Tribe, 'Economic Property and the Theorisation of Ground Rent', *Economy and Society* 6, no. 1, February 1977, pp. 69–88; Allan J. Scott, 'Land and Land-rent: An Interpretative Review of the French Literature', in *Progress in Geography: International Review of Current Research* (St. Martin's Press, New York, 1976) pp. 101–46; and Matthew Edel, 'Marx's Theory of Rent: Urban Applications', *Kapitalistate*, nos. 4–5, 1976, pp. 100–24.

28. Underlying the recent debates on Marxian rent theory is the controversy on value between the neo-Ricardians and the orthodox Marxists. Neo-Ricardians, notably represented by Arghiri Emmanuel, argue that Marx's transformation from values to prices is incorrect and that most of his major propositions can be made without recourse to his theory of labour value. See Arghiri Emmanuel, *Unequal Exchange: A Study of the Imperialism of Trade* (Monthly Review Press, New York, 1972) chap. 5, especially Appendix V. But, G.A. Cohen's 'The Labour Theory of Value and the Concept of Exploitation', *Philosophy and Public Affairs* 8, no. 4, Summer 1979, pp. 338–60, and Geoff Hodgson's 'A Theory of Exploitation Without the Labour Theory of Value', *Science and Society* 44, no. 3 Fall 1980, pp. 257–73, also argue that the labour value concept is not essential to the theory of the capitalist economy.

29. See Karl Marx's *A Contribution to the Critique of Political Economy* (Progress Publishers, Moscow, 1977) pp. 61–3.

The immediately pertinent of Marx's four objections to the labour theory of value is the fourth one concerning the exchange-value of natural resources; but it would be useful briefly to note the first three objections as well:

1. given that labour-time is the intrinsic measure of value, how can wages be explained on the basis of the labour theory of value? Marx claimed to provide the answer to this question in his theory of wage-labour;

2. coupled with the first problem was the second — how does production on the basis of exchange-value solely determined by labour-time lead to the result that the exchange-value of labour is less than the exchange-value of its product? This problem was solved by Marx in his analysis of capital;

3. how can the fact of the constantly fluctuating price of commodities be reconciled with the labour theory? His solution was in the theory of competition.

30. *Ibid.*, p. 63.

31. Marx, *Capital*, vol. 3, chap. 37.

32. To Marx, contrary to 'vulgar economists', rent was not a return to land as a factor of production. Rent was a price; and land was a use value. Land, a use value, can have a price without having value; but, in this case, the price cannot signify the contribution that the use value made to the value of social production, for land, a use value that is not a product of human labour, could have no value.

Land-rent, i.e., rent as the price of land, defines land as a commodity, a use-value which has a value whose monetary expression is its price. But a use-value which is not the product of labour cannot have a value; in other words, it cannot be defined as the materialisation of a definite quantity of social labour, as the social expression of a certain quantity of labour. It is nothing of the kind. Only if it is the product of concrete labour can use-value take the form of exchange-value — become a commodity. Only under this condition can concrete labour, for its part, be expressed as social labour, value. Land and price are incommensurable magnitudes, nevertheless, they are supposed to bear a certain relation to each other. Here a thing which has no value has a price. (Marx, *Theories of Surplus Value*, vol. 3, p. 520.)

Marx regarded it as one of Ricardo's great achievements to have penetrated beneath this irrational form in search of the relation between value and rent and agreed with him that rent, seen as a return to land as a factor of production, was inconsistent with the labour theory of value.

Marx continued:

. . . the price of things which have in themselves no value, i.e., are not the product of labour, such as land, or which at least cannot be reproduced by labour such as antiques and works of art by certain masters, etc., may be determined by more fortuitous combinations. In order to sell a thing, nothing more is required than its capacity to be monopolised and alienated.' (Marx, *Capital*, vol. 3, p. 633.)

33. 'All ground-rent is surplus-value, the product of surplus-labour'. *Ibid.*, p. 634.
34. See *Capital*, chaps. 37–47.

Some writers choose to associate a third form of rent, 'monopoly rent', to Marx even though he neither used that coinage nor did he discuss it specifically as a normal form. Absolute rent and differential rent were, to Marx, 'the only normal ones'.

Apart from them the rent can be based only upon an actual monopoly price, which is determined neither by the price of production nor by value of commodities, but by the buyers' needs and ability to pay. Its analysis belongs under the theory of competition, where the actual movement of market-price is considered. (*Capital*, p. 764.)

To the best of the present writer's knowledge, this is the closest that Marx came to discussing what has been identified by some writers as Marx's monopoly rent, and as one of his specific forms of rent. One such work that identified monopoly rent as one of Marx's specific forms of rent is Mathew Edel, 'Rent Theory and Working Class Strategy: Marx, George, and the "Urban Crisis" ', *Review of Radical Political Economy* 9, no. 4, 1977, pp. 1–15.

35. The two qualifications were as follows: first, in place of Ricardo's statement, 'rent is always the difference between the produce obtained by the employment of two equal quantities of capital and labour', Marx suggested that 'differential rent' is always the difference between the produce obtained by the employment of two equal quantities of capital and labour 'on equal areas of land, in so far as it is a matter of ground-rent and not surplus-profit in general'. Second, Marx agreed with Ricardo that 'whatever diminishes the inequality in the produce obtained on the same or on new land, tends to lower rent, and whatever increases that inequality, necessarily produces an opposite effect and tends to raise it'. However, according to Marx, besides fertility and location, which Ricardo had identified as the only causes of these diminishing or increasing inequalities, there were other causes, including:

a) 'the distribution of taxes, depending on whether it operates uniformly or not';

b) 'the inequalities arising from a difference in agricultural development in different parts of the country, since this line of production, owing to its traditional character, evens out with more difficulty than manufacture'; and

c) 'the inequality in distribution of capital among capitalist tenants.' Marx concluded: 'Since the invasion of agriculture by the capitalist mode of production, transformation of independently producing peasants into wage-workers, is in fact the last conquest of this mode of production, these inequalities are greater here than in any other line of production.' See Marx, *Capital*, pp. 649–50.

36. *Ibid..*, chap. 39.

37. *Ibid.*, chaps. 40–44, which are an exhaustive analysis of DR II in cases with constant, falling, and rising 'price of production'. The technical details of that exposition, replete with numerical tables will, however, not be considered in any detail here.

38. *Ibid.*

39. Marx, *Capital*, vol. 3, p. 651.

40. See Karl Marx, *The Poverty of Philosophy* (Progress Publishers, Moscow, 1973) p. 141:

> Fertility is not so natural a quality as might be thought; it is closely bound up with the social relations of the time. A piece of land may be very fertile for corn growing, and yet the market price may decide the cultivator to turn it into an artificial pasture land and thus render it infertile.

41. Marx, *Capital*, vol. 3, p. 659.

42. The difference between Ricardo's and Marx's differential rent stems from their different treatments of the question of value, one of the fundamental bases of Marx's critique of classical political economy. What was important for Marx's differential rent was the worst production process in use, i.e., the most expensive in terms of labour time, not, as Ricardo saw it, the worst land in use. For an elaboration on the difference between Marx's and Ricardo's differential rent and of the influence of rent relations on the law of value, see Ball, 'Differential Rent and the Role of Landed Property'.

43. Marx, *Capital*, vol. 3, p. 675.

44. *Ibid.*, p. 680.

45. *Ibid.*, p. 675.

46. *Ibid.*; my emphases.

47. See *Ibid.*, chap. 45. With absolute rent, Marx changes the focus of his critique from the relation of rent and the rate of profit to Ricardo's concept of value. Marx's absolute rent was the theoretical consequence of his argument on value. and of his method of transforming values into prices. His notion of absolute rent was the culmination of his attack on Ricardo's failure to distinguish between constant and variable capital, and, therefore, between values and prices of production. Marx's absolute rent depends on (1) the tendency of commodities to exchange at their value, and the modification of this tendency towards exchange at prices of production as a result of the free flow of capital between branches; (2) the presence of low organic compositions of capital in those branches yielding absolute rent; and (3) the reproduction of the comparative monopoly power of landed property against capital in those branches. The main objections to Marx's concept of absolute rent have centred on these three conditions of absolute rent. See Murray, 'Value and Theory of Rent', pp. 107–12, for a summary of these objections.

48. Marx, *Capital*, vol. 3, p. 762.

49. *Ibid.*, p. 755; emphasis in original.

50. *Ibid.*, p. 634.

51. *Ibid.*, p. 614. In his *A Contribution to the Critique of Political Economy*, p. 202, Marx wrote: 'Modern large-scale landed property has been brought about not only by modern trade and modern industry, but also by the application of the latter to agriculture.'

According to Murray, the principal features of modern landed property were:

1. property rights could be bought and sold;

2. the landlord was transformed from an active agent in production to an unproductive one in distribution;

3. the landlord's payment in rent was no longer directly residual payment in cash from a capitalist farmer; and

4. landholding was stripped of its former political and social power derived from its direct role in production.

See Murray, 'Value and Theory of Rent', p. 113.

52. The supply of labour is ensured by establishing the kind of property rights on land that would separate workers from their means of subsistence.

It is the modern landed proprietor himself who clears the land of its 'excess mouths, tears the children of the earth from the breast on which they were raised . . . the colliers, serfs, bondsmen, tenants for life, cottagers, etc., become day labourers, wage labourers'. See Karl Marx, *Grundrisse: Foundations of the Critique of Political Economy* (Vintage Books, New York, 1973) p. 276.

53. Capital ensured the supply of food to feed wage workers in the new towns by introducing capitalist relations on the land, transforming agriculture into industrial agronomy, and totally separating land as an instrument of production from landed property.

The rationalizing of agriculture, on the one hand, which makes it for the first time capable of operating on a social scale, and the reduction *ad absurdum* of property on land, on the other, are the great achievements of the capitalist mode of production. Like all of its other historical advances, it also attained these by first completely impoverishing the direct producers. (*Capital*, vol. 3, p. 618.)

54. The intimate relation between wage labour, capital, and modern landed property was most clearly demonstrated during colonial expansion when capital moved to new territory where no landed institutions existed. In volume 1 of *Capital*, Marx cites E.G. Wakefield's story about one Mr. Peel, who took with him, from England to a new settlement on Swan River, West Australia, means of subsistence and of production worth some £50,000, including 3,000 working men, women, and children. However, because land was freely available, 'unhappy Mr. Peel who had provided for everything except the export of English modes of production to Swan River . . . was left without a servant to make his bed or fetch him water from the river'. According to Marx, Wakefield's suggestion was that the British government should create modern landed property that would then put an artificially high price on colonial land, put a stop to proletarian settlement, and provide a fund from the sale of land to finance further migration of 'have-nothings' (workers) from Europe to the new areas of accumulation. That was 'the great secret' of what, according to Marx, Wakefield had called 'systematic colonization'. See Karl Marx, *Capital: Volume 1, A Critical Analysis of Capitalist Production* (International Publishers, New York, 1977) chap. 33.

55. Murray, 'Value and Theory of Rent', p. 114.

56. In spite of the fact that Marx's landlord deducted absolute rent as well as differential rent in contrast to Ricardo's more modest deduction.

57. Marx, *Capital*, vol. 3, p. 773.

58. *Ibid.*, p. 798.

59. *Ibid.*, p. 799; my emphasis.

60. *Ibid.*, p. 800; my emphasis.

61. The notion of the average rate of profit is not a vague conception but has a sound analytic grounding in Marxian economics, being central to capitalist production. For Marx's treatment of the subject, see *Capital*, chaps. 8–10.

62. Petter Nore, 'Oil and State: A Study of Nationalization in the Oil Industry', in Petter Nore and Terisa Turner (eds.) *Oil and Class Struggle* (Zed Press, London, 1980) p. 70.

63. Jean Marie Chevalier, 'Theoretical Elements for an Introduction to Petroleum Economics', in A.P. Jacquemin and H.W. deJong (eds.) *Markets, Corporate Behavior and the State* (Martinus Nijhoff, The Hague, 1976) p. 292.

64. Marx, *Capital*, vol. 3, p. 646.

65. *Ibid.*, p. 645.

66. *Ibid.*

67. Taki Rifai, *The Pricing of Crude Oil* (Praeger Publishers, New York, 1975), p. 84.

68. Chevalier, 'Theoretical Elements for an Introduction to Petroleum Economics', p. 284.

69. See Mohssen Massarrat, 'The Energy Crisis: The Struggle for the Redistribution of Surplus Profit from Oil', in Petter Nore and Terisa Turner (eds.), *Oil and Class Struggle* (Zed Press, London, 1980, chap 3; and Nore, 'Oil and State', chap. 4.

70. Nore, 'Oil and State', p. 70.

71. *Ibid.*

72. See Allen J. Scott, 'Land and Land-Rent: An Interpretative Review of the French Literature', in *Progress in Geography: International Review of Current Research* (St. Martin's Press, New York, 1976) pp. 101–46.

73. *Ibid.*

74. *Ibid.*

75. In other words, in today's world mining, there is apparently a surplus profit (after differential rent) arising from the limited supply of, and increasing demand for, minerals. However, it is certainly not 'created' by Third World landlord governments because the market price of minerals is largely determined by mechanisms in the industrialized world. While, for convenience, it may be called absolute rent, this surplus profit is, therefore, certainly not Marxian absolute rent.

76. In Chapter 4, I refer to 'the struggle over absolute rent from oil' precisely in order to underline the point that, had there been Marxian absolute rent today (in the sense of a surplus profit *created* only by the landlord through his monopoly power), there would not be such a struggle, in the first place, over an income that, by Marx's definition, it should be the prerogative of the landlord to appropriate. Marx's exposition of the notion of absolute rent did not conceive of the capitalist struggling with the landlord over this form of surplus value. According to him, since land (natural resources) is limited and appropriated, then in an elementary way, it therefore does not represent a field of activity accessible to capital, and this is why, to him, absolute rent existed. In referring to the struggle over absolute rent, I am, therefore, pointing to the inconsistency that in today's world mining — as opposed

to Marx's nineteenth century agriculture — what is new is that there is a definite sharing of this surplus profit (which may be called absolute rent but is not Marxian absolute rent) arising from the limited supply of, and increasing demand for, minerals. This struggle takes place today precisely because today's 'landlords' (Third World minerals-exporting governments) do not have Marx's requisite 'monopoly over private property', that is, over minerals.

77. Dorothea Mezger, *Copper in the World Economy* (Monthly Review Press, New York, 1980) pp. 57–8.

78. Michael Tanzer, *The Race for Resources: Continuing Struggle Over Minerals and Fuels* (Monthly Review Press, New York, 1980) pp. 50–1.

79. *Ibid.*, p. 52.

80. Since there is a rather extensive literature on the power of MNCs, it is not necessary to dwell on this issue here. For an introduction to the subject, see the following: Norman Girvan, *Corporate Imperialism: Conflict and Expropriation* (M. E. Sharpe, Inc., New York, 1976); Edith Penrose, *The Large International Firm in Developing Countries: The Petroleum Industry* (Greenwood Press, Westport, Conn., 1968); Michael Tanzer, *The Energy Crisis: World Struggle Over Power and Wealth* (Monthly Review Press, New York, 1974); and Hugo Radice (ed.) *International Firms and Modern Imperialism* (Penguin Books, Inc., Baltimore, 1975).

2. The Struggle over Surplus Profits: Mining MNCs' Defensive Strategies vs. Landlord Governments' Limited Options

Introduction

In the extractive sphere, if the landowner appropriates that part of surplus value called rent, the capitalist's excess profits (and his rate of accumulation of capital) will be reduced accordingly. Rent, the excess surplus value from international mining today, is relevant to accumulation in the centre of the world capitalist system as well as in the periphery. On the one hand, Third World landlord governments of mono-cultural economies are in dire need of, and dependent on, this surplus value to pursue their peripheral accumulation; on the other hand, if all this surplus value is captured by these governments, one can argue that accumulation will not take place at a 'rapid' or 'maximum' rate in the metropolis, since metropolitan mining MNCs would then receive only the normal, average, rate of profit.

An important implication of Marx's rent theory is that the essence of today's so-called minerals crisis is the struggle between the principal actors involved in world mining (metropolitan mining MNCs and Third World landlord governments) as to who will acquire the larger shares of the enormous excess surplus value, or rent. I suggest that, in this struggle, the power of the former far surpasses that of the latter.

Metropolitan Mining Capital's Constraints on Modern Landed Property's Rent-appropriating Potential

The capitalist continually seeks to surpass the potential fetter he perceives from his dependence upon land, which is subject to private ownership. In the history of the world capitalist economy, two specific methods are used: (1) expanding metropolitan mining capitalists' territory beyond landed property's jurisdiction, and (2) attacking the material basis of rent, through technological innovation, by increasing the productivity of low-grade deposits of the advanced countries, and decreasing the significance of minerals as elements in the labour process.

Capitalist Expansion
While Marx had assumed a theoretically closed economy regarding landed property, that assumption is not relevant to the relationship between mining

MNCs, that is, monopoly capital, and Third World minerals-exporting governments today. While it can be argued that Marx's assumption is still relevant in a limited sense today (because certain areas of the globe — on land, at sea, in wastes and marshes — have always been separated from capitalist production by barriers of nature), contemporary technology has broken down these barriers and opened up 'new lands' to capital. Capital then tends to expand to these new lands in order to avoid the impact of landed property (absolute rent), and to exact this surplus profit, as well as to appropriate differential rent.[1]

Historically, capital tends to extend geographically beyond the range over which the institution of landed property holds sway. The material basis of colonization can be understood in terms of capital's urge to acquire new land in foreign areas where the institution of landed property is either non-existent or can easily be appropriated and/or subjugated. In other words, colonization and imperialism are motivated not only by under-consumption or the falling rate of profit as some have argued,[2] but also by capital's relation to the institution of landed property. An accurate account of capital's efforts to supplant the fetter of landed property in the contemporary world must begin with the period of colonial conquest.

In opening up colonies, and thereby laying claim to new land, capital established and acquired the rights of landed property and became, *de facto*, a landlord itself, that is, a potential recipient of rent. The difference between the potential benefits of colonization, that is, benefits derived from capital's acquisition of the rights of landed property, and capital's 'costs' of opening up the colonies (including administrative and other costs of 'civilizing' the poor bastards) constituted what one can roughly call 'the colonizer's rent'.[3]

Capitalist expansion is thus rooted in two contradictory structures — capital and landed property. Because of the problem of rent, this expansion initially tends to claim particular new areas, since they offer a 'colonizer's rent' inaccessible to late-arriving capital. It is against this background of rent that we can understand why trade is said to follow the flag, and why the capitalist class is particularly concerned with establishing influence over the state as the regulator, allocator, and enforcer of property rights.[4]

The benefits of colonization, that is, colonial capital's acquisition of the 'rights' of landed property on 'new land', derive from the new proprietor (having escaped from the restraints on landed property at home) gaining access to rent in foreign lands. This rent may be absolute or differential in form.

Absolute rent on new mining land depends on the absence of further new mining land at the given level of technology.[5] If further new land is available, new capital will equalize profit rates between the extractive and manufacturing spheres, in which case the new landed proprietor would be unable to establish his control as a fetter. If, on the other hand, further new mining land is not available (and if the product of the new land can be sold above its price of production without cutting out the previous marginal land), then even the new proprietor will enjoy an absolute rent on new land. In other words, the greater the monopoly on the newly colonized land, the greater the likelihood that capital will receive absolute rent by virtue of its new proprietorial 'rights'.[6] It is only in this distorted context that 'landed property' can be said to have 'created' rent in the extractive sector. Note, however, that it was colonial capital, not modern landed property, that is, Third World landlord governments, that created and appropriated such absolute rent.

Colonizing capital may also derive its benefits from privileged access to differential rent on new mining land, especially where the new deposit is more productive than average and is introduced into production as an intra-marginal mine. 'New lands' can earn differential rent because the particular deposit may have, from the point of view of expanding capital, a unique 'stored up fertility'.[7] Wage-labour would likely be cheap in pre-capitalist, subsistence areas since part of the subsistence costs may be borne in the pre-capitalist area. Moreover, mining can be organized in an optimal manner, that is, production can be laid out according to the current level of technology and the mine geared to the best use of fixed capital and available labour.

Capital's historical tendency to move to new lands has thus allowed it to establish a topographical and social organization of production that would not have been possible within the established capitalist order.[8] The creation, by colonization, of the great plantation and mineral-exporting economies (mono-culture) on new lands in the 19th Century continues to benefit both agri-business and mining capital in Senegal, Kenya, Brazil, Bolivia, Honduras (plantation economies), and in Nigeria, Zambia, Zaire, Algeria, and Saudi Arabia (minerals-exporting economies). In all cases, the benefit is access to rent. More specifically, in expanding geographically, capital escaped the fetter of the local class of landed proprietors, acquired the rights of landed property in foreign lands and, itself, became a rent-receiver.

From the perspective of rent, colonial violence against pre-capitalist societies cannot, therefore, be viewed as an accidental phenomenon in the development of capitalism, for all formal rights over distant territories had to be secured by conquering capital.[9] While colonial landed property thus brought with it the violence of exclusive rights, violence is not the exclusive form of relations between capitalist and pre-capitalist modes of production today; the original market violence of colonial capital has effectively reduced the power of pre-capitalist economies so that even when they become politically independent, exploitation continues. Today, the 'egalitarian independence' of the neo-colonialist's law of contracts (modern concession agreements), more than gunboat diplomacy, binds them to metropolitan capital.[10] By nurturing comprador (intermediary) elements within the ruling classes in pre-capitalist societies, the colonists made gunboat diplomacy a less immediate strategy in the neo-colonial period.

'Neo-colonial' indicates that, in the transition from colonialism to independence, political power transfers to classes closely linked to those foreign interests that formerly controlled the colonial state. 'Comprador' is Portuguese for buyer. Professional intermediaries who dealt with the foreign trading houses in the coastal enclaves during colonization were dubbed 'comprador elements' by Chinese Marxists. As used here, comprador describes those professional intermediaries who organize the access of foreign mining companies to the Third World's minerals in the neo-colonial period, that is, after the 'abolition' of colonial landed property and the introduction of 'modern landed property'. Nigerian middlemen, for example, many of whom occupy government positions and control the state, constitute comprador elements.[11]

Comprador elements are likely to have a negative impact on the ability of Third World governments to appropriate rents at a maximum scale. With respect to DR I, the negative effect would be likely to arise from a government's dependency on metropolitan mining firms (especially those from the 'mother country') to exploit their rich mines. Such governments typically offer secure, lengthy, and lucrative concessions in their contracts. This is the old (extra) favourable-investment-climate situation, under which the host government may not be able to appropriate DR II, if it existed in today's world. Also, Third World landlord governments, run by comprador elements, are not likely to be willing to operate minerals cartels, and are, therefore, unlikely to impose a monopoly charge, or absolute rent, on the capitalist world's demand for their depletable resources.

The significance of landed property is central to any adequate analysis of the minerals problem in today's world capitalist economy. It explains the constant search for extensive rent by the metropolitan mining companies. For example, following the era of colonization, exploration has today been pushed to Alaska, Antarctica, the continental shelf, and the ocean bed, where the benefits of landed property offer an 'early bird's worm', that is, surplus value, or rent, not available to latecomers. The significance of landed property also explains MNCs' collusion on monopoly pricing as well as their symbiotic relations with their home governments and, in the neo-colonial period, with Third World comprador elements.

In summary, in capitalism, the contradiction between capital and modern landed property appears in the sphere of distribution; it reflects capital's struggle to bypass the disadvantages it perceived in its relation with modern landed property in the extractive sphere. Capitalist expansion, so far discussed, is one way by which metropolitan mining capital has attempted to overcome the disadvantages of modern landed property.

Expansion alone, however, may offer capital only a temporary solution.[12] For example, in the case of the Third World, as soon as social relations develop in pre-capitalist societies, the optimal compradorial arrangements on new lands set up earlier may, from capital's point of view, cease to be optimal. In other words, the compradorial elements created in a colonial period can become capital's fetters in the neo-colonial period. Two examples of pliant governments turned radical are Allende in Chile, in the case of copper, and contemporary Libya under Qaddafi, in the case of oil.

Metropolitan capital's conquest of landed property, by geographical extension and capitalist inclusion, is probably temporary, and certainly limited by the given area of feasible mineral deposits. Hence until capital is able completely to eliminate the importance of land or natural resources in the capitalist production process, landed property, and the landlord's rent, will remain significant as a potential threat to capital and its accumulation.

Technological Innovation

From the standpoint of eliminating the fetter capital perceives of landed property's power, there are limits to capitalist expansion. Capital has, therefore, with the aid of technology, not only expanded territorially but also attacked the very material basis of rent by raising productivity of poor mineral lands in the advanced countries, and by decreasing the significance of land or natural resources. In sum, in addition to expanding territorially, capital is, in the neo-colonial period, also concerned with developing new techniques of recovery and new methods of transforming natural resources. Finding new products that are freely available or open to appropriation at low cost (without the burdens of the landlord's rent) are included in this concern.

Capital's efforts to raise productivity of low-grade mineral land in order to attack the material basis of the landlord's rent are related to the application of technological innovation in mining today. An excellent example is the open-pit mining technique which, as noted in Chapter 2, now permits the profitable working of low-grade deposits mostly found in the traditional minerals-consuming countries like the U.S. and Canada. The profitable working of these deposits is likely to reduce some of the potential benefits, that is, DR I, from the labour-cost differential that the Third World's mines would normally enjoy *vis-à-vis* those in the advanced countries. The use of the open-pit mining technique in the advanced countries, making 'scarce' materials now relatively plentiful, can also reduce the scarcity value of the minerals mostly produced in Third World countries, thereby eliminating the basis for them to exact monopoly charges, or absolute rents, on these minerals.

With regard to capital's effort to decrease the significance of minerals, the following developments are noteworthy: development of substitute materials, scrap recovery, and ocean mining. In a sense, these developments reduce the scarcity value of minerals and weaken the ability of landlord governments to operate effective minerals cartels and impose a charge on global minerals demand. (See Chapter 5 for a full discussion of these developments in the case of copper.)

These methods of attacking the material basis of rent cannot, individually, be regarded as a panacea for metropolitan mining MNCs because of the obvious costs involved. But, taken together, they constitute a complete package of defensive strategies to deal with the disadvantages monopoly capital perceives in its relation with modern landed property in the development of capitalism. It must be borne in mind that included in these strategies is, most importantly, the colonizers' early nurturing of comprador elements who today rule neo-colonial economies and are, typically, interested in organizing access to the Third World's minerals in favour of metropolitan mining MNCs. With such a package of strategies, economic nationalism in the Third World notwithstanding, the continual drainage of differential rent from the Third World is ensured and potential monopoly power of Third World landlord governments is neutralized.

The Technological Dependence of Third World Landlord Governments

The development of new dominant social classes in the Third World has occasionally led Third World landlord governments to show an interest in claiming a growing share of the wealth produced from mining. Nevertheless, specifically with respect to differential rent, their ultimate aim must be completely to exclude metropolitan companies from all stages of minerals production. And in a partial attempt to attain this objective, they have attempted to nationalize their minerals industries.

But, as Chapter 6 will argue in the case of copper, it has also become evident that through the entrenched MNCs' ability to manipulate technological innovations, even nationalizations have turned out to be quite conducive to their super-profitable investments. This is a result of the technological dependence of Third World landlord governments on metropolitan mining MNCs for the operation of their mines.

It is not only the development of new means of production by MNCs, but also their ability to link them together into a complex network, that contributes to the continued technological dependence of Third World landlord governments. In this respect, large engineering firms from the metropolis (often subsidiaries of private mining MNCs operating in the Third World) can connect the different means of production into complex installations so that the private mining MNCs can secure parts from their home bases or from associated companies, which only they can supply.[13]

Given the technological underdevelopment of Third World minerals-exporting countries, the dubious process of 'technological transfer', which has often followed in their neo-colonial relations with metropolitan mining MNCs, has enabled MNCs effectively to control these countries. Third World nationalization policies often apply to improving local skills and indigenous research and development capabilities. Initially, at least, foreigners must supply these services. Even where, under nationalization, ownership or control legally lies with the national mining enterprises of host governments, the suppliers of technology from the metropolis are in a position to specify such restrictive conditions as to assure virtual control over these enterprises, including social and economic structures. In particular, the monopolistic prices charged for technology and management by metropolitan mining MNCs are an important means of extracting a good proportion of the differential rent accruable to Third World governments.

With regard to technology transfer in general, it is interesting to note Patel's four categories of its costs, with respect to the Third World's dependence. First, there are 'direct costs' for patents, licences, know-how, trademarks, and technical services.[14] These direct costs, according to him, are 'the tip of the iceberg' compared to a second type, 'indirect costs', which form a much larger part of the total costs and are borne in various ways. They include payments for (1) overpricing of imports of intermediate products and equipment; (2) profits in the capitalization of know-how; (3) a portion of repatriated profits of the wholly-owned subsidiaries or joint ventures; (4) the price 'mark-ups' for technology included in the costs of imported capital goods and equipment.[15]

Beyond direct and indirect costs, Patel identified a third category of 'not easily perceived real costs' or 'benefits forgone'. These costs result from (1) limitations imposed in transfer arrangements; (2) the transfer of wrong or inappropriate technology; (3) inadequate or delayed transfer; (4) the non-transfer of technology; and (5) the longer term influence of imported technology on deflecting national policies away from the sound development of local technological capabilities.[16]

Finally, the 'cost of non-transfer' of technology may be a fourth type. This type of cost exists because, while it is generally believed that once a project has been located in a particular country a transfer of technology immediately takes place, in many cases even the basic elements of technology are actually not transferred at all. According to Patel,

> the petroleum industry is a classic example of such a practice — but not the only one. For instance, most of the mineral-ore processing and metal-producing plants come into this category, as well as plantations, and even industries employing such traditional and well-known technology as textile manufacturing. In all these cases, what are euphemistically called payments for the 'transfer' of technology are really payments for its non-transfer.[17]

Host, Landlord, Governments' Practical Difficulty with Maximizing DR I

According to Marx, private property in land simply enables the landowner to appropriate DR I from the capitalist. Today, however, the appropriation of the full DR I by Third World landlord governments is no longer automatic. This situation results from the structure of the international capitalist division of labour, which was created by the prevailing technology monopolized by mining MNCs from the advanced countries.

In general, it appears that the restrictions usually entailed in technology transfer impose severe burdens on Third World governments. The process can jeopardize the development of skilled personnel and domestic research and development, as well as the structuring of integrated rent-related domestic policies. Moreover, the costs of the so-called technological transfer are difficult to determine in absolute figures. Methods of determining at least the order of magnitude of these costs remain to be developed, and the very secrecy of both corporate and government data has not helped the Third World's rent-appropriating efforts. Because of the Third World's technological dependence, appropriating the full amount of differential rent in international mining is an important problem for landlord governments.

More explicitly, while it is theoretically easy to explain the emergence of DR I in international mining today, it is practically difficult for the host government to identify precisely, let alone maximize, this rent. This problem arises because there are usually substantial leaks of differential rents to metropolitan suppliers. Because of the problem of ascertaining arms-length market prices, it would be difficult for Third World governments to measure DR I as an addition to these prices.

The pricing of the services offered by mining MNCs to host governments is particularly complex.[18] For example, mining projects are usually situated in underdeveloped areas lacking infrastructural facilities that are often supplied solely by one metropolitan mining company to the host government. The company assuming the full cost of infrastructural facilities usually becomes a monopoly supplier; pricing possibilities could conceivably range from implicit or explicit subsidies to the mining company, to attempts to capture (through high charges) a part of the DR I accruable to the host government.

Large metropolitan mining firms have non-market access to material inputs, through their subsidiaries and associated companies. These firms often tend to price such inputs above arms-length prices in a given host country in order to build up their equity *vis-à-vis* local partners or, if they face unfavourable tax conditions, for tax purposes. But if, alternatively, they face a relatively favourable tax situation, they may underprice materials inputs in order to lower their overall tax liability, assuming national tax regulations and international tax agreements permit this.[19]

It is also difficult to determine the appropriate price of capital, since equity capital is usually part of a package containing not only arrangements for management, but also provisions for technology and access to markets.[20] Because large mineral investments often take the form of a relatively low equity share complemented by large loans from bank consortia, insurance companies, and other large financial institutions, it is not usually possible to determine a competitive market price for such capital since each financial package is unique and the capital is considered 'risk capital'.

Wages and salaries involve further distortions.[21] New mineral deposits tend to be located in 'isolated' areas in underdeveloped countries; managers and other specialized staff usually have to be brought from abroad and financially compensated for isolation. Their remuneration may, therefore, also include elements of DR I accruable to the host government.

Minerals, with the exception of precious metals such as gold and diamonds, are generally heavy and bulky. Transport costs between mines and market can thus be substantial, making the distance of a particular deposit from the market a significant factor in determining the size of DR I. However, international shipping today is hardly competitive, and there is considerable backward integration by MNCs into ship ownership and chartering. Market transport prices, which are today determined by non-competitive factors, may likely cut into the size of DR I from a Third World government's rich mine.[22]

In sum, because landlord governments of peripheralized countries seriously lack the facilities and expertise so crucial in today's international mining business, their dependence on metropolitan mining MNCs in these areas is obviously very costly to them. More specifically, as Chapter 6 will show in the case of copper-exporting countries, the cost of such dependence to the host government is likely to be the drainage of significant portions of DR I by metropolitan copper MNCs. On the whole, while, in the context of today's world mining business, Third World governments are important landowners, serious practical constraints in the international political economy tend to limit their traditional landlord's potential power to capture the landlord's rent.

Metropolitan Mining MNCs' Monopoly in the Supply of Minerals Investment

Today, a few large, vertically and horizontally integrated mineral MNCs from the metropolis dominate the international mining industries. Post-colonial minerals-exporting governments have been made to believe that only these large international minerals firms control exploration technology, have the capital for exploration and development, and can afford the risk of minerals exploration. And although these beliefs (described in Chapter 7 as myths) have been largely penetrated by Third World governments, their exploitative effects still persist, precisely because of the nature of the international capitalist power structure within which these governments find themselves to be subjugated. In that sense, the large metropolitan mining MNCs can be said to enjoy a monopoly in the supply of mineral investments to the Third World. Under such circumstances, they are not likely simply to surrender the entire excess surplus profits to host landlord governments. More explicitly, the high prices charged by the large minerals firms for the supply of technology and management services can be said to constitute monopoly prices, that is, a means for them to drain most of the differential rent from the Third World. Clearly, this situation is unlike the one that influenced Marx's notion of differential rent, that is, where capitalists were effectively competing for access to the landlord's land, enabling the landowner to capture differential rent, while leaving the capitalist with just the average profit. It would thus be useful, at this point, to put the metropolitan mining firms' monopoly in the supply of mineral investment to the Third World today into specific focus.

To the extent that there is competition at all among metropolitan mining MNCs, it exists among only a few large firms. Third World governments wishing to have their mineral deposits developed have had to deal with one of these companies. The tendency towards monopolistic organization has, furthermore, been increased by the regional concentration of the activities of some of the major firms. The presence of competition in the supply of mineral investment is, therefore, minimal.

If Third World minerals-exporting governments, as owners of important mineral resources were able to cede access to their resources in a competitive market, they would, theoretically, be in a position to exact charges for their resources equal to the potential differential rent inherent in the comparative advantages of their rich minerals. However, because these governments depend on monopolistic MNCs for the supply of minerals investment, an asymmetric relationship has arisen between the two, in which the former's differential rents are now determined through a distorted, and an indirect, process that allows the monopolistic foreign investors to share in this rent with the governments.

Monopolistic elements are involved in the supply of mineral investment because the circumstances of today's international capitalist power structure dictate that if a metropolitan mining company were to abandon negotiations with a Third World host government over the terms of a mining agreement, the government would most likely be unable to negotiate with other investors and receive terms (that is, differential rent) comparable to the best that the first company would be prepared to offer. More explicitly, from the point of view of a host government, monopolistic elements may enter the supply price of foreign investment because of barriers against access to technology, facilities, and markets, or because the foreign firm owns the managerial qualities necessary to establish the mining project. This type of monopolistic organization may vary between industries and regions and through time. In the minerals industries, one firm can have exclusive access to new technology when recent innovation has, for example, led to the development of previously 'unprofitable' mineral deposits. Deep offshore petroleum mining and deep sea mining are recent examples of this monopoly. Also, in some cases, such as trade in bauxite and alumina, monopoly in extraction may arise from a firm's monopoly in processing and marketing.[23]

Even where the foreign investor does not have a monopoly control over technology or access to markets, the host government may still be constrained from dealing with other companies by a second type of monopoly. This may happen when a particular company, usually from the mother country, has tenure in the relevant mineral properties. This arrangement is usually protected by the foreign investors' imposed morality of the sanctity of contracts within the mineral industries. If, for example, through his holding of a mining lease, the foreign investor has been granted an exclusive right to develop some resource, the host government may not be able, for fear of establishing a history of breaching contracts, to deal with other potential investors even where such investors may offer better terms. And even where the host government does not grant an investor an exclusive right to develop the property, the mere granting of a prospecting authority, in effect, carries with it an implicit tenure or, at least, some priority in negotiations.[24]

The situation in the minerals industries today, in which host governments are forced to maintain agreements with a single foreign investor, establishes an effective monopoly for the companies *vis-à-vis* host governments. This is because even if the government does not offer absolute tenure to the first investor, it must offer terms that, to foreign investors as a group, would give a sufficiently large share of income (differential rent) to compensate for exploration expenditure.

According to the logic of foreign investors, if prospecting authority did not at least involve an implication of tenure, and therefore of differential rent, the benefits of exploration would not justify the investment. The option open to the host government is thus between undertaking the exploration itself or granting rights to mine with tenure, that is, sharing differential rent with the foreign investor.

It is the initial granting of absolute tenure with exploration rights by Third World landlord governments that entrenched the foreign investors' monopoly *vis-à-vis* host governments in future investment negotiations during and after the exploration phase. This element of monopoly is likely to persist, since host governments are dealing with the operators of established mines, and because of the governments' fear of breaking contracts with these operators, and thereby losing business confidence with others. These structural constraints imply that host Third World landlord governments will tend to offer extra-favourable investment conditions, which means offering super profits, that is, differential rents plus average profits, to foreign mining firms. In other words, Third World landlord governments will probably fail to maximize differential rent in international mining today.

The Limited Policy Options Open to Host Landlord Governments Today

This chapter began with the assertion that rent, an excess surplus value in international mining today, is relevant to accumulation in both the centre and periphery of the world capitalist economy, and that the struggle over this surplus value constitutes the essence of today's so-called minerals crisis. So far I have argued that, in this struggle, capitalist expansion and technological innovation are two significant means metropolitan mining capitalists have historically adopted to counter whatever there is of the potential producer, or rent-maximizing, power of Third World landlord governments. I have also noted the implication of host governments' technological dependence on metropolitan mining MNCs, their practical difficulty in identifying differential rent, and metropolitan mining MNCs' monopoly in the capitalist exploitation of the Third World's rich mineral deposits.

With the above in mind, the next pertinent question then becomes: what can Third World landlord governments do, under the circumstances, with respect to rent-appropriation? Hence, I shall review the limited policy options open to these governments with respect to their chances to appropriate, as rents, the surplus profits from international mining today.

The Importance of Information

Ideally, with respect to differential rent, the most obvious way for a Third World landlord government to maximize this excess surplus value is for it effectively to control and run its mines. And, for Third World governments to exact an absolute rent on the world's increasing demand for minerals, they must be able to operate effective minerals cartels. However, unlike the imposition of an absolute rent, which requires monopoly power, the capture of the full amount of differential rent by host. Third World, governments does not necessarily require monopoly or collusion among them, even though it would not damage their chances to do so. The one general and fundamental prerequisite for forming an effective, rent-related, minerals policy in the Third World is the acquisition of crucial minerals industry information.

If a Third World landlord government is to be able to identify, in order to capture, the full DR I, it must be knowledgeable about the quality of its mines and the size of its reserves. This information can be acquired through basic geological survey work.

If Third World governments had the resources to undertake such basic survey work, they would be in a good position to assess, first hand, the size of the potential surplus profit they can capture as DR I from their mines. However, the survey institutions of Third World host governments, especially compared to those of the advanced countries, typically lack experience, sophisticated staff, and buoyant financial resources.[25] Hence, they are largely dependent on metropolitan mining MNCs even for basic exploration work.

Because metropolitan mining firms consider exploration the riskiest part of the mining process, the host governments' acquisition of sophisticated knowledge about the geological characteristics of natural resources will probably have the effect of eliminating most, if not all, of the bases of the high charges metropolitan MNCs presently impose on them for 'risk and uncertainty' at the exploration stage. From the standpoint of host governments, these high charges constitute disguised sources that drain DR I from the Third World.

Large oligopolistic mining MNCs dominate the capitalist exploitation of the Third World's rich mines. Third World host governments must acquire information about how to deal with these formidable entities in order to capture the landlord's rent involved. The best way to do this is, obviously, to study the various minerals concession agreements these companies have written and accumulated over time. However, according to Smith, throughout the first half of this century and beyond, minerals agreements negotiated with MNCs and Third World governments were notoriously unavailable for public, or third party, inspection.[26] Withholding this information has weakened the chances of host governments to draw up efficient concession terms; it has also distorted the very literature on minerals concessions.

In order to deal intelligently with the exploiting company, it is important that the host government be well informed about what entities are affiliated with the company. Typically, a complex maze arises from relationships among metropolitan mining MNCs where ownership and control extend vertically and horizontally through a number of international companies. In view of this, the structuring of efficient concession terms would also require that the host government know how to decipher complex financial transactions of metropolitan mining MNCs. The ability and tendency of these companies to understate profits and expenses would be particularly detrimental to host governments' efforts to capture differential rents.

With respect to absolute rent, information on marketing outlets and trade patterns, and the role of dominant MNCs in the industry, are critical for assessing the prospects of Third World landlord governments to operate minerals cartels. For example, if Third World landlord governments wish to operate minerals cartels they must know whether their particular resource is widely available, how badly the minerals-consuming countries need it, and the economics and state of the art of the available technology for making its substitutes or for recovering it in scrap. It would appear that not only have Third World landlord governments not found answers to these pertinent questions, but they have not even systematically sought them.

In summary, with respect to both differential and absolute rent, a crucial problem facing all Third World landlord governments is lack of access to pertinent information needed for effective decision-making, including (1) data on the mine, including the quality and quantity of ore, and the international market for the ore; (2) data on the company or companies with whom the government is negotiating; (3) data on the projected cash flow from the mine under different sets of assumptions about various contractual arrangements; (4) data on the operating company's structure for the purpose of monitoring transfer pricing and other financial arrangements; (5) data on market and industry development; (6) information on minerals policies and issues in the most advanced mineral-exporting countries, and analyses of the current relations among these countries, mining MNCs, and consuming countries; (7) information on policies and issues in other less advanced mineral-exporting countries (particularly recent entrants) and analyses of the relations among these countries, mining MNCs, and consuming countries; (8) information on mechanisms for maximizing mineral income and controlling the transfer of profits by mining MNCs from host-countries to other jurisdictions (through transfer-pricing and related tax avoidance devices); (9) information on the role of state companies in mineral production and control, and the socio-political context in which these entities operate; and (10) case studies that examine the role of minerals in medium- and long-range national development and reveal the possibilities and problems inherent in managing mineral wealth.[27]

Acquisition of these kinds of knowledge, including mineral processing, can be facilitated by encouraging exchange of information and joint research and development efforts among Third World landlord governments. There is also a need for coordinated minerals-related training and multidisciplinary research institutions. As Smith has observed, in a field long dominated by lawyers and economists, there is much that can be contributed by environmentalists, sociologists, and anthropologists, sources that have not yet been tapped by landlord governments. Their input will be necessary in developing comprehensive studies.[28] The objective of coordinated minerals-related research institutions could be primarily to put together case histories of major mineral projects and to examine the full range of decisions about past mineral development projects. Third World landlord governments need access to a depository of such valuable information in order to make intelligent and rational decisions regarding contract drafting.

Third World landlord governments can also probably gain access to some minerals industry information through regional or international organizations like the United Nation's Center on Transnational Corporations.[29] Such organizations are, however, unlikely to be able to put together the complete packages of information that individual governments would need.

One means of gathering mineral industry information might be Third World producers' associations. In fact, in the long run, the information-gathering role, not the cartel-quality, of Third World producers' associations may be the most important and commendable function they could perform. Notice how Mikdashi described the benefits derived by the Organization of Petroleum Exporting Countries' (OPEC's) members, in 1974, from the organization's information-gathering activities:

> The [OPEC] Secretariat has . . . attempted to induce member governments to seek terms and adopt policies and practices *vis-à-vis* concessionary companies in line with the best economic terms prevailing in various member countries. One study commissioned by OPEC analyzed, on a comparative basis, members' posted prices, royalties, taxes, transit and port dues, guarantees and timing of payments, and other economic benefits offered to host countries. The best terms were to be used as guidelines by host governments in their negotiations with concessionaires. Information, studies, and advice have produced far-reaching economic benefits, essentially in the form of improved fiscal terms claimed, and eventually obtained, from oil operators.
>
> The contribution of OPEC to its member countries, especially those with limited oil experience, is notable in the areas of analyzing conditions in the international petroleum industry, offering advice, and training nationals in the technical and economic aspects of the industry. The OPEC Secretariat has performed a useful function in acting as a clearinghouse and in filling gaps of information on oil markets. Detailed, accurate, and increasingly comprehensive information, supplied on a regular basis, assists top officials of OPEC governments in formulating appropriate policies and regulations, whether dealing with the oil sector or with other related sectors of the economy — especially in view of the general unwillingness of their concessionaires to supply them with certain data in technical and economic matters (e.g., prices realized on oil exports). International companies classify such information as trade secrets, bearing in mind that national companies of host countries are their active competitors.[30]

In summary, the science and technology of the internationalized minerals industries are developed in the capitalist heartlands of the West; and the benefits of their exclusive property rights are being appropriated and defended at the world's extremities. Since critical minerals industry data are controlled by metropolitan mining MNCs, an important problem facing Third World landlord governments is how to gain access to them. Third World governments can focus their efforts to structure effective, rent-oriented, minerals policies on a greater exchange of information, joint research and development efforts, and coordinated minerals-related training and research institutions.

While some of the critical information will become available to host governments as domestic personnel become more sophisticated in dealing with foreign investors, the learning process involved in the acquisition of the full range of minerals industry information is, however, a slow one. And since the critical data are controlled by metropolitan mining MNCs, the attraction of foreign technical assistance, in the form of accounting firms and business and legal advisers, will characterize Third World policy for some time to come.

Some Policy Options

Ownership and Control

I have noted that an important constraint facing Third World landlord governments wishing to appropriate differential rents is how to identify the exact amount of the excess surplus value arising from the higher productivity of their rich mines. And it is apparent that metropolitan mining MNCs, because they dominate the operations of the Third World's mines, supply their minerals investments at monopolistic prices which, most likely, include differential rent, the excess surplus value arising from the Third World's rich deposits.

In order to capture all the differential rent in international mining today, the landlord government must, therefore, own and run its mines. Hence, the importance of the recent move in the Third World towards the nationalization of their minerals industries.

To begin with, nationalization, as a policy option, is only indirectly relevant to the imposition of an absolute rent in international mining today. The indirect effect can come, perhaps, through the increased confidence of landlord governments as they accumulate knowledge of the minerals industries, which could follow from the process of nationalization. For example, the only time the copper-exporting governments showed any real interest in collusion to curtail production and raise the price of copper was (in 1974) soon after they completed the nationalization of their copper industries.

On the other hand, assuming free competition among metropolitan mining MNCs that operate in the Third World, nationalizations (national state ownership of extraction) would place Third World landlord governments in a position to receive, as differential rent, the excess profits from the more favourable productivity of their mines, that is, leaving the operating MNC with only the average profit. However, for Third World landlord governments of mono-cultural economies, it is a difficult task to substitute fully and effectively for the metropolitan mining MNCs that have historically dominated their international mining industries. To do so, they need to develop indigenous, sophisticated managerial, technical, and marketing capabilities. This demands early and careful planning and investment by the governments in relevant education, and research and development.

It is quite conceivable that serious, careful, and truly nationalist planning and development of educational policy and strategy in the Third World can eventually result in landlord governments gaining autonomy in the crucial spheres involved in the international mining business. However, while investments in education can enhance authentic national ownership of minerals production and, thereby, the chances of Third World governments to appropriate differential rents, such educational investments typically have long gestation. Therefore, from the beginning, Third World landlord governments have been forced to rely quite heavily on foreign investors and 'experts'.

While the most obvious way for a Third World landlord government to appropriate the full differential rent is to control its own mines, the extent of this control today is minimal. As Chapter 6 will show, in the case of copper-exporting countries, the meagre extent of this control can be further appreciated by reviewing their efforts to attain it through nationalizations.

Governments of copper- (as well as oil-) exporting countries have tried to gain some control over the exploitation of their resources by means of partial or total nationalizations. Neither of these means has, however, succeeded in effectively controlling the large metropolitan mining MNCs that dominate their minerals industries. At best, nationalizations ultimately resulted in the setting up of joint ventures, in the nominal transfer of ownership to the Third World government, and in the formation of state mining corporations. However, even after formal nationalizations in the Third World, metropolitan mining MNCs still control, through their subsidiaries and holding companies, a considerable part of the exploration, extraction, transportation, processing, and marketing facilities. Under the circumstances, they can afford to capture, as super profit, most of the extra surplus value (differential rent) from the Third World's rich mines. For example, instead of showing these extra profits in the books of the subsidiaries directly engaged in the extraction of minerals in the Third World, the MNCs can conceal them in the accounts of their purchasing and processing affiliates.

This is not to argue that nationalizations have, practically, not improved the chances of Third World governments to capture larger shares of differential rents. On the contrary, one cannot deny the importance of nationalization as at least the beginning of a necessary learning process for the host government. The accumulated knowledge and increased confidence resulting from the mere nominal transfer of ownership to the state must, on the whole, improve the chances of Third World governments to appropriate larger portions of differential rent.

The point is, however, that differential rent is an excess profit, the total amount of which can be appropriated by the landlord government without affecting the level of its minerals production. In order to appropriate this excess profit, Third World landlord governments must strive for greater autonomy in the exploitation of their rich mines. Towards that aim, nationalizations are, however, not a panacea, but at best a necessary first step.

Production-sharing and Contracting Agreements
The next policy option that I wish to identify in this section, only because a few minerals-exporting governments have been known to focus on it, is known as 'production-sharing and contracting agreements'. Some exporting governments have introduced these new arrangements designed, as one writer puts it, to 'preserve the spirit of the income and profits tax, retain the advantages of private operation, and reduce political risks'.[31] Production-sharing and

contracting agreements were first introduced in Indonesia and, more recently, in Peru, both in petroleum production.

In production-sharing, the foreign investor supplies foreign exchange investment, management and export markets. The payment of interests and profits, including the repayment of capital, is predetermined and takes the form of a *share of output at agreed prices*.[32] Ownership and control ostensibly remain in national hands. According to the original model, which was developed in Indonesia, the foreign contractors financed all expenditures and recovered costs from up to 40 percent of production valued at the world market price. The remaining oil was divided between the contractor and PERTAMANIA, Indonesia's state oil company, and the taxes were paid by PERTAMANIA. There was also a distinction made between 'domestic oil', for which a very low price was received by the contractor, and 'profit oil', valued at the world market price.

During the 1970s, a purer form of production-sharing, involving no recovery of capital or operating cost, was adopted in several Peruvian petroleum contracts; here foreign contractors financed all expenditures, and production was split at the wellhead between the government enterprise, PETROPERU, and the foreign operator. The profit was split fifty-fifty, with PETROPERU paying the income tax on the foreign operator's share.[33]

With respect to production-contracting, a variance of production-sharing agreements, foreign investors operate on an *output-share* basis.[34] Ownership, again, remains in national hands. While both approaches can be useful in overcoming some of the usual difficulties of appropriating rent (estimating operating costs and input prices), they are not feasible precisely because in effect, they avoid the issue of rent. And while the government does receive some of the resource, it often ends up simply selling it back to the dominant MNCs at 'market', that is, exploitative, prices. Mikesell correctly observed this drawback about production-sharing agreements:

> By making the agreements appear to the public as contracts to explore and produce minerals in return for a share of the output, they are not well designed to capture a share of the rent or to encourage production of a marginal ore body. *The share going to the government simply serves as a tax based on output rather than a tax on surplus over cost.* Although the production-sharing principle is becoming more widely used in petroleum, it is less feasible in mining since such a large share of the gross output of mines must be reserved for operating costs and debt service.[35]

Although a production-sharing agreement may provide some political advantages to host governments, as a policy option it is not designed either to capture the surplus profit from the comparative advantages of their rich resources (DR I), or to levy a charge on the global demand for their minerals (absolute rent). Because these arrangements typically seem to open up the foreign investment package by having a substantive public ownership share in mineral exploitation, the advantages to the government are mostly political.

On the whole, production-sharing and contractual agreements would seem to be mostly suitable to comprador elements who would wish to appear to be satisfying the public sentiment with regard to developing Third World mineral resources for the benefit of nationals, but who would not have the strength or will to tax the foreign operator to the utmost or to abolish him altogether. Far from being designed to capture the maximum differential rent in international mining today, these arrangements precisely provide a favourable basis for sharing this surplus value with metropolitan mining MNCs. Moreover, from the standpoint of Third World governments, they have the major disadvantage of requiring extremely sophisticated negotiation and supervision to obtain even limited objectives.

Auctioning of Exploitation Rights
The auctioning of exploitation rights is yet another minerals-related policy option. As the name implies, a landlord government invites metropolitan mining MNCs to submit bids to exploit its rich mines. Theoretically, the government can then choose the highest bidder, that is, the MNC that would be willing to receive only the average, but not super, profit. In other words, if effective competition existed among mining MNCs, this device would put the host government in a good position to maximize differential rent.

The auctioning of exploitation rights does not appear to be directly related to the appropriation of absolute rent. And, with respect to the appropriation of differential rent, the practical difficulty with this infrequently used option from the standpoint of the host government, is precisely that it assumes that effective competition does exist when, in reality, there are very few bidders. The auctioning of exploitation rights can be effective only if the number of potential bidders is large. Furthermore, with this approach, because of the host government's lack of relevant information, its uncertainty about the quality and size of its reserves might become a particularly costly factor.

Taxation
Although the participation of Third World state mining corporations in their own mines is increasing, high entry barriers in marketing and other spheres of the international mining business limit such involvement. Moreover, even though it is increasingly becoming possible to contract out the managerial and technical parts of the production process, the historical sense of dependence on metropolitan mining firms prohibits host governments from pursuing this option. Thus, the role of metropolitan mining MNCs is likely to remain a significant factor, and hence also will the role of taxation,[36] the fourth minerals policy option I wish to discuss in this section.

From the standpoint of host landlord governments, the primary objective of taxation in mining should be to capture all the differential rent while allowing the foreign mining capitalist to receive only the average profit. Generally, this is a difficult task, since competition among metropolitan mining MNCs is imperfect, the tax-collector-government's knowledge of the industry is inferior to that of the foreign mining investor, and transfer pricing is the rule rather than the exception.

Taxation can take many forms in the mining business. Three decades ago, 'royalties', the oldest form of taxation, constituted the principal source of government revenues from resource projects. Royalties can be based on tonnage of minerals mined (or sold), or on sales revenue.

There are two forms of royalties in the mining business. The first, known as the 'specific royalty', that is, a tax on tonnage of minerals produced, is the older form. Its main advantage lies in its ease of calculation and collection, including the assurance of a stable income for the host government.[37] However, this advantage may not be sufficient to overcome its disadvantage of not differentiating among minerals of varying quality, so that a host government applying it may not benefit from the comparative advantages of its rich ores (differential rent), or from a rise in prices (absolute rent).

Alternatively, there is a second form of royalties known as '*ad valorem* royalty', that is, a tax based on sales revenues. *Ad valorem* taxes are more, if only indirectly, related to changes in ore quality and commodity prices. It is primarily because an *ad valorem* tax *can* tax, if only indirectly and imprecisely, both differential and absolute rent that it may be seen as the preferred form of royalties. In addition, the *ad valorem* tax is relatively more easily administered than the specific royalty tax, though it is somewhat more demanding on the usually scant administrative capabilities of the host government. Also, an *ad valorem* tax is relatively stable, though less so than the specific royalty.[38]

On balance, the most important justification of a royalty tax as a host government's minerals policy option is that it provides a modest income from a major mineral development, regardless of the manipulated 'vagaries' of corporate profits via the transfer pricing normally shown under conventional accounting procedures. However, from the standpoint of capturing *all* the landlord's rent from the capitalist exploitation of natural resources, the royalty tax suffers a major drawback because it is not precisely related to the idea of an excess surplus value over normal costs, including the average profit on the capital invested. In this sense, a royalty may or may not capture rents. Nevertheless, while the royalty tax has serious limitations, its assurance of stable income and its ease of collection can perhaps encourage its use, especially as a supplement to other systems of taxation in mining.

A second form of taxation often adopted by host governments is known as the 'income and excess profits tax'. This form was adopted precisely to minimize the metropolitan mining MNCs' tax burden while at the same time attempting indirectly to capture some mining rent. Because it liberally allows for all sorts of 'exploitation' and 'development' expenditures, its main advantages are likely to favour the foreign mining operators. Like the royalty tax, the income and excess profits tax is not finely tuned to capturing all the excess surplus value from international mining today. Because of the host government's problem with access to relevant mineral industry information, and also because of the MNCs' tendency towards transfer pricing, this kind of taxation is not likely, especially by itself, to take Third World landlord governments beyond the exploitative situation in which they presently find themselves.

Furthermore, it would be difficult precisely to calculate corporate incomes and profits and, therefore, to tax away any excess profits as rents. Above all, the income and excess profits tax has the disadvantage of potentially causing revenue instability. For example, in 1971, when Zambia first changed from the royalty tax system to an income and excess profits tax system, the country's mineral tax revenues were known to have dropped by almost 50 percent, very likely due to the supposed fall in corporate profits, which were said to have resulted from a fall in copper demand.[39]

Generally, any landlord government with a substantial MNC involvement in its minerals project, that is, a host government, must compare the levels of its income tax with those of the MNCs' home governments. If the host government's taxes are lower than the home government's, the host government will, most likely (under double tax agreements and *de facto* tax arrangements), be transferring not only its rents but also its share of income taxes to the MNC's home government.

A new and more innovative approach to mineral taxation in Third World countries now seeks to unify the objectives of appropriating normal rents and of taxing 'quasi-rents' and normal profits. This approach was introduced in Papua New Guinea in 1976, during its agreement with foreign investors for the development of the Ok Tedi Copper ore body. It taxes earnings, but only after the investor has realized a certain minimum 'internal' rate of return on his investment. The approach was labelled the 'resource-rent-tax' by Garnaut and Clunies Ross, who first outlined its basic scheme.[40]

In essence, Garnaut and Clunies Ross propose a yearly calculation of the accumulated value of the mineral investment at an agreed upon minimum rate of discount, say 15 percent. During the exploration and construction periods, the annual present values will be negative, becoming positive in some future year following the initiation of production.

The resource-rent-tax is 'triggered' only when the accumulated present value of the investment becomes a positive figure. This amount is then taxed at a specified rate that will apply each year thereafter. (If there is a 'loss' in subsequent years, no taxes are levied until the accumulated present value again becomes positive.)

In Papua New Guinea's case, the resource-rent-tax prescribes that the foreign investor pay a corporate tax set initially at 35 percent, with a provision for deducting all capital expenditures from earnings at an annual rate of 25 percent.[41] According to Mikesell, there is also a provision for

a 70 percent excess profits tax, with excess profits in any tax year, calculated as the amount by which the accumulated present value of net cash receipts are equal to the sum of all sales proceeds and other receipts taken into account in determining taxable income less the sum of all capital expenditures and other payments that would be allowable deductions, except interest payments, plus the amount of normal corporate income tax actually paid in any tax year. Whenever the accumulated present value of the net cash receipts since the initial investments is positive, this amount will be taxed at 70 percent. The rate of accumulation at the option of the foreign investor is: a) 20 percent or b) the interest rate on Aaa domestic bonds, plus 10 percentage points . . . the choice made is binding during the term of the agreement.[42]

The resource-rent-tax attempts to take into account the metropolitan mining MNC's risk aversion, as well as the fluctuations in its costs and prices of fixed products. In essence, it is a profits tax that begins to be levied by the host government at a high rate when a certain threshold rate of return to investment has been realized by the MNC. Only if we naïvely assume that the discount rate used for calculating the present value of a mineral investment in any way begins accurately to represent the cost of capital could the approach be said to constitute an effective tax on differential rent. But I suggest that it does not.

The important advantage of the resource-rent-tax might, in fact, ultimately favour the metropolitan MNCs that operate in the Third World. From their standpoint, the advantage of this approach is that 'bargaining' over the distribution of benefits would be conducted on the basis of the 'discount cash flow' (DCF) method rather than the notion of an average rate of profit and rent.

Because the resource-rent-tax approach precisely caters to the metropolitan mining MNCs' notion of 'risk', different foreign operators in the Third World will apply different DCF rates, depending on their arbitrary and subjective definitions of the costs of capital and the risk of entrepreneurship. This very notion of risk, central in the resource-rent-tax approach, is what has historically made the task of calculating the true cost of capital (and, therefore, of capturing the full rent from mining) difficult or impossible for host governments with limited knowledge of the operations of international minerals industries.

Another problem is that this approach typically grants long tax holidays to the exploiting MNC. Not only is this a potentially unpopular political move in the Third World but, like an income tax, it would allow the MNC easily to shift excess profits to tax havens.

Also, as long as the accumulated present value of expenditures and receipts does not reach a positive figure, the resource-rent-tax approach does not allow the host government any minerals revenue.[43] Such a situation can exist even when corporate earnings, as a percentage of invested capital, are quite high. Moreover, the resource-rent-tax approach also requires a strong direct tax administration.

But the resource-rent-tax is less demanding of the host government's administrative resources than most taxes. And, since it is administratively similar to an income tax, any country with an income tax system can, practically, afford to employ it. Moreover, the resource-rent-tax can be combined with royalties, a practice that would yield some basic return to the host government until the accumulated present value of the stream of expenditures and earnings become positive. No doubt, the new resource-rent-tax approach has good potential for helping host governments capture mining rents; but its potential is yet to be fully appreciated and developed.

Another form of taxation in mining focuses on the value of the final product.

The 'tax on final product' approach was pioneered in Jamaica in an attempt to tax bauxite in proportion to the market value of aluminium. This bold measure was necessitated by the absence of an open price for bauxite.[44]

To the extent that the scarcity value of a mineral will ultimately express itself in the price of its final products, the levying of a tax in proportion to the value of the final product may help a landlord government to capture absolute rent. Especially if this tax can be uniformly applied by host governments, it can represent a meaningful way for them to share in some of the major benefits hitherto inaccessible to them.

The problem with this approach is, however, that like most existing tax systems in the Third World, while it might include some element of rent, it does so only very imprecisely and indirectly. Moreover, there is a wide range of final-product uses derivable from primary resources; and it would be difficult for a host government to determine the exact value of the relevant final product on which to base the tax. Furthermore, this approach is not yet likely to be efficient because of Third World governments' difficulty in acquiring relevant minerals industry information.

With respect to Third World minerals-related policy in general, and to taxation in particular, it is important to distinguish the concept of rent, as expounded in Chapter 2, from general taxation. As I have noted in this section, while a host government may impose a variety of taxes upon a foreign mineral operator as a means of collecting some or all of the excess surplus value in mining, such taxes are, in principle, different from the general taxes imposed upon industry and individuals in order to pay for the state's services. General income tax, designed to operate as a charge upon all income-producing activities conducted within the jurisdiction of the host government, is the most significant type of payment in the latter category.

In contrast, taxes aimed at rent collection must be seen as compensation to the landlord government for mining a publicly-owned asset, which is a depletable natural resource. Even though the two taxes are related, the point is that the collection of rent and the general taxation of a mining activity run by a foreign operator should be viewed separately.

An effective, long-term, articulation of this rent mentality requires courageous and committed nationalist leadership in the Third World. In a Third World resource regime informed by the rent-mentality, one would expect to find a tax system that is tuned as finely as possible to the appropriation of rent. The primary objective of such a regime would then be to fully tax potential differential rent (the difference between total revenue and total costs, including the payment of an average profit on the foreign capitalist's outlay).

The theoretical justification of a rent-mentality regime based on land-ownership is its emphasis on the full appropriation of an excess surplus value that it can collect without jeopardizing the operations of its mines. By allowing for a normal (average) profit for the mining capitalist, the regime would theoretically have ensured that the foreign investor's perceived risk is not increased beyond what it would be in the absence of taxation. The focus on a 'full tax on potential differential rent' is also economically justified.

This approach requires a strong, committed, and sophisticated direct administration and supervision. A Third World landlord regime that is imbued with the rent-mentality must have tax administrators and supervisors who understand and believe that while the foreign mining operator would prefer to receive any differential rent in addition to his average profits, satisfying this preference is not a necessary condition for obtaining his investment. Conceding all or part of the Third World's differential rent to the foreign mining operator would not induce him to invest more in a particular host country because, in order to have attracted the profit-oriented operator in the first place, his payment would have been fixed at the average profitable level at least.

One important problem that would practically confront a tax system aimed at appropriating the full potential differential rent from mining concerns would be ascertaining the applicable actual revenues and costs, including the average rate of profit. And since a host government is not likely to wait until the conclusion of a mining operation before calculating its differential rent (so that it would be in a better position to calculate revenues and costs), potential differential rent would have to be calculated on the basis of expected revenues and costs. With this approach the host government would probably face the usual problem of how to ascertain the fair supply price of capital, including the administrative nightmare of deciding which costs are deductible and which are not. Also, because revenues and costs must be estimated before all the characteristics of the host government's mineral deposits are fully known, the usual element of uncertainty would still exist.

Now, even though in general the amount of rent garnered by a Third World landlord government is not independent of the chosen tax methods, the primary objective of this discussion on taxation has been not to compare the relative merits of different methods, but rather to identify available forms of taxation, an important policy option on which Third World landlord governments have mostly focused their rent-appropriating efforts. In conclusion, if taxation is, generally, to become an effective policy option, an important task facing Third World landlord governments is how to design and coordinate their individual tax policies. Since governments that attract metropolitan mining MNCs by offering them very low tax rates are likely to be relinquishing their chances of appropriating rents, the importance of coordinating tax policies among Third World landlord governments is obvious.

Coordinating these tax policies can, however, be a herculean task because of typically limited knowledge of the minerals industry, widely heterogeneous economies and development priorities. It specifically demands that, as a group, either they ensure that individual host governments impose similar taxes on foreign operators and increase the taxes by roughly the same magnitude, or they prevent the foreign operators from shifting their sources of supply from higher to lower tax regimes by refusing to expand output in the higher tax regimes. However, standardization of tax conditions among Third World landlord governments (to avoid the shifting of supply by foreign mining operators by reason of tax advantage) has been shown, with OPEC countries as an example, to be achievable through the help of producers' associations. By passing a resolution in 1965 not to grant new oil rights to any petroleum companies operating in Libya that did not comply with that country's new decree relating to the calculation of taxes.[45] OPEC members successfully prevented those companies operating in Libya which refused to accept an increase in the tax rate in that country from shifting their output to other countries.

Third World Minerals Cartels

The final policy option considered here is the operation of minerals cartels by Third World landlord governments. Since OPEC's initial successful price increases over a decade ago, concern has been expressed about the possibility that other Third World producers' associations can, through cartelization, receive monopoly gains, or absolute rent. And while oil would probably not be the exception, we must understand that factors affecting the formation of successful cartels vary among minerals.

In general, three factors influence the potential of Third World landlord governments to benefit from cartelization: the degree to which their producers' associations dominate the market, substitution possibilities for their minerals, and the political problem of achieving cohesion and cooperation (see Chapters 4 and 5).

Briefly stated, the degree to which the producers' association dominates the market will partly determine the short-term supply elasticity of the mineral. Substitution possibilities determine the elasticity of demand as well as, in part, that of supply. The two factors together determine the producers' association's potential to exact monopoly charges, or absolute rent, through cartelization, that is, curtailing production in order to increase prices. And if there are considerable differences among Third World landlord governments (with respect to such basic factors as their ideological preferences, ore quality, size of minerals reserves, and foreign exchange reserves and expenditures) the political problem of achieving producer collusion will be equally difficult.

It is doubtful that the organization of successful minerals cartels is as possible for all Third World landlord governments as it earlier appeared to be for OPEC governments. Many important non-fuel minerals are produced by oligopolistic mining MNCs from the metropole, MNCs which also control the distribution of them. Advanced countries produce over 60 percent of the total output of major non-fuel minerals;[46] Third World landlord governments produce only a few. Even for copper and bauxite, where production is fairly concentrated in the Third World, new deposits can be brought into production fairly quickly. Substitutes are also more easily available for many non-fuel minerals than they are for petroleum. A Third World resource cartel for these minerals would require stringent production controls (which its members probably could not afford) if it is substantially to increase relative prices, and, therefore, absolute rent.

More fundamentally, successful cartelization by Third World landlord governments would require detailed and sophisticated knowledge of the world minerals industry and market. More precisely, successful cartelization will require the ability to determine the 'safe' price level at which the development of substitutes for a particular mineral or the opening up of new mines will no longer attract major consumers of the mineral. As a means of encouraging and maintaining group cohesion among Third World minerals exporting governments, it would also be useful if their producers' associations provided comprehensive analyses of the mining industries and markets in order to reveal the potential gains, if any, from cartelization. Until such knowledge becomes accumulated and used systematically by Third World landlord governments, the question of their exaction of absolute rent will remain an uncertain proposition.

This is not to argue that Third World producers' associations are not useful. On the contrary, while collusion is commonly appreciated only in terms of the ability of Third World producers' associations to operate successful cartels (to curtail minerals production in order to exact monopoly prices, or absolute rent), Third World producer cooperation may actually take at least three other major forms that are not necessarily restricted to the exaction of absolute rent. First, tax policies may be coordinated by host, landlord governments, either overtly or by price leadership, in order to facilitate individual host governments' appropriation of larger portions of differential rent. Second, landlord governments may exchange crucial minerals industry information as a precondition for individually making intelligent, rent-related decisions. And, third, landlord governments may coordinate joint research and development efforts in order to obtain the technological independence necessary to individually run their mines. Such independence will facilitate their ability to capture the full differential rent involved. To the extent that it is partly because of their ignorance about the minerals industries that the exaction of absolute rent is yet an uncertain proposition for Third World landlord governments, their cooperation in these areas, rather than their efforts at cartelization, *per se*, should, perhaps, receive their prior attention.

In this section, I have noted that the rent-maximizing options open to Third World minerals-exporting governments are limited. But even within these limited options their choices are rarely made on qualitative grounds alone. Because of the non-homogeneity of their development priorities, the perceptions of the benefits and costs associated with alternative means of tapping rents will differ from country to country and, because of periodic changes in government leadership, from time to time. It would, therefore, be difficult to prescribe an optimal rent-collecting approach applicable to all Third World landlord governments. The intention of the discussion so far has not, therefore, been to prescribe an optimal approach but to underline the limitedness of policy options.

Some general statements may, nevertheless, still be made by way of synthesizing the discussion here. First, without the authentic national ownership and operation of their mines, an important rent-appropriating problem facing Third World governments is the difficulty of identifying rent. It may, therefore, be desirable to rely on a royalty system, despite its drawbacks.

especially if used as a supplement to other forms of taxation. An important advantage of the royalty system may be its relative ease of administration and the stability of revenue it affords.

Second, the resource-rent-tax, despite its inherent tax holidays, may be combined with a specific royalty in the early years and still retain its advantage of encouraging exploration and development. Moreover, in principle, a resource-rent-tax can be operated by any country that has an income or profits tax system.

Third, a major factor limiting the exaction of rents by Third World governments is their relative lack of sophistication with respect to the complex details of the technology, management and marketing of their minerals. Production-sharing and contracting agreements may, therefore, be justified and encouraged, especially if temporarily adopted at a cautious pace as a means of ensuring government and domestic participation in the mining industry. Such participation can facilitate the accumulation of knowledge about the industry, the nation's mineral reserves, and its long-term needs and capacities for mineral exploration and exploitation, all crucial information for the identification and maximization of rent.

Fourth, Third World governments that attract foreign mining investors by offering them relatively lower tax rates are likely to be giving up the landlord's rents. The call for host governments to co-ordinate their tax policies and strategies is sound advice. Obviously, too, host governments need individually to develop and integrate their information-sharing and research and development activities. While there are yet few examples of such integrated activities by Third World governments, if focused well the activities can eliminate the basis of the high and uncertain costs presently associated with foreign operators in the mining sector.

Fifth, most Third World producers' associations would not be able to operate successful minerals cartels. But the importance of their potential function of disseminating information to landlord governments must not be overlooked.

Summary and Conclusion

This chapter was premised on the understanding that the essence of the so-called minerals crisis is the struggle between metropolitan mining MNCs (backed by their home governments) and Third World landlord governments over rent, the enormous surplus profit involved in international mining today. My contention is that, in this struggle, the power of the former far surpasses that of the latter.

Thus, the primary objective here was to underline the structural constraints facing Third World landlord governments with respect to appropriating mining rents in full. As I have noted, capitalist expansion and the manipulation of technological innovation are two important means that metropolitan mining capitalists have historically used to overcome the landlord's fetter, which they perceive from their dependence on natural resources. Against the expansive defensive strategies of large and powerful metropolitan mining MNCs, the chances of Third World landlord governments maximizing rent-collection in today's world are limited, as a review of some policy options that are open to them has revealed. To the extent that the chances of Third World governments to capture rents in full are limited, the metropolitan mining MNCs that dominate the capitalist exploitation of their rich mines are likely to be receiving above average, or super, profits, that is, including differential and absolute rents. These MNCs cannot, therefore, be considered to be in a real crisis situation today, since their super profits are not effectively threatened by the rent-maximizing, or producer, power of Third World landlord governments.

Notes

1. See Robin Murray, 'Value and Theory of Rent', *Capital and Class* 4, 1978, pp. 11–13 for a detailed presentation of this kind of argument in the case of contemporary agriculture.

2. For an introduction to the debate on the necessity of imperialism and capital accumulation on a world scale, see the following: Harry Magdoff, *The Age of Imperialism: The Economics of U.S. Foreign Policy* (Monthly Review Press, New York, 1969); Harry Magdoff, *Imperialism: From the Colonial Age to the Present* (Monthly Review Press, New York, 1978) chaps. 10 and 11; Al Szymanski, 'Capital Accumulation on a World Scale and the Necessity of Imperialism', *The Insurgent Sociologist* 7, no. 2, Spring 1977, pp. 35–53; S.M. Miller, Roy Bennett and Cyril Alapatt, 'Does the U.S. Economy Require Imperialism', *Social Policy* 1, no. 2, September–October 1970, pp. 13–19; and Heather Dean, 'Scarce Resources: The Dynamics of U.S. Imperialism', in K.T. Fann and Donald C. Hodges (eds.) *Readings in U.S. Imperialism* (P. Sargent Publishers, Boston, 1971) chap. 9.

3. This is similar to what Murray terms 'founder's rent', following Hilferding's concept of 'founder's benefit'. Murray, 'Value and Theory of Rent', p. 13.

4. *Ibid.*

5. *Ibid.*

6. *Ibid.*

7. *Ibid.*

8. *Ibid.*

9. *Ibid.*

10. *Ibid.*

11. For a good account of the impact of the compradorial role of elements of the ruling class of an important Third World landlord government, see Terisa Turner, 'Nigeria: Imperialism, Oil Technology and the Comprador State', in Petter Nore and Terisa Turner (eds.) *Oil and Class Struggle* (Zed Press, London, 1980) chap. 10.

12. This is because any extension of capital and its attendant social relations will also require the extension of landed property. Marx's account of Mr. Peel's experience at Swan River testifies to this phenomenon. Capital, in surpassing landed property by territorial expansion, is forced to create it anew on 'new land'. Capital thus acts, in a sense, as a vanguard for the territorial expansion of landed property.

13. For an account of the significance of metropolitan engineering firms in the copper industry, see Dorothea Mezger, *Copper in the World Economy* (Monthly

Review Press, New York, 1980) pp. 70–3.

14. See Surrendra Patel, 'The Technological Dependence of Developing Countries', *The Journal of Modern African Studies* 12, no. 1, 1974, p. 9.

15. *Ibid.*, pp. 10–11.

16. *Ibid.*, p. 12.

17. *Ibid.*, p. 13.

18. See Helen Hughes, 'Economic Rents, the Distribution of Gains from Mineral Exploitation, and Mineral Development Policy', *World Development* 3, nos. 11, 12, 1975, pp. 814–15.

19. *Ibid.*

20. *Ibid.*

21. *Ibid.*

22. *Ibid.*

23. See Ross Garnaut and Anthony Clunies Ross, 'Relationships Between Governments and Mining Investors', *Materials and Society* 5, no. 4, 1981, p. 442.

24. *Ibid.*

25. Hughes, 'Economic Rents', p. 817.

26. David N. Smith, 'Information Sharing and Bargaining: Institutional Problems and Implications', in Gerald Garvey and Lou Ann Garvey (eds.), *International Resource Flows*, D.C. Heath and Co., Lexington, Mass. 1977, p. 88.

27. David N. Smith, 'New Eyes for Old: The Future, Present and Past in the Evolution of Mineral Agreements', *Materials and Society* 5, no. 4, 1981, p. 419.

28. *Ibid.*

29. *Ibid.*

30. Zuhayr Mikdashi, 'Cooperation Among Oil Exporting Countries with Special Reference to Arab Countries', *International Organization* 28, no. 1, Winter 1975, pp. 24–5.

31. Gobind Nankani, *Development Problems of Mineral-Exporting Countries* (The World Bank, Washington, 1979) p. 91.

32. Hughes, 'Economic Rents', p. 820.

33. See Raymond Mikesell, 'Options for Packaging Agreements to Meet Host Government and Foreign Investor Financial Goals', *Materials and Society* 5, no. 4, 1981, p. 453. According to him, more recently, the PERTAMANIA contracts with U.S. contractors were revised so that the foreign contractor pays Indonesian income tax on his own net earnings in order to meet the U.S. Treasury Department's conditions for the creditability of foreign taxes against tax liabilities. The Peruvian government's production-sharing agreements have also been renegotiated to provide for payment, by the foreign contractor, of his Peruvian tax liabilities.

34. Hughes, 'Economic Rents', p. 820.

35. Mikesell, 'Options for Packaging Agreements', p. 453; my emphasis.

36. The best of the rather new and scant literature on the important subject of taxation in the minerals industries includes the following: Malcolm Gillis *et al.*, *Taxation and Mining: Nonfuel Minerals in Bolivia and Other Countries* (Ballinger Publishing Co., Cambridge, Mass., 1978); Malcolm Gillis and Ralph E. Beals, *Tax and Investment Policies for Hard Minerals: Public and Multinational Enterprises in Indonesia* (Ballinger Publishing Co., Cambridge, Mass., 1980); Craig Emerson, 'Taxing Natural Resource Projects', *Natural Resources Forum* 4, no. 2, April 1980, pp. 123–45; George Polanyi, 'The Taxation of Profits from Middle East Oil Production: Some Implications for Oil Prices and Taxation Policy', *The Economic*

Journal 76, no. 304, December 1966, pp. 768–85; Robert L. McGeorge, 'Approaches to State Taxation of the Mining Industry', *Natural Resources Journal* 10, no. 1, 1970, pp. 156–70; Ross Garnaut and Anthony Clunies Ross, 'Uncertainty, Risk Aversion and the Taxing of Natural Resources Projects', *The Economic Journal* 85, no. 338, 1975, pp. 272–87; and Charles J. Johnson, 'Taking the Take But Not the Risk', *Materials and Society* 5, no. 4, 1981, pp. 455–69.

37. Hughes, 'Economic Rents', p. 818.

38. Nankani, *Development Problems*, p. 90.

39. *Ibid.*, p. 91.

40. See Ross Garnaut and Anthony Clunies Ross, 'A New Tax for Natural Resource Projects', in Michael Crommelin and Andrew R. Thompson (eds.) *Mineral Leasing as an Instrument of Public Policy* (University of British Columbia Press, Vancouver, 1974) pp. 78–91; and Ross Garnaut and Anthony Clunies Ross, 'Neutrality of the Resource Rent Tax', *The Economic Record* 55, no. 150, September 1979, pp. 193–201.

41. Mikesell, 'Options for Packaging Agreements', p. 451.

42. *Ibid.*, pp. 451–3.

43. *Ibid.*, p. 451. See also Emerson, 'Taxing Natural Resource Projects'.

44. Nankani, *Development Problems*, p. 92.

45. According to Mikesell, 'The Libyan government's decree of November 30, 1965 required that profits be computed on the basis of "posted prices" less discounts agreed upon rather than on "realized prices" as was provided under the concession agreements with the petroleum companies. In addition, royalties were to be treated as an expense and not as a credit against income taxes. Since the new Libyan legislation violated the contracts with the petroleum companies, some of the companies failed to comply with the law. OPEC's action apparently helped induce the companies to comply.' See Raymond Mikesell, *Nonfuel Minerals: U.S. Investment Policies Abroad* (Sage Publications, Beverly Hills, 1975) pp. 91–2.

46. Alexander Sutulov, *Minerals in World Affairs* (The University of Utah Printing Services, Salt Lake City, 1972) p. 49.

3. Absolute Rent and the Limited Prospects of Third World Producers' Associations

Introduction

The Marxian rent approach is very useful for appreciating the pattern that the distribution of the wealth from international mining could, theoretically, assume in today's world. First, if Third World landlord governments had an absolute monopoly in today's world minerals industries, *vis-à-vis* metropolitan minerals-consuming countries and their mining MNCs, these governments would be in a position to exact a monopoly charge, or absolute rent, on the increasing global demand for their minerals. Second, if competition among metropolitan mining MNCs were freely allowed, and if Third World landlord governments authentically controlled the crucial production facilities and expertise needed today they could capture the excess surplus profits from their mines as differential rents.

This and the following chapter discuss the limited prospects for Third World producers' associations as related to absolute rent in contemporary world mining. The underlying thesis is that these prospects are limited because Third World landlord governments do not have an absolute monopoly over minerals, and cannot operate effective minerals cartels for any reasonable length of time.

In this era of Third World economic nationalism, producers' associations are the most important and visible international symbol of the influence of modern landed property in today's world mining business. In view of the asymmetry and exploitation that have historically characterized relationships between Third World landlord governments and metropolitan mining MNCs and their home governments, these producers' associations may be seen as cooperative efforts by landlord governments to develop, as a group, countervailing measures that would allow them to capture increasing shares of the surplus profits, or absolute rent, in mining today. However, for these governments whose economies vary immensely in basic attributes and expectations, the inherent political problem of achieving producer cooperation can be compounded.

Heterogeneity: The Basic Difficulty with Cooperating

An important political barrier to cooperation among producers' associations'

members is their ideological heterogeneity. Considerable ideological homogeneity and other shared goals can be helpful in arriving at agreements on
prices and on principles of market allocations. Members must also have a
political consensus on general and specific views regarding matters of foreign
policy (especially *vis-à-vis* industrialized minerals-consuming countries and
their large MNCs) if they are to take effective concerted action.

Attempts by governments of ideologically diverse nations to take collusive
action in producers' associations are likely to fail if they lack shared political
perspectives. In the case of OPEC, political diversity and lack of shared
perspectives seriously inhibited effective cooperation among its member
governments in the first decade of the organization's existence.[1] The
governments of Indonesia, Iran, Kuwait and Saudi Arabia, the original
founders of OPEC, share few political values and perspectives; and lacking
trust and agreement, OPEC members today still internally dispute market
shares.

Ideological homogeneity among members of producers' associations in the
non-fuel minerals sphere is even less likely than among OPEC members.
Copper is, for example, produced in large quantities in the United States,
Canada, Chile, Zambia, Zaire, and Peru. It would be difficult to imagine a
more disparate collection of polities than these if their governments were all in
the same producers' association. And while the governments of the latter four
countries which are members of a Third World producers' association do meet
regularly to talk about copper prices, there is little likelihood of a real
cooperative effort among them to raise prices significantly. In fact, their
organization, like OPEC, has been most effective in conducting studies and
disseminating information, not in concerted actions to raise prices.[2]

Similar political ideologies and cultures might facilitate communications
and exchange of information among members of producers' associations, as
well as help convince more governments to join, and therefore strengthen
cooperation within existing associations.

Mutual understanding and unity of purpose are also political factors
relevant for cooperation in Third World producers' associations. Unity can be
provided by shared historical experiences or by shared perceptions of the
advanced countries as the common enemy of landlord governments. Or, in the
absence of such unity, an external factor may act as a catalyst that will
neutralize initial disagreements in the group.[3]

The Arab–Israeli conflict provided such a catalyst in the case of OPEC, a
catalyst which helped overcome existing mistrust within the group. There is
little doubt that the community of Arab governments, expressed institutionally
and politically in the Arab League and OAPEC,[4] played an important role in
cementing the platform necessary for the successful actions taken by OPEC,
because they agreed that the United States (and the industrialized world in
general) was their common enemy, in view of U.S. pro-Israeli foreign policy.
Petroleum was, therefore, first withheld from selected industrial countries by
OPEC for political, rather than economic reasons. And the crisis atmosphere,
and the divisions and weaknesses that the embargo revealed in the

industrialized world, contributed to the rapid implementation of a new price structure in the world petroleum market that would have been impossible without years of protracted bickering between OPEC members and their industrialized customers.[5] A new price structure having been established, and the economic pay offs (increased shares of absolute rent) having become clear to all participants, the new-found 'OPEC solidarity' appeared firmly established.

Whether or not there are similar external factors that can act as a catalyst in producers' associations in the non-fuel minerals markets is purely speculative. At present, it does not appear that the level of trust among members of such organizations is high.[6]

The recognition of mutual self-interest among members of a Third World producers' association is a third political factor that can facilitate collusion. Mutual feelings or beliefs that their economies and polities have the same destinies are essential for cooperation. For Third World landlord governments, whose economies are mono-cultural, agreeing to restrict production in order to raise prices represents a potentially risky course of action. Without perceived common interests, it would be difficult for such governments to take such risks within producers' associations because simply by breaking ranks, any one member can maximize short-run gains and make long-term arrangements at the expense of others. This point is especially relevant for Third World landlord governments whose economies are at various levels of economic development, and who may, therefore, very well perceive their interests to be mutually antagonistic, rather than congruent.

In general, the political problem of achieving cooperation among members of Third World producers' associations will be great if there are significant differences among them with respect to basic conditions and expectations. While most of their economies do share certain similarities and historical experiences (that is, their forceful incorporation into the world capitalist economy and their poverty), they vary immensely with respect to the sizes of their populations, extent of minerals endowment, stage of minerals exploitation, the level of human resource development, and the sophistication of economic and social infrastructure. Effective cooperation among the governments of such heterogeneous economies is likely to be problematic.

Third World Landlord Government Cartels?

The assumption of a closed economy in Marx's treatment of absolute rent, where there existed a general and effective landlord's monopoly over land, is not valid in contemporary international political economy. Moreover, Third World landlord governments, unlike the English landed gentry that Marx had observed, do not constitute an organized class with a clear perception of a common political goal based on their recognition of an identity of interests arising from land ownership.

Unlike the monopoly power that Marx ascribed to the English landlords in his exposition of rent theory, the power of Third World landlord governments, that is, modern landed property, is limited with respect to the exaction of absolute rent on the increasing global demand for their minerals. This tendency can be appreciated by revealing the very limited prospects of Third World landlord governments to operate successful minerals cartels in their producers' associations.

Above all, it is important to understand that, conceptually, Third World producers' associations are not cartels *per se*, in the classical sense of the term. Their description, by most observers, as production-curtailing and price-raising institutions capable of dislocating the normal operations of the world capitalist economy (of which they are actually a peripheral appendage) naïvely obscures the very limited producer, or rent-exacting, power of these landlord governments in today's world. It is this limitation I want to underline in this chapter.

Attempts at operating cartels have arisen periodically in many industries throughout the 20th Century. In 1975, one study identified as many as 51 cartel agreements in 18 industries involved in international commodity trade.[7] Briefly defined, a cartel, in the classical sense, is a group of commercial enterprises that agree to control the prices, production, or marketing of a commodity in order to restrict competition and maximize collective profits.

While efforts at cartelization are not new to the metal industries, what is new today is that governments of the major mineral-exporting countries are now interested in setting up producers' associations.[8] And whether or not Third World producers' associations express any of the above mentioned goals of a typical cartel, they have nevertheless been broadly perceived as cartels, especially by the advanced countries. Three factors can be identified that have contributed to this misplaced fear of the threat of cartelization by Third World producers' associations.[9]

First, following the Arab–Israeli War of 5 October, 1973, oil-exporting governments within OPEC were able unilaterally to raise the price of Persian Gulf crude oil by almost 400 percent during the last quarter of 1973. This price increase, which actually had little to do with OPEC's monopoly power, produced a tremendous boost in the interests and expectations of other non-fuel minerals-exporting governments to form OPEC-type organizations, and therefore increased concerns in the advanced minerals-consuming countries about the threat of possible cartel action by these Third World governments.

Second, following the widespread news about shortages in 1973, including studies like the Club of Rome's *Limits to Growth*,[10] which focused attention on the finiteness of resources, governments in exporting countries became more convinced that they held valuable depletable resources over which they might extract greater gains, in the form of absolute rent, from the consuming countries. The impact of this news about minerals scarcity encouraged the formation of producers' associations as a symbol of their newly discovered power, which further increased fears in the industrialized world about cartel action by Third World landlord governments.

Third, increased concern about Third World cartels also derived from the initiatives and rhetoric of Third World governments to introduce a new international economic order, where, hopefully, the minerals-exporting governments would be receiving much higher returns for their exports. An obvious symbolism in this movement towards a new world order was the increased effort to form producers' associations, which, in the consuming countries, were generally described and feared as cartels.

It is important to understand, however, that the nature of agreements among governments of nation-states is very different from that among competing commercial firms.[11] Whereas, in the case of the latter, a model of a rational economic man seeking to maximize profits appears to be an adequate basis of analysis, in the former, assumptions about economic rationality are often not enough, and political factors seem to be emphasized instead. OPEC, the forerunner of Third World producers' associations, itself provides a good example of the significance of the political factor in agreements among nations. For example, it was the political conflict in the Middle East in late 1973 that led to OPEC's oil embargo, which facilitated OPEC's so-called success in raising the price of oil in the first place, and which later encouraged the formation of OPEC-type, Third World, producers' associations in the bauxite, copper, iron-ore, mercury, tin, and tungsten industries.

There are differences of opinion as to the extent to which the so-called OPEC success at cartelization can be emulated by other Third World producers' associations. Some writers have pointed to a number of factors in international politics and economics to conclude that OPEC will be the forerunner of the movement towards a new international economic order, featuring a variety of Third World, non-fuel cartels aimed at destroying the existing international capitalist system of imperialism.[12] Others have pointed to different forces, also operating in the international political economy, that have historically broken up cartel arrangements and they have expressed scepticism about the possibilities for Third World governments to cooperate, for a substantial length of time, in any OPEC-like operations.[13] While the latter conclusion is, from my point of view, more correct, both analyses are wrong because of their common assumption that Third World producers' associations are cartels. In some cases, a Third World producers' association may indirectly and temporarily, at best, have the effect of a cartel but, conceptually, it must *not* be considered as a cartel in the classical sense.

In the interest of forming meaningful policy, there is a need to clarify and to emphasize that, conceptually, Third World producers' associations are not cartels. In particular, there is a need to demonstrate that even OPEC, the supposed forerunner of Third World cartels, is itself not a cartel. Before discussing the general limitations of Third World producers' associations in the non-fuel sector to operate as cartels, I will first summarize the essence of the notion of collusion according to cartel theory, and then relate this notion to OPEC's case in order to argue that that organization was not, and is not likely to be, an effective cartel.

Non-collusion within OPEC

Cartel theorists have made some generalizations about the complex requirements and costs of forming and policing a collusion.[14] First, the larger the number of sellers in a cartel, the more difficult it would be for them to agree on the price structure and the greater the probability that cheating would not be detected; it would also be difficult for the cartel to know, and to penalize, just who is chiselling. On the other hand, if the number of sellers in a cartel is relatively small, the influence of the action of any individual member on the rest of the cartel members would be greater. The probability of chiselling would be reduced if the members of a cartel recognized interdependence among themselves; violations of cartel agreements could be easily detected and the chiseller punished, or members could have his net gain eliminated by themselves resorting to cheating.

Second, the more complex the industry's product structure, the greater would be the chances of disagreement on price structures among sellers. If, however, the elasticity of substitution between any pairs of a firm's products is infinite, product differentiation would become impossible, and the only way an individual producer could increase his net return would, under the circumstances, be to collude with others — an automatic cartel situation. The homogeneity of a cartel's product is an important prerequisite for collusion to take place among its members, especially if the costs of collusion are not prohibitive and if the number of sellers in the cartel is not large.

Third, the larger the number of buyers of the cartel's product, the more difficult it would be for any one seller in the cartel to increase his share of the market (through advertising, price reductions, product improvement, credit terms, etc.), without the knowledge of other members of the cartel. In general, cheating by cartel members would be harder to detect and punish, given fewer and larger buyers of the cartel's product.

Fourth, customers' loyalty to sellers within a cartel can be an important cost factor in collusion among cartel members. The less erratic the shift of customers among sellers in the cartel, the easier it would be to detect chiselling, and the smaller would be the chances of competitive price cutting among cartel members.

In summary, the essence of the cartel model is this: if the benefits of collusion are perceived to be greater than the costs, collusion will occur among cartel members; if the costs of collusion are perceived to be greater than the benefits, then competition would prevail among them. Every collusive agreement, whether in perfect form or made through an implicit understanding, will create at least two problems for a cartel. First, there would be an external problem of how to predict, and if possible discourage, production by non-members. Second, there would be an internal problem of how to share the net gains from collusion and how to prevent these gains from falling to zero as a result of the potentially high costs of policing cheaters among cartel members.[15]

An ideal cartel would establish a monopoly price and rate of product output that would maximize the wealth of the entire group of sellers or producers in the cartel. When each member of an organization has completely surrendered his power and functions to make management decisions to a joint sales agency, one may speak of a perfect collusion, or what is sometimes referred to as a centralized cartel.

Perfect collusions, however, especially among governments of nation-states, are rare and problematic. There are important differences between commercial enterprises' and governments' prospects at cartelization that are not usually emphasized in the literature that treats Third World producers' associations as cartels. For example, decisions regarding the sharing of production and surplus revenues gained through collusion can be made more difficult in the case of governments of nation-states, as political entities, than in the case of firms controlling known shares in a well-understood market. In the case of commercial firms, collusion most often takes place among established firms familiar with, and knowledgeable about, others who join in the collusive activities. This is crucial because predictability of the behaviour of others is essential in appreciating the risks involved in cartel action; if there is little confidence that other firms will abide by cartel agreements, it would be futile to even initiate any kind of market-sharing arrangements among the cartel's members.

Those who, in 1973, predicted that OPEC would immediately crumble were most likely considering the inherent difficulties of reaching agreements on profit-sharing and production quotas in such an organization composed of diverse nations. It must have been apparent to them that, especially in that case (an organization of nation-states), individual members would not likely be willing to surrender their economic and political decisions (their new found 'sovereignty') to the OPEC organization.

It is important to underline that because of the difficult task of collusion characteristic of cartels, the emergence and survival of OPEC, a Third World producers' association, suggests that the organization is something other than a typical cartel. Whatever gains it is supposedly making today are, therefore, not a function of its collusive activities or its elimination of competition.

One reason why OPEC cannot be said to be an effective cartel is because it has not succeeded in setting output quotas for its members. In fact, all attempts within OPEC towards production-quota and demand prorationing were abandoned in the early 1960s, long before the organization became thought of as 'an effective cartel', that is, one that eliminated competition in the world oil market. Oil-exporting governments could not find a satisfactory method for fixing output quotas. While Venezuela, then the largest exporter within OPEC, wanted to use historical levels of output as the base for setting output quotas, Iran preferred population, and Saudi Arabia and Kuwait favoured proven reserves.[16] OPEC does not now stipulate output quotas for its members, even though, when compared with its historical levels, output within the organization is certainly being restricted (to keep the price at its current levels).[17]

The only time oil-exporting governments within OPEC agreed to act in concert to reduce output was in the last three months of 1973, following the 5

October 1973, Arab–Israeli war. On 5 November 1973, the OAPEC members of OPEC declared that they would cut their oil outputs by 25 percent of their September 1973 levels, and by 5 percent each successive month until they realized their political objectives.[18] It is, however, important to note that the non-Arab members of OPEC did not participate in the output reductions and that output in Iran, Indonesia, and Nigeria actually rose during the Arab oil embargo. Moreover, the actual reductions by OAPEC were far less than their declared targets. As compared to their output levels during September 1973 (the month immediately preceding the three-month embargo period from October through December 1973), the production levels of the OAPEC members of OPEC actually fell by only 17.5 percent, instead of by 35 percent as planned. And, with respect to OPEC as a whole, production during the embargo only fell, on the average, by about 8 percent from the organization's September 1973 level.[19]

It is almost certain that without the emotional atmosphere associated with the Arab–Israeli war, any collective efforts to reduce outputs by oil-exporting governments would have failed. Moreover, other factors external to OPEC's monopoly power were responsible for even this example of a limited collusive action by OPEC's Arab oil exporters. First, so-called 'independents' and newcomers (Phillips, AMOCO, Occidental and the state-owned companies of France, Italy, and Japan) emerged as important buyers of crude oil and threatened the monopoly power of the 'majors' that dominated the oil industry, encouraging the governments of oil-exporting countries to challenge them. Second, the tightness of the oil market in the 1970–73 period (caused by actual demand being greater than projected demand), had reduced the chances that the oil companies would be able to unite and to boycott OPEC oil at that time. For example, while, in 1954, the oil companies that were nationalized in Iran were able to enlist the support of other members of the 'Seven Sisters' in blackmailing Iranian crude oil (resulting in the overthrow of the Mossadegh regime), by the early 1970s, oil buyers had increased in number, with relatively more divergent interests that did not allow them to frustrate oil-exporting governments' attempts to control their own natural resources.[20]

In other words, the so-called OPEC success in the early 1970s was facilitated by unique structural changes in the international oil industry during that period. Even though these changes had greatly enhanced the oil-exporting governments' perception of their producer power *vis-à-vis* oil MNCs, the effects of the changes were short-lived. By the winter of 1975–76, the companies had recovered their influence and control of the prices at which they purchased oil from host governments.[21]

Another reason why OPEC cannot be considered a cartel is because its pricing policies are not binding on its members. Some writers describe OPEC as a cartel because it meets periodically to 'fix' prices. But, even when, in 1973, the organization finally established the right to set oil prices 'unilaterally', that is, without 'negotiations' with the oil companies, it did not compel its individual members to abide by its pricing decisions.

OPEC's periodic meetings to set prices are not unique in Third World producers' associations, for the exporters of many other raw materials meet regularly to set prices, but the mere setting of prices is not enough to ensure that such prices will prevail. Indeed, today, most OPEC governments charge prices different from those officially announced periodically by OPEC. Moreover, unlike a cartel, there are no rewards for abiding by the organization's so-called official prices, no penalties are imposed for violating them, and no side-payments of any kind are made to prevent members from departing from the organization's 'official' prices. And while some Arab members of OPEC have been known to make payments to Syria, Egypt, and Jordan, none of these countries is a member of OPEC. Furthermore, the pricing decisions are made, not by a central agency, as would have been the case if OPEC were a cartel, but by OPEC's oil ministers[22] (perhaps the most influential comprador elements in the oil-exporting countries) who represent their various governments.

If, as some writers have argued, OPEC became an effective cartel in October 1973, one would also expect that it would reduce its members' output during periods of market weakness to maintain an optimal cartel price. Records from 1974 to 1977, however, show that output during 1974 (when the market was strong and clearly qualified as a seller's market) actually expanded. The governments of six OPEC member countries (Saudi Arabia, Iraq, Libya, Indonesia, United Arab Emirates, and Algeria) produced roughly 50 percent of OPEC's total output, expanding production so much so that their market shares increased from 52.2 percent to 58.8 percent of OPEC's production. And, in that same period, the OPEC governments of Kuwait, Iran, Venezuela, Nigeria, Ecuador, Gabon, and Qatar reduced output such that their market shares declined from 47.8 percent to 41.2 percent of OPEC's total output.[23] This pattern is not the kind of record one would expect to find in an effectively collusive cartel.

OPEC country output and market shares can also be divided into 'saver countries' and 'spender countries'.[24] The governments of saver countries (Saudi Arabia, Kuwait, Libya, and the United Arab Emirates) have less immediate need for cash and, therefore, consider future revenues more heavily in calculating the equity value of their resources. They also possess rather large reserves of oil so that resource depletion is less of a constraint for them. The governments of OPEC's spender countries have, on the other hand, a greater immediate need for cash and thus value current revenues more heavily. These countries include Algeria, Ecuador, Iran, Nigeria, and Venezuela, countries whose smaller oil reserves may begin to run out in the not-too-distant future. This dichotomy within OPEC's membership causes conflict regarding their best output or pricing strategy.

If OPEC were a cartel, one would expect that its saver countries would be willing to bear the burden of output reductions, so that spender countries could maintain or increase their levels of output. However, the governments of OPEC saver countries in fact expanded output and market shares at the expense of the spender countries. In 1974, these saver countries together produced over 14 million barrels of oil per day, and their market share within OPEC was 46.3 percent; by 1977 their daily output had increased to over 15 million barrels and their market share to 48.9 percent. On the other hand, the governments of the spender countries within OPEC produced 13.8 million barrels of oil per day and held 44.9 percent of OPEC's market shares in 1974; by 1977 their daily output had dropped to just 13 million barrels and their market share to 41.7 percent.[25] Again, this record does not correspond to standard models of collusive behaviour; there is no evidence that OPEC coordinated control over output, with constant market shares, between 1974 and 1977.

It has often been said that OPEC is a cartel because Saudi Arabia is its price leader. The significance of the price leadership model in cartel theory is that the large firm is aware of its economic power and would exploit it, through price leadership, in the interest of all the cartel's members.

According to this model, the Saudi Arabian government would set what it considers to be an optimal price while the smaller oil-exporting governments within OPEC would sell as much as they want at that price. But, neither the behaviour of the Saudi Arabian government nor that of the other oil-exporting governments confirms the predictions of the price leadership model in OPEC. Moreover, if the Saudi Arabian government were able to set the OPEC oil price, that price could be expected to serve mainly the interests of that government, not those of all the other OPEC members, as would be expected of a centralized cartel composed of commercial firms.

Even if Saudi Arabia were, indeed, more interested in high oil prices than other smaller oil exporters, its government would have to bear the brunt of OPEC's output cutbacks (to allow these other oil-exporters to expand output without causing severe gluts or price reductions in the market) and would, obviously, not be able to pursue such a benevolent policy indefinitely. The point is that models of price leadership in a dominant firm are, in cartel theory, strictly short-run analyses. Besides, conceptually, the Saudi Arabian government would find it difficult, if not impossible, to perform as a price leader in OPEC if its government were more interested in higher prices than the smaller oil exporters.

But OPEC is not a cartel, and the government of Saudi Arabia is not its price leader. While that government does, indeed, have some power significantly to influence the world oil price (for example, about 12 million barrels were produced daily between 1974 and 1977), it has not used this power to increase oil prices, but rather to avert increases, or at best keep them as small as possible.[26] If, during that period, that government had been interested in dramatic price increases, or in at least preventing price reductions, it would have reduced its outputs when the market was weak, while allowing all other smaller OPEC governments to expand theirs if they wished.[27] On the contrary, however, over time, the Saudi Arabian government has increased its absolute oil output as well as its market share both within OPEC and in the total world market. For example, in 1974, the government's daily oil output was about 8.5 million barrels and its share of OPEC's market was 28 percent; by 1977, however, its daily output had increased to 9.2 million barrels and its share of OPEC's market to 30 percent.[28]

In fact, as one writer has pointed out, in the early days of OPEC, no government within the organization doubted that the Saudi Arabian government would be more interested in increasing its output to the level that would make price rises impossible. And, as expected, throughout 1976, when most OPEC members wanted to raise the price of oil from its 1975 levels, the Saudi Arabian government refused, instead increasing its rate of production by 21 percent from its 1975 levels, so as effectively to frustrate any such price increases by other oil-exporters in OPEC.[29] Also, in autumn 1978, when the Iranian revolution resulted in cutbacks in oil output, the price of oil rose sharply. The Saudi Arabian government then raised its oil output from an announced target of 8.5 million barrels per day, obviously in order to avoid price increases.[30] By the beginning of the 1980s, however, the government seemed to have lost most of its power, probably, according to Johany, because it could not afford to increase its rate of output beyond 10 million barrels per day without causing serious damage to its oil fields.[31]

So far, I have argued here that OPEC is not a cartel, that is, an organization whose primary role is to restrict oil output in order to raise prices for its members. Even though substantial absolute rents are created in the oil industry, OPEC, a Third World producers' association, has not, therefore, been able to establish and sustain systematic, long-term, price increases and to capture these rents for its landlord member governments.

Most of the so-called OPEC success is, in fact, related to the existence of vertically integrated companies in the oil industry who make it possible for the oil-exporting governments to increase their oil revenues by raising taxes on the international oil firms. These companies, in turn, pass on the increased taxes to consumers in the form of higher prices. This 'OPEC approach' had made it unnecessary for its members to reach agreements on production or export quotas (except, of course, as was noted earlier, in October 1973 when limited restrictions were imposed by the Arab members within OPEC for largely political reasons). Hence, the international oil firms have been called 'OPEC's tax collectors' by one notable oil industry expert.[32]

According to Adelman, OPEC sets its price by raising its member governments' taxes on metropolitan oil firms per barrel of oil. Those taxes, like all excise taxes, are treated as a cost and become a floor to price. Without this OPEC tax system, Adelman argues, the 'cartel' would crumble because

> the floor to price would then be not the tax-plus-cost, but only bare cost. The producing nations would need to set and obey production quotas. Otherwise, they would inevitably chisel and bring prices down by selling incremental amounts at discount prices. Each seller nation would be forced to chisel to retain markets because it could no longer be assured of the collaboration of all the other sellers. Every cartel has in time been destroyed by one then some members chiseling and cheating; without the instrument of the multinational companies and the cooperation of the consuming countries, OPEC would be an ordinary cartel.[33]

Adelman suggests that vertical integration in the oil industry enables the oil-exporting governments to increase their revenues; this factor clearly explains the survival of OPEC. I agree with his argument. However, Adelman, like most economists, was wrong, conceptually, in assuming OPEC to be a cartel.

The point is that despite 'the instrument of the multinational companies and the cooperation of the consuming countries', nothing bars any sovereign government member of OPEC from simply reducing its tax rate by an incremental amount. Since oil price is high, the OPEC member faces a highly elastic demand curve and can increase its revenues by instituting a small tax reduction. While it is certainly true that an oil company will not reduce the selling price of oil if a large percentage of that price represents OPEC countries' taxes, there is nothing to prevent an oil-exporting sovereign government within OPEC from reducing its tax rate in order to increase its market share.[34]

Moreover, despite the opportunity to tax metropolitan oil companies, oil-exporting governments in OPEC still face a serious problem: that metropolitan oil firms will shift their production and investment facilities from high-taxing host countries to lower-taxing areas. The oil MNCs can accomplish this move unless OPEC members prevent them by fixing, or increasing, their formerly various taxes by roughly the same amount. Apart from OPEC's gesture in 1965 (by passing a resolution that its members not grant new oil rights to petroleum companies operating in Libya that did not comply with that government's new decree relating to the calculation of taxes), apparently no further efforts have been made systematically to standardize taxes among OPEC members for this purpose. Above all, it is important to bear in mind that, commendable as the OPEC approach is (from the point of view of the organization's survival), it nevertheless constitutes an income tax system which, as was pointed out in the previous chapter, is not designed to maximize either differential or absolute rent.

Finally, in addition to vertical integration in the oil industry, OPEC's survival may also be attributed to factors external to OPEC, including a high concentration of world petroleum production in the OPEC countries, an inelastic demand for the product, and a high rate of growth in world demand for petroleum. This unique combination of conditions is not exactly approximated in any producers' association organized by Third World governments in the non-fuel minerals industries. Nevertheless, in attempting to estimate the potential, or actual, impact of Third World producers' associations in the non-fuel minerals industries, economists have tended to use OPEC as a model,[35] and wrongly view these newer organizations as price-raising, output-restricting, cartels, albeit constituted by nation-states, not private firms.

On the whole, the political and economic differences between OPEC-member governments would make it difficult, if not impossible, for OPEC to act as a central cartel with the power to set prices and allocate production quotas while effectively monitoring violators of such agreements. According to an informed oil industry analyst, OPEC's primary function has been the collection of technical and economic data.[36] And while substantial absolute rents are created in the oil industry, OPEC's prices are not the kind of 'monopoly prices' that would enable its member governments efficiently to capture this form of surplus profits.

But the above observation is not meant to suggest that OPEC, a Third World producers' association, is useless. On the contrary, the organization's function of collecting technical and economic data may, in the long run, be an important factor that will enhance the chances of individual OPEC landlord governments to capture increasing shares of both absolute and differential rents. Also, OPEC must be commended for its relative longevity that is unlike a cartel. And, from the standpoint of individual landlord governments, the political clout they enjoy via membership in a renowned and symbolic international institution such as OPEC must not be discounted.

Above all, compared to Third World producers' associations in the non-fuel minerals sphere, the OPEC organization (with the better prospects for cartelization) has the better potential for capturing significant shares of absolute rents for its member governments. But before I discuss the more limited prospects of cartelization by Third World producers' associations in the nonfuel minerals sphere, it would be useful first to underline the point that, because of OPEC's weakness as a cartel, the surplus profit from oil is not the prerogative only of the oil-exporting governments to capture.

The Distribution of the Surplus Profit (Absolute Rent) from OPEC's Oil

In the context of the world energy market, crude oil represents only one source of energy, measured in calories. Because of capitalist value formation, it is the marginal production of energy — not of oil — that determines the final price of oil to the consumer. In other words, the price of oil to the final consumer will be above the individual price of production (cost price plus the average profit) of oil in the world, but equal to the price of production of the marginal energy form on a world scale.

Disregarding other less significant forms of energy in the world such as oil shale, natural gas, nuclear energy, etc. (because of their relatively small share in providing energy for the world), coal and crude oil are the two main sources of energy today. And even disregarding the obvious advantages of oil compared to coal (for example, oil is less costly to process and provides highly valuable by-products) and merely considering the mass of calories that they both contain, the individual price of production of a ton of coal is several times that of a ton of crude oil. In other words, because of coal's particularly unfavourable use-value form, it is more costly to produce a given unit of energy from coal than it is to produce the same mass of calories from crude oil, making coal the marginal energy form in the world today.

The actual world market price of crude oil is thus governed by the individual price of coal production and the great demand for coal in the world energy market.

Even before the so-called energy crisis (in 1972, for example), the average market price of oil in Western Europe, then $72.80 per ton, was about four times the total costs of production, transportation, processing, and distribution, including the average profit, all of which came to $18.90 per ton.[37] This, as Massarrat also recognized, indicates that the world market price of oil is not determined on the basis of its actual individual price of production, but by the actual production costs of coal (oil's closest substitute) in the industrialized countries. This cost is many times higher than the actual production costs of oil in the OPEC countries.

As *The Economist* reported, before the 1971 Teheran and Tripoli Agreement, the total cost of oil was believed to be about £5 per ton delivered to Western European markets. In Britain, at that time, a ton of coal cost, on the average, between £7 and £8 to produce. Since the energy equivalent of one ton of oil is about 1.5 tons of coal, the cost of oil's closest substitute was, therefore, between £10 and £12 per ton.[38] This cost differential can be considerably greater if we take into account the fact that coal production in Britain is not the least efficient, or most marginal, within Western Europe.

The point of this analysis is that it is obvious that substantial surplus profits, or absolute rents, are created in the international oil industry today. If collusion within OPEC could be effectively implemented, the rewards to its member governments could be substantial. This reward, or increasing shares of absolute rent, could be obtained if the OPEC organization priced oil just below the price of the cheapest substitute for oil, that is, coal.

If OPEC were an effective cartel, the substantial absolute rent in the international oil industry today would be captured by its member governments as monopoly gains. However, because of the inability of the governments to exploit their producer power, only a modest amount of this surplus was, for a long time, actually captured by them.

As a result of OPEC governments' weakness at operating an effective cartel, before the so-called energy crisis they failed to capture a large part of the surplus profit from oil. Instead, even today, this surplus is shared by the governments of the industrialized countries and their oil MNCs. The governments of the industrialized countries can capture part of this surplus profit in the form of petroleum taxes on that part of the annual crude oil production of the OPEC countries that they actually imported. And their oil MNCs can capture part of the surplus as excess, or super, profits from that part of OPEC's oil production that they control in their concessionary areas.

According to *The Economist*, before the so-called oil crisis of December 1973, the market price of refined oil in Western Europe was about $14.50 per barrel. The consumer governments' take of this amount, in the form of petroleum taxes, was $7.46, or 51 percent. The oil MNCs received $4.79, or 33 percent of the price above their average profits, that is, in the form of super profits, while the remaining $2.30, or only 16 percent of the price, went to the OPEC governments as royalty taxes.[39]

In the struggle over the distribution of the absolute rent from oil, the posted price has acquired a decisive significance and must therefore be distinguished from the market price for oil.[40] Up until the end of the 1960s, the posted price was the basis for calculating the taxes and royalties to be paid to the oil-exporting governments. By means of the very low levels of the posted price for oil, which was dictated by the oil MNCs, they were able to keep the oil-exporting governments' share of the oil surplus very low. The market price of oil is, on the other hand, determined in the world market in competition with other sources of energy.

Only with the development of modern landed property were the oil-exporting governments first able, through the formation of OPEC, to organize their *de facto* monopoly power and thus convert the posted price mechanism into their own self-interested tool for capturing larger shares of the surplus profits from oil.[41] By drastically increasing the posted price for oil at the end of 1973, the OPEC governments were able dramatically to increase their share of the total surplus profit from oil as absolute rent.

Table 4 shows this change in the pattern of the distribution of the surplus profit from OPEC's oil sold in the Organization for Economic Cooperation and Development (OECD) oil-consuming countries before and after the famous OPEC price hike of 1973. The table shows that the bulk of this surplus has historically been realized by the governments of the oil-consuming countries and their oil MNCs. After the tremendous leap in the posted price of oil in 1974, however, the oil-exporting governments' share of the total surplus profit increased more than thirteen times compared to 1960 when they received only \$4.88 per ton. During this same period, on the other hand, both the oil MNCs' super profit and the consuming governments' petroleum taxes increased only by approximately two times. Also, after the increase in the posted price of oil, the oil-exporting governments were able to capture absolute rent, the magnitude of which was actually higher than the total surplus profit that, in 1972, that is, before the energy crisis, had been created from the production of one ton of oil and appropriated by the parties concerned.[42]

From the standpoint of the Western industrialized countries, such a drastic reallocation of wealth in favour of the OPEC, oil-exporting governments implied the withdrawal of a part of the surplus value hitherto at the disposal of their national aggregate capital. In other words, the reallocation of wealth meant a decrease in the proportion of the total surplus profit going to the oil MNCs, though the absolute sizes of their super profits increased. The possible decline in the MNCs' rate of profit must have aggravated, at least temporarily, the inherent crisis of capitalist production[43] in the oil sphere.

What is to be emphasized is, however, that oil-exporting governments have not succeeded in capturing the total amount of the oil surplus as absolute rent, even though this could be done by increasing the posted price to the level of the actual price of oil in the world market.[44] This is partly a result of the weakness of OPEC governments to exploit their *de facto* monopoly power as owners of an important resource.

Moreover, as chief consumers of OPEC's oil, the industrialized governments' defensive strategy or monopoly power, *vis-à-vis* the OPEC governments' monopoly inherent in their ownership of the oil wells, must be noted. For example, at the end of 1974, the OECD governments set up the International Energy Agency (IEA) whose function was primarily to abolish competition,

Table 4

The Distribution of OPEC's Surplus Oil Profit between OPEC Governments, Oil MNCs, and OECD Oil Importing Governments

Year	Total Surplus Profit From a Ton of Oil (Dollars per ton sold)	OPEC Governments' Share in Taxes		Oil MNCs' Share in Super Profits		Oil-Importing Governments' Share in Petroleum Taxes	
		(Dollars per ton sold)	(Percentage of Total Surplus)	(Dollars per ton sold)	(Percentage of Total Surplus)	(Dollars per ton sold)	(Percentage of Total Surplus)
1950	19.50	2.16	11	4.95	25	12.40	64
1955	50.79	2.50	11	5.39	11	39.90	78
1960	38.79	4.88	12	5.49	14	28.60	74
1962	33.89	4.99	15	5.70	17	23.20	68
1964	40.77	5.75	14	5.62	14	29.40	72
1966	41.09	6.04	15	6.05	15	29.00	70
1968	41.25	6.29	15	6.16	15	28.80	70
1970	41.55	6.26	15	6.14	15	29.00	70
1971	49.31	8.17	17	5.94	12	35.20	71
1972	59.13	10.14	17	5.69	9	43.30	74
1973	79.01	14.64	18	8.67	11	55.70	71
1974	137.91	63.02	46	14.09	10	60.80	44
1975	150.20	62.78	42	13.22	9	74.20	49

Source: Adapted from M. Massarrat. 'The Energy Crisis: The Struggle for the Redistribution of Surplus Profit From Oil'. in Petter Nore and Terisa Turner (eds.) *Oil and Class Struggle*. (Zed Press, London. 1980) p. 55.

resulting from the energy crisis between the consumer governments. The agency's long-term objective is to enforce a uniform strategy for the defence of the common interests of the OECD governments *vis-à-vis* OPEC governments. Its tasks include guaranteeing the supply of oil to all its member governments, coordinating measures to reduce consumption of OPEC's oil, establishing an information system on the oil market, and drawing up and implementing a long-term cooperation programme for a more rational use of energy and for the production of alternative sources of energy.[45]

Even without the platform of the IEA, the OECD governments individually have at their disposal well-developed national institutions, including tariffs and petroleum taxes, which they can use to set limits to whatever monopoly power the OPEC governments may have. Thus, even if the OPEC governments were able (because they own the oil wells) to enforce further increases in their shares of the oil surplus by, for example, reducing the quantity of oil and increasing its price, the OECD governments can react defensively to this move on a purely economic level by reducing their consumption of OPEC's oil and by increasing their petroleum taxes (assuming the OECD governments are not capable of, or interested in, significantly increasing production from alternative sources of energy).[46]

The threat of the perceived power of the OECD governments *vis-à-vis* OPEC governments will be magnified if, in addition to the economic levers at their disposal, the former's military and political power are also taken into account. Even disregarding the perception of the threat of force from the United States against OPEC governments, it is apparent that the other OECD governments have ultimately counteracted any economic monopoly power of OPEC through massive political pressure on individual OPEC governments who are their dependent allies.[47]

On the whole, the defensive strategies of the industrialized world have fostered splits within the ranks of OPEC. In this respect, within OPEC, the ruling class of Saudi Arabia has proved to be the most important ally of imperialism and the industrialized countries' governments. For example, as Massarrat put it,

> when one group of OPEC [governments] grouped around Iran announced a 30 percent increase in the posted price for oil from 1 October 1975, Yamani, the Saudi Arabian oil minister, firmly rejected it and pleaded instead for the freezing of the price. By threatening to leave OPEC, increase its production and offer its oil at a cheaper rate on the world market than the other OPEC [governments], Saudi Arabia succeeded in keeping the increase down — officially to 10 percent, but in reality to 6.8 percent.[48]

Saudi Arabia's (and others') divisive policies within OPEC are due to political pressure of the OECD governments, especially that of the United States. The crucial weakness of OPEC as a cartel has its roots in these divisive policies of its members.

In sum, because of a number of special circumstances that led to their first price hike, OPEC governments have succeeded in capturing large shares of the oil surplus as absolute rent. However, partly because of the Saudi Arabian government's refusal to curtail production, OPEC could not sustain this price hike for long. Nevertheless, other attempts at collusion, though temporary, have been made within OPEC to raise prices. At best, one can conclude that OPEC has only succeeded temporarily as a cartel in capturing absolute rents for its oil-exporting member governments. And since, from the standpoint of cartelization, the unique advantages that are offered by oil as a commodity are better than those offered by non-fuel minerals, the chances of Third World landlord governments appropriating absolute rent in these spheres through their producers' associations are even more limited than they are in the petroleum sphere.

The Limited Prospects of Cartelization by Third World Producers' Associations in the Non-fuel Minerals Sphere

Not only is OPEC not a cartel, but as a producers' association it is different from others in terms of the unique opportunities and constraints facing them. The prospects for the success of Third World producers' associations capturing absolute rent in the non-fuel minerals industries (from the standpoint of cartelization) are far less promising than in petroleum, for a number of reasons. First, the world demand for non-fuel minerals has not grown at any rate close to the rate of growth in demand for petroleum.[49] Second, members of Third World producers' associations in the non-fuel minerals sphere are generally poorer and more urgently in need of foreign exchange income than OPEC members and are, therefore, more likely to cheat and thus frustrate any cartel objectives of their organization. Third, there are readily-available substitutes for most non-fuel minerals whereas, in the case of OPEC and petroleum, energy substitutes are not as readily available. Fourth, there is a substantial difference in the distribution of world reserves of petroleum from that of most non-fuel minerals. While the bulk of petroleum reserves are located in the OPEC countries, with a very heavy concentration in a few Middle East countries, the locations of non-fuel minerals are more widely distributed around the world; and compared to petroleum, there is less concentration of reserves and productive capacities of non-fuel minerals in Third World countries. At this point, it will be useful briefly to discuss some specific conditions that explain why Third World producers' associations' prospects of operating effective cartels in the non-fuel minerals industries are limited.

The likelihood that the major exporters of a mineral can establish a cartel and maintain artificially high prices and output restrictions, that is, capture absolute rent, may depend on, (1) how large a share of the minerals' world reserves, output and export they control; (2) how little the demand for their minerals falls as their price rises; (3) how little the supply from sources outside their organization increases as the price of their mineral rises; and (4) how strong are the bonds among the countries, which would lend cohesion to their organization and prevent its members from cheating or leaving it.[50]

A general overview of these conditions will be presented in this section, and in the next chapter, on the copper industry, a more elaborate picture of this tendency will be presented.

First, as Table 5 shows, for most non-fuel minerals, the number of major producing and exporting governments is not great and the known reserves tend to be concentrated in the major producing countries. To the extent that the problems of organizing producers' cartels will tend to increase with the number of participants, the table suggests that, for many non-fuel minerals, it should not be too difficult to form cartels. With respect to the concentration of exports, one study has noted that in 1972, for the four largest countries exporting 18 commodities known to be important to national security and industrial processes, all but two were found to have concentration levels of at least 60 percent of world mineral exports, while none had a concentration level of less than 48 percent.[51]

There are, however, some qualifications. First, for some metals, the existence of secondary production can effectively erode a group of exporting governments' control over supply. For example, in 1975, 23 percent of the copper, and 47 percent of the lead consumed by the United States was produced from scrap.[52] Furthermore, as Table 5 shows, the industrialized countries of the West, and the Soviet Union, are the major producers of a considerable number of metals. Obviously, the governments of such countries are unlikely formally to join a Third World producers' organization in a cartel action to raise prices.

Second, with regard to the effect of price increases on the demand for minerals, the prospects of cartel-like producers' associations can be considered good if their minerals have a low price elasticity of demand, that is, if the demand for the commodity changes relatively little in response to substantial price changes. On this score, while, in the short run (for one year), the demand for most minerals is quite insensitive to price changes, in the longer term (three to five years), the demand is usually more responsive — in the opposite direction — to changes in their own prices, as well as in the price of substitutes.[53] This tendency exists in the minerals industry because, while minerals are used in producing other goods, it takes time and considerable investment to change production processes.

The third characteristic of a successful cartel-like producers' association is that expansion potential, particularly that outside the organization, should be relatively small over the price range being considered. The responsiveness of mineral supplies (outside the control of a producers' association) to increases in price, like the responsiveness of demand to price increases, tends to be low in the short run and high in the long run. And while it takes several years to develop major new mineral deposits, it is still possible (as has been the case in the United States over the post-war period), to accumulate sizeable strategic stockpiles that could constitute substantial short-run responses (for example, by the United States) to possible increases in price by the major exporters of the Third World. The estimated market value of strategic materials held in U.S. government inventories as of 30 June, 1975, was $2.7 billion, including $1.2 billion held against government objectives and $6.0 billion in excess of these objectives.[54]

Cohesion among members of Third World producers' associations is another characteristic of success for cartels. But, on the whole, cohesion in the non-fuel minerals industry has been weak, most cohesive efforts seldom lasting for more than five years. A number of factors may frustrate the efforts of producers' associations, many of whose members depend heavily on mineral exports for tax revenues and foreign exchange earnings. There may be disagreements over market shares. While the governments with large undeveloped reserves that hope to increase their mineral exports in order to stimulate domestic development are unlikely to adhere to cartel-like agreements that may thwart these aspirations, more established exporting governments may not be willing to accommodate plans that would result in a decline in their own share of world markets. Moreover, because mineral production in many of these countries is an important source of government revenue, foreign exchange, sales for domestic support industries and employment, falling world demand for their commodities during downswings in the business cycle may put unbearable pressure on some governments to cut price (either overtly or covertly) in order to keep their production and capacity utilization from falling too drastically.

Furthermore, in general, the governments of many non-fuel minerals-exporting countries have conflicting political ideologies that could make it difficult for them to establish and maintain cartel-like organizations. For example, as Table 5 shows, the major producers of fluorspar are Mexico, the Soviet Union, Spain and Thailand, while the major producers of the platinum group of minerals are South Africa, the Soviet Union, and Canada. The governments of these countries, including the Soviet Union, South Africa, Rhodesia and Turkey, which together produce the bulk of the world's chromium, would be strange bedfellows in Third World organizations designed to raise the price of fluorspar, platinum and chromium. And, given South Africa's political and economic orientation, its government is unlikely to force the world price of chromium upward by a special tax on chromium consumers, nor is it likely to join Gabon, Zaire, and Brazil in order to raise the price of manganese.

Even though some advanced countries (Canada and Australia, for example) have been known indirectly to show some interest in, or sympathy for, Third World producers' associations in the non-fuel area, this is not sufficient to argue for the possibility of effective Third World minerals cartels in the future. In the case of Australia, there was a move by its government to join three recently formed associations of bauxite, iron ore and tungsten producers.[55] The significance of this move must, however, be weighed in light of the Australian government's continued independence in making minerals policies, compared with the largely comprador policies of most Third World countries. It appears quite unlikely that the Australian government will become a part of any strong cartel action severely to restrict supplies from the industrialized world in order to drive prices above market levels, and to increase the absolute rent of Third World governments. On the contrary, even if Australia does join a producers' association, it is very clear that its government's role will represent a

Table 5

Percentage of World Production and Reserves of Selected Minerals Shared by the Four Largest Producing Countries, 1975

Mineral Commodity	Share of World Production	Share of World Reserves	Countries
Bauxite	64	62	Australia, Jamaica, Guinea, Surinam
Chromium[a]	70	96	Soviet Union, South Africa, Rhodesia, Philippines
Cobalt[b]	90	64	Zaire, Zambia, Canada, Morocco
Copper	53	57	United States, Chile, Canada, Soviet Union
Fluorspar	51	42	Mexico, Soviet Union, Spain, Thailand
Gold[b]	84	88	South Africa, Canada, United States, Australia
Iron ore	55	61	Soviet Union, Australia, United States, Brazil
Lead[b]	59	77	United States, Australia, Canada, Mexico
Manganese[b]	78	95	South Africa, Gabon, Brazil, Australia
Mercury	65	65	Spain, Soviet Union, China, Italy
Molybdenum[b]	99	98	United States, Canada, Chile, Peru
Nickel[b]	63	65	Canada, New Caledonia[c]
Phosphate rock[b]	81	88	United States, Morocco, Spanish Sahara, Tunisia
Platinum group	99	99	South Africa, Soviet Union, Canada[c]
Potash[b]	90	95	Canada, West Germany, United States, France

Table 5 Continued

Mineral Commodity	Share of World Production	Share of World Reserves	Countries
Silver	53	60	Peru, Mexico, Canada, United States
Tin	65	48	Malaysia, Soviet Union, Indonesia, Bolivia
Vanadium[a]	85	96	South Africa, United States, Soviet Union, Chile
Zinc	43	57	Canada, Australia, United States, Peru

[a]Figures are based on 1974 data.
[b]Calculated for non-communist countries only.
[c]For nickel, figures are for two largest producers; for platinum for the three largest.

Source: John E. Tilton, *The Future of Nonfuel Minerals* (The Brookings Institution, Washington, D.C., 1977) p. 83.

moderating, rather than a radical or an anti-imperialist, force within such an organization.

In summary, when the purpose is to raise the price of non-fuel mineral exports permanently above the competitive level in order to capture absolute rent, the likelihood that a single exporter can, through unilateral action, manipulate the market and achieve this aim will be greater if (1) its share of world reserves, output and export is large; (2) the elasticity of demand for its commodity is low; and (3) the price elasticity of alternative supply is low. When a group of exporters collectively pursues the same objective of raising prices through cartel or other forms of collusive behaviour, these three conditions for success apply, but a fourth is also essential: (4) there must be sufficient cohesion to keep the group together so as to prevent members from bypassing the cartel. Such cohesion will vary with, among other factors, the dissimilarity of the political and economic objectives of the participants; differences in their production costs; the degree of their dependence on exports for government revenues, domestic employment, and foreign exchange; and the effectiveness of economic and political counterpressure from advanced-country importers.

While the role of political forces on cartel behaviour is difficult to predict, it is clear that it adds a substantial element of uncertainty to the analyses of, and conclusions about, the producer power of Third World producers' associations. With that point in mind, the following conclusions can be made with respect to the prospects of non-fuel minerals cartels run by Third World governments.

Most Third World non-fuel minerals-exporting governments do not pose a threat to the major importing governments, particularly the United States. While the global political and economic climate seems to be conducive to the formation and survival of Third World producers' associations in the non-fuel minerals area, these associations can at best succeed as cartels only for a few years. This is so because increases in prices have little effect in the short run either on the demand for, or on the supply of, many non-fuel minerals, whereas in the long run the price elasticities of supply and demand tend to be high. Thus, even if cohesion exists in a particular producers' association, its members may eventually find the demand for their export commodities falling, as producers outside their organization increase their production and as consumers switch to alternative materials. In other words, cohesive or not, a Third World producers' association that is attempting to raise prices in the non-fuel minerals sphere may ultimately have to abandon its artificially high price or lose its markets entirely.

Summary and Conclusion

This chapter has argued that the prospects of Third World landlord governments capturing absolute rents in today's world are limited. This is so because they do not have an absolute monopoly over minerals and cannot operate effective minerals cartels in the world economy for any significant length of time.

In the case of oil, its final price — that is, the amount paid by the individual consumer — is clearly not exclusively in the control of the oil-exporting governments. Rather, because of the enormous power of oil MNCs, including the influence of their metropolitan oil-consuming home governments, the total surplus profit arising from the increasing global demand for OPEC's oil is shared by OPEC governments, the oil MNCs, and their home governments. Only recently in the history of OPEC has the organization been able, if only temporarily (by increasing the posted price of oil), to capture larger shares of the surplus profits from oil as absolute rent.

OPEC has not been able to exploit its *de facto* monopoly power as an organization of the exporters of an important natural resource. But, compared to Third World producers' associations in the non-fuel minerals sphere, OPEC's natural monopoly advantages — and, therefore, its prospects at cartelization — are better. The chances that Third World exporters of non-fuel minerals will be able, through cartelization in their producers' associations, to capture large shares of the absolute rent from world mining are, therefore, likely to be more limited than OPEC's chances appear to be in the case of oil.

At present, there is a paucity of scholarly and comprehensive analyses of the capability of Third World producers' associations, other than OPEC's in the world oil industry. In order to provide a more detailed analysis of the very limited prospects of a Third World producers' association in the non-fuel minerals sphere capturing absolute rents for its members through cartelization, the following chapter focuses on the world copper industry (copper being the most valuable mineral in the non-fuel minerals sphere today).

Notes

1. Dennis Pirages, *The New Context of International Relations: Global Ecopolitics* (Duxbury Press, North Scituate, 1978) p. 153.

2. Zuhayr Mikdashi, *The International Politics of Natural Resources* (Cornell University Press, New York, 1976) p. 88.

3. Pirages, *The New Context of International Relations*, p. 152.

4. OAPEC stands for the Organization of Arab Petroleum Exporting Countries.

5. See Michael Tanzer, *The Political Economy of International Oil and the Underdeveloped Countries* (Beacon Press, Boston, 1969) pp. 70–5.

6. See H. Jon Rosenbaum and William Tyler, 'South-South Relations: The Economic and Political Context of Interaction Among Developing Countries', *International Organization* 29, no. 1, Winter 1975, pp. 243–74.

7. See Paul Leo Eckbo, 'OPEC and the Experience of Previous International Commodity Cartels', MIT Energy Laboratory Working Paper, No. 75-008WP, August 1975.

8. For an introduction to these organizations, see Mikdashi, *The International Politics of Natural Resources;* Kenneth Clarifield *et al., Eight Mineral Cartels: The New Challenge to Industrialized Nations* (McGraw-Hill, New York, 1975); and Helge Hveem, *The Political Economy of Third World Producer Associations* (Universitetsforlaget, Oslo, 1977).

9. See Charles J. Johnson, 'Cartels in Minerals and Metal Supply', *Mining Congress Journal* 62, no. 1, January 1976, p. 30.

10. See Donella H. Meadows *et al., The Limits to Growth: A Report for the Club of Rome's Project on the Predicament of Mankind* (Universe Books, New York, 1974).

11. Writers in this field rarely appreciate this difference. For a discussion of general cartel theory, including its limited applicability to organizations composed of nation-states, see David Bobrow and Robert Kudrle, 'Theory, Policy, and Resource Cartels: The Case of OPEC', *Journal of Conflict Resolution* 20, no. 1, March 1976, pp. 3–56.

12. See C. Fred Bergsten, 'The Threat From the Third World', *Foreign Policy*, no. 11, Summer 1973, pp. 102–24; and Zuhayr Mikdashi, 'Collusion Could Work', *Foreign Policy*, no. 14, Spring 1974, pp. 57–68.

13. See Stephen Krasner, 'Oil is the Exception', *Foreign Policy*, no. 14, Spring 1974, pp. 68–84.

14. See George J. Stigler, *The Organization of Industry* (Richard D. Irwin, Inc., Homewood, Ill., 1968) chap. 5; Mancur Olson, *The Logic of Collective Action* (Harvard University Press, Cambridge, Mass., 1965); S. Groennings, E.W. Kelly, and M. Leiserson (eds.) *The Study of Coalition Behavior* (Holt, Rinehart and Winston, New York, 1970); Ervin Hexner, *International Cartels* (The University of Northern Carolina Press, Chapel Hill, 1946); and Ali D. Johany, *The Myth of the OPEC Cartel: The Role of Saudi Arabia* (John Wiley and Sons, Ltd., New York, 1980).

15. Johany, *The Myth of the OPEC Cartel*, p. 25.

16. Zuhayr Mikdashi, *The Community of Oil Exporting Countries* (Cornell University Press, New York, 1972) pp. 30–68.

17. Johany, *The Myth of the OPEC Cartel*, p. 27.

18. *Ibid.*, p. 45.

19. *Ibid.*, p. 48.

20. *Ibid.*, pp. 46–48.

21. Louis Turner, *Oil Companies in the International System* (George Allen and Unwin Ltd., London, 1980) p. 131.

22. Johany, *The Myth of the OPEC Cartel*, p. 27.

23. Walter J. Mead, 'An Economic Analysis of Crude Oil Price Behavior in the 1970s', *Journal of Energy and Development* 4, no. 2, Spring 1979, p. 220.

24. See Robert R. Pindyk, 'OPEC's Threat to the West', *Foreign Policy*, no. 30, Spring 1978, p. 39.

25. Mead, 'An Economic Analysis', p. 220.

26. Johany, *The Myth of the OPEC Cartel*, p. 49.

27. *Ibid.* The Saudi Arabian government can do this since the demand for oil is considered highly inelastic and since the marginal cost of producing oil in Saudi Arabia is considered constant.

28. Mead, 'An Economic Analysis', p. 221.

29. Johany, *The Myth of the OPEC Cartel*, p. 50.

30. *Ibid.*, p. 51.

31. *Ibid.*

32. See M.A. Adelman, 'Is the Oil Shortage Real? Oil Companies as OPEC Tax Collectors', *Foreign Policy*, no. 9, Winter 1972–73, pp. 69–107.

33. *Ibid.*, p. 87.

34. Johany, *The Myth of the OPEC Cartel*, p. 51.

35. See, for example, Theodore Panayotou, 'OPEC as a Model for Copper

Exporters: Potential Gains and Cartel Behavior', *The Development Economies* 17, no. 2, June 1979, pp. 203–19; Robert A. Pindyk, 'Gains to Producers for the Cartelization of Exhaustible Resources', *The Review of Economics and Statistics* 60, no. 2, May 1978, pp. 238–51; and Marian Radetzki, 'The Potential for Monopolistic Commodity Pricing by Developing Countries', in G.K. Helleiner (ed.) *A World Divided: The Less Developed Countries in the International Economy* (Cambridge University Press, New York, 1976) chap. 3.

36. See Zuhayr Mikdashi, 'The OPEC Process', *Daedalus* 104, no. 4, Fall 1975, pp. 104–28.

37. Mohssen Massarrat, 'The Energy Crisis: The Struggle for the Redistribution of Surplus Profit from Oil', in Petter Nore and Terisa Turner (eds.) *Oil and Class Struggle* (Zed Press, London, 1980) pp. 48, 49.

38. *The Economist*, 20 April 1976, p. 36.

39. *Ibid.*

40. Massarrat, 'The Energy Crisis', p. 47.

41. *Ibid.*, p. 54.

42. *Ibid.*

43. *Ibid.*, p. 59.

44. *Ibid.*

45. *Ibid.*

46. *Ibid.*, p. 61.

47. *Ibid.*

48. *Ibid.*

49. See Michael Tanzer, *The Race for Resources: Continuing Struggles Over Minerals and Fuels* (Monthly Review Press, New York, 1980) chap. 2.

50. On the potentials of new cartel-like producers' associations, see John E. Tilton, *The Future of Nonfuel Minerals* (The Brookings Institution, Washington, D.C., 1977) chap. 6; and Pirages, *The New Context of International Relations*, Chap. 5.

51. Johnson, 'Cartels in Minerals', p. 31.

52. Tilton, *The Future of Nonfuel Minerals*, p. 82.

53. *Ibid.*, p. 52.

54. *Stockpile Report to the Congress* (GSA, Washington, D.C., 1975) p. 1. On the role of national stockpiles as a U.S. policy tool, see *Raw Materials and Foreign Policy* (International Economic Studies Institute, Washington, D.C., 1976) chap. 11.

55. Johnson, 'Cartels in Minerals', p. 34.

4. Third World Producers' Association in the World Copper Industry

Introduction

Chapter 4 introduced the thesis that Third World landlord governments cannot, through their producers' associations, capture as absolute rents the full surplus profits from the sale of their resources because they have neither the common identity of interests characteristic of a landowning class nor a systematic and concerted monopoly over mineral resources. This chapter extends that thesis, specifically focusing on CIPEC,[1] the first producers' association in the history of the international copper industry that is constituted exclusively of Third World landlord governments.

To provide a useful framework to introduce CIPEC, this chapter begins with a historical review of earlier international attempts to control the copper industry, and goes on to analyse CIPEC's weakness as a supply-curtailing, price-raising cartel. The following section describes the uncartel-like impact of CIPEC's policy-output since the organization's inception, and concludes that CIPEC has not been able to operate as an effective cartel in the copper industry. CIPEC governments, like OPEC governments, are not likely to be able to capture, as absolute rents, the entire surplus profits involved in international mining today, even though OPEC governments' prospects do appear, on balance, to be better than CIPEC governments'.

History of the International Regulation of the Copper Market Prior to CIPEC

The international importance of copper, and attempts to control the market of the 'red metal', date back to ancient times. As Adelaide Walters wrote more than forty years ago,

> the history of the copper trade can be traced back to ancient man's search for better implements and materials. Even then, the copper trade assumed an international character as it followed the development of civilization in Europe, India, China . . .
> In 1548, an international copper cartel was formed which did not differ much in its structural aspects from modern international marketing organizations.

Scarcity of supply, poor transportation facilities, and, last but not least, the protective measures of the almost insolvent Holy Roman Emperor gave this monopoly its peculiar powers. This cartel controlled the bulk of production and trade in this commodity all over Europe. The marketing controls were so stringent as to stir up an anti-monopolistic movement which was quelled only by the efforts of the Emperor himself.[2]

Although copper was important during that period, its uses obviously remained limited. By the 19th Century, however, with the onset of the Industrial Revolution, the importance of copper as a conductor of heat and electricity dramatically increased. The story of copper is, according to Skelton,

> a tabloid of modern economic history in which are concentrated man's technical triumphs and the remarkable growth of material production on one hand, and his frequent blundering with the problems of regulating and distributing these gains on the other. Political history, too, including the current wave of economic nationalism, is reflected in a metal which is one of the basic requirements of both war and industry, and which, through the necessity of physical location, must be international in movement. All these features are exaggerated in the violent fluctuations of the copper industry and present striking illustrations of the continuous struggle man carries on against nature and fellow man.[3]

Copper shares with many widely traded metals and minerals a history of marked price instability.[4] Copper-producing companies, copper consumers, and more recently, governments have many times attempted to stabilize and regulate copper prices by a variety of means. Generally, the ability to regulate prices effectively can be derived from monopoly or oligopoly control of either the selling or buying side of the copper market.

From the 1800s to date, a total of eleven schemes have been designed to control the copper market, including one by CIPEC. It would be useful to review these earlier attempts at controlling the market before discussing the inception of CIPEC in 1967.[5]

First, in the early 1800s, the British, who controlled copper supply, formed the Swansea Smelters' Association in Wales for the purpose of governing the copper market. This association controlled the price of copper from 1800 to 1870, and operated the very rich Morwellam mines in Cornwall, which, at their zenith, yielded over 17 percent copper content.[6] Furthermore, because Swansea was the principal smelting centre in the world, it benefited from a low sales price for minerals and concentrates imported from Chile and Spain. Swansea became so prominent as a smelting centre that the association regulated not only the world price of copper, but also the price of ores it purchased. This regulation continued until Chilean suppliers built their own domestic smelting industry. The gradual decay of Swansea's power followed the eventual depletion of Cornish ore reserves and the development of the copper industry in the United States, where smelters had been constructed on the East Coast. The supply of concentrates and minerals to Swansea declined markedly after 1860, and by 1876, when the London Metal Exchange (LME) was formed, the Swansea Smelters' Association had completely lost its influence over prices.

The decline of the British (Welsh) dominance of the copper industry was followed by the emergence of the United States as the world's largest producer of copper. Production, then controlled by Calumet and Hecla (C&H), was concentrated in the copper deposits of Michigan, where the copper content approached 20 percent in the 1880s.[7] From the mid 19th Century to 1880, C&H together with what was known as the Lake Pools, through whom it was operating, accounted for some 75 percent of U.S. copper output.[8] During that period, they managed to keep the copper price somewhat above 20 cents per pound.[9] According to *Copper Studies*, C&H was helped by a high protective tariff imposed in 1869.[10] Its effectiveness was, however, temporary; the net impact of its high price was to encourage exploration and development of mines by other companies. The first threat, in 1882, came from the Anaconda Silver Mining Company, which had begun working the rich ores in Butte, Montana. By the late 1880s, C&H had cut its prices in half to thwart Anaconda's competition. The attempt proved abortive, however, as Anaconda and other companies in Montana continued to increase production. By 1887, production in Montana had exceeded that in Michigan, and the operations of C&H, the second attempt to control the market, came to an end.[11]

By the end of the 1880s, depressed and falling prices caused world copper production to stagnate (with the exception of that in Spain and the United States). This opened the way for the third spectacular effort to control copper prices, an attempt in 1887, in France, under the leadership of the famous M. Secretan. He acted through the *Société Industrielle et Commerciale des Métaux* and had the backing of such international bankers as the Baring Brothers, Rothschilds, and the Comptoir d'Escompte.[12] By the middle of 1888, Secretan had managed to contract for over 75 percent of total world output, including that of C&H and Anaconda in Michigan and Montana, on three-year contracts at a price of approximately 14 cents per pound, while selling at over 18 cents per pound.[13] The effect of the high price was to create a flood of new mine production and recovered scrap. As Skelton put it,

> Copper Buddhas and cooking utensils from the Orient voyaged to Europe to swell the flood, and the scrap flow was much larger than Secretan estimated....
>
> Stocks of copper continued to increase and finally, in March 1889, the crash came. The large loans to the Société Industrielle et Commerciale des Métaux began to be called, and the stock market broke as Secretan started unloading his Rio Tinto and other holdings. The manager of the Comptoir d'Escompte committed suicide, and within a fortnight copper dropped to [7.6c per pound], and the former 900-franc shares of the Société Industrielle et Commerciale des Métaux collapsed to 27, and Secretan's brokers announced that they could not meet their commitments.[14]

The Secretan demise was, perhaps, the inevitable consequence of a purely financial control of the copper market, that is, without sufficient structural control. Secretan's effort to control the copper market, like that of the Swansea Association before it, merely encouraged a vigorous growth of world copper output, causing prices once again to fall.

Secretan's experience did not discourage other attempts to regulate the copper market. The fourth major move came from the United States, whose copper production was becoming dominant in world markets. In 1892, the first of two pre-World War I associations of copper-producing companies, the American Producers' Association (APA), was formed. Made up of several companies, its objective was to limit production and exports in order to support prices. APA agreed to restrict U.S. production to 146,000 long tons and its exports to 40,000 long tons between July of 1892 and 1893.[15] It endeavoured to persuade the major European producers that were operating in Germany, Spain, Portugal, Mexico, and the Cape Colony to reduce their output by 15 percent in an effort to internationalize the regulation. The Europeans, however, obliged by reducing their output by only 5 percent, which barely affected the price.[16] APA's attempts to negotiate subsequent production restrictions failed, and the association served mainly as an information-gatherer until it broke up in the early 1900s.

As the fourth scheme to control the copper market came to an end, and even before the copper industry had completely recovered from the last *débâcle*, foundations were being laid for a fifth effort. As Skelton put it, 'Standard Oil interests, fresh from profitable victories in the oil industry, had turned to copper as a likely medium for new triumphs'.[17] Standard Oil, including National City Bank interests, proceeded to acquire control of Anaconda and to form the Amalgamated Copper Company (ACC) in April 1899, in an effort to combat the depressed copper prices then prevalent. Comparing ACC's market control strategy to earlier schemes, *Copper Studies* observed:

> The Swansea Smelters had used brute strength to control the world market, the Lake Pools took advantage of their natural near-monopoly of U.S. copper output and the opportunist entrepreneur Secretan used commercial astuteness. The Amalgamated Copper Company, however, acting as a holding company for its copper interests, pursued a vigorous policy of acquisition.[18]

The company controlled some 25 percent of world copper output by 1900. It received, however, limited support from foreign companies in its attempts to cut supply, and the price of copper rose from about 12 cents per pound to 18 cents per pound. Inspired by the artificially high prices, copper production soon rose dramatically in a pattern similar to that of C&H and Secretan. Consumption soon fell drastically, the recovery of scrap increased, and output from producers outside the organization grew substantially. By 1903, ACC gave up its attempts to control the copper price, which then fell to its original 12 cents per pound level.[19]

The copper industry had hardly recovered from Amalgamated's failure before it embarked on a sixth price-raising attempt. In 1909, the Copper Producers' Association (CPA), the second U.S. association of producing companies to try to regulate the copper market, was formed.[20] Members included the Phelps-Dodge Corporation, C&H, American Smelter and Refining Company, and Amalgamated. The environment, though, hardly called for collusive price control. World demand was growing steadily as the electrical industry emerged as a large-scale outlet for copper. While the world prepared for war, the consumption of copper became abnormally high as the demand for armaments increased in the West. Nevertheless, CPA attempted to peg prices and to limit output when market conditions weakened, but always with minimal success. Furthermore, vast reserves of low-grade porphyry ores had been discovered outside the United States in South America and Africa, and were being exploited by companies which had little identity of interests with their U.S. counterparts and which, therefore, refused to cooperate with them. In 1915, CPA disbanded.

The First World War profoundly affected the copper market. Because of inordinate demands placed on the industry during the war, there was a fundamental and structural imbalance in the market when hostilities eventually ceased. During the four years of the war, almost 6 million tons of copper had been produced — more than half of all copper produced in the entire 19th Century.[21] The rise in world copper production capacity involved the extraordinary growth of production in Africa and South America. Moreover, since about 2 million tons went directly into munitions, according to Skelton, a substantial proportion of this soon reappeared in the market as scrap; the world had to pay 75 percent more for this 6 million tons than it had paid for the previous 6 million tons produced.[22] Furthermore, the war greatly stimulated the use of substitutes for copper as well as techniques for scrap recovery, especially in Germany, following the embargo of the Triple Alliance. According to Skelton,

> At least half a million tons of copper must have been recovered from scrap during the war, making Germany the second largest producer in the world.
> The use of both zinc and aluminium as substitutes, and the production of aluminium, were greatly stimulated in Germany. The war was the beginning of active government encouragement of copper's growing competitor, aluminium, in countries which lacked copper resources.[23]

A common feature of the pre-World War I schemes for controlling the world copper market was that the attainment of higher prices was considered the important criterion for success. But, in every case, the pursuit of higher prices depressed consumption, stimulated scrap recovery, and encouraged production outside the producers' association. At the end of World War I, the international copper industry faced stocks of copper that were too high in terms of new productive capacity in the world, and in terms of a vast scrap potential.

Since the immediate period before the war was one of abnormally high copper consumption and the war itself had dramatically raised copper consumption, the possibility of returning to normal patterns of consumption in the face of these huge stockpiles frightened the industry. The first signs of falling demand, high stockpiles, and excessive capacity were witnessed in 1914.[24] That year, in an effort to combat the coming crisis, the Copper Export Association (CEA), comprising major copper producers, was formed. This seventh scheme, controlling 95 percent of American production and 65 percent of world output, was founded under the Webb-Pomerene Act, which allowed

American companies to cartelize exports so long as the cartelization did not affect the U.S. domestic industry.[25] The task of CEA was to liquidate the tremendous wartime stockpiles of copper and to regulate production. Its operations included such features as a common selling agency (for exports), a fixed price for foreign sales, and the allocation of shares for export.[26]

From the producers' point of view, CEA was a relatively successful venture in copper regulation since it did accomplish its primary goal of stock disposal. Unlike previous arrangements that aimed to achieve high prices, CEA, which simply wanted to liquidate the surplus stocks of copper in an orderly fashion, experienced in the process a real price decline of between 35 and 40 percent from pre-war levels.[27] By 1923, as Skelton observed,

> the war surplus of both primary and secondary copper (with the exception of a reserve of scrap copper held by the French Government for munitions purposes) had been liquidated, and the sharp depression of 1921 had been successfully weathered, thanks to a drastically lowered production and a very large consumption.[28]

Two important factors explain the unique success of CEA. First, the large, low-cost producers in the United States had borne the brunt of the sacrifices involved in liquidating the war stocks, instead of trying to exploit the situation by displacing the smaller, high-cost producers. In 1921, the output of the large producers had been cut to 20 percent of their 1918 level, while that of other smaller producers had fallen by less than 50 percent.[29] This was the first attempt by copper producers at joint maximization, in the sense of seeking to further the welfare of the industry as a whole even at the expense of individual firms. Second, a fortuitous combination of circumstances was working in CEA's favour. For example, the level of consumption of new copper, though reviving slowly, was beyond expectations, especially in Europe where huge stocks and scrap piles would have constituted a definite threat to the market.[30] Also, Japan, once a net exporter, had become a net importer of copper primarily because of the tremendous expansion in Japanese industrial development.[31] Furthermore, after 1918, with Australian output declining even faster than American output, largely because of labour difficulties, CEA was virtually free of competition.[32]

Having successfully reduced wartime excess copper capacity to somewhat manageable proportions, and having sold the last of its stock, the association disbanded in 1923, following dissensions that had begun to grow between the purely domestic producers and those with foreign holdings.[33] No formal attempts were made to control the international copper market between 1924 and 1926. To replace the CEA (and most likely to take advantage of the privileged anti-trust status under the Webb-Pomerene Act), an eighth marketing scheme, Copper Exporters, Inc. (CEI), was formed in 1926, with membership including not only the major U.S. producers but also (among others) Rio Tinto, Union Minière, and British Metals Corporation.[34] This was the first time a Webb-Pomerene Assocation included members from outside the United States. It thus represented one of the first truly international attempts at price control, and perhaps therefore avoided, to some extent, one of the major institutional weaknesses of previous regulatory schemes, that is, the threat of the presence of strong non-member producers. The group accounted for some 95 percent of world copper production and, starting with a favourable market condition of low stocks and rising consumption, its position seemed strong.[35] Members agreed on a group selling price, but output restrictions (necessary only in weak market periods) were only loosely enforced.[36] Copper prices doubled, between 1928 and March 1929, to 24 cents per pound. When the price subsequently dropped to 18 cents per pound, it was successfully kept at that level for a year, despite wild fluctuations in demand and inventory, representing one of the most spectacular single episodes of copper price stabilization.[37]

Both the buoyancy of copper prices at the end of the 1920s and the generally favourable conditions that had persisted in the mid-decade soon encouraged the growth of production from non-CEI members. By 1930, the copper price had broken and by 1932, it had been halved.[38] Hasty efforts to negotiate production cutbacks failed and, in 1932, foreign companies withdrew from CEI. American producers finally took unilateral protectionist action by imposing a tariff on copper imports. This measure sounded the death knell of CEI. Controlling only 32 percent of world production, CEI disbanded in 1932 in circumstances similar to other attempts at market control during the previous century.[39]

Yet another (ninth) marketing scheme was, however, soon underway in the copper industry. In fact, U.S. producers were said to have proposed it as early as 1933. Walters explains it in this way:

> At the London Monetary and Economic Conference in 1933 an attempt was made to find a workable basis for cooperation on the international copper market. In a report of the sub-committee of the Monetary and Economic Conference appears the following statement: "The delegation of the United States of America calls attention to the desirability of considering plans for the coordination by the international agreement of the production and marketing of copper . . . Accordingly, it is proposed that the Governments of the copper-producing countries submit to the Secretary-General of the Monetary and Economic Conference, before September 15, 1933, their views and proposals concerning the organization of the production of copper and of the international trade in this product, with a view to the summoning of a suitable meeting to examine whether it is possible and expedient to conclude an agreement" . . .
>
> Occasional attempts were made by copper producers, American and foreign, to reach an understanding on some kind of cooperative marketing control, but no definitive undertaking was launched until . . . 1935.[40]

At least four factors constituted favourable circumstances in the latter part of 1934, for the ninth attempt at a 'cooperative marketing control' of copper.[41] First, copper stocks, although reduced from the 1932 to 1933 levels, were still far above the requirements of consumers. As long as stocks remained excessive and production continued to surpass consumption, the major copper producers could hardly hope to produce enough 'profitable returns'. Second, ownership was concentrated in the hands of a few (European and U.S.) producers. Third, the relative power position of the major copper producers on the world market had been virtually established. Because Rhodesian mines did not begin large-scale production until the early 1930s, their capacities had been uncertain before 1935. Capacities of the Canadian and Chilean copper mines, however, had been developed during the 1920s and were more certain. Fourth, the major producers had a number of shared interests and experiences. They all had heavy plant investments. Also, they needed to sell large quantities of copper in order to operate their mines profitably. Most of them had cooperated previously in the copper market, and many had interlocking corporate connections.[42]

In December 1934, initial discussions were begun for an agreement between European copper producers and U.S. producers who were, ostensibly, acting as representatives of their foreign holdings.[43] After some months of negotiations in New York and London, the European and American copper producers signed an agreement on 28 March, 1935, forming the International Copper Cartel (ICC). The agreement, relating to copper on the world market outside the United States, was titled 'Memorandum of Provisions Covering Producers'.[44] It was to remain in effect until 1938, when it was renewed until 1941.

The cartel consisted of five full members and two associate members. The full members were:

1. Rhokana Corporation (British holding in Rhodesia);
2. Mufulira Copper Mines, Ltd., and Roan Antelope Copper Mines Ltd. (British holdings in Rhodesia);
3. Union Minière du Haut Katanga (Belgian holding in Belgian Congo);
4. Braden Copper Company (American (Kennecott) holding in Chile); and
5. Chile Exploration Company and Andes Copper Mining Company (American (Anaconda) holdings in Chile and Mexico, respectively).

The associate members were:

1. Compagnie du Mines du Bor (French holding in Yugoslavia) and
2. Rio Tinto Company, Ltd. (British holding in Spain).

Each full member had one vote; the associate members could not vote but were free to attend all the meetings.[45]

The objective of the ICC, as stated in the first paragraph of the memorandum, reads: 'The purpose of the above mentioned producers in participating in this memorandum is to bring about better conditions in the production, distribution and marketing of copper throughout the world outside of the United States . . .'[46] A 20 percent production cutback was imposed for 1 May 1935, and was increased to 35 percent by June of the same year. The scheme of ICC included imposition of production quotas, regulation of trade policies, and exchange of information.[47] The most important provision regarding trade practices was that the members would sell only to consumers, not to middlemen, in order to restrict speculation and sharp price fluctuations.

Its Control Committee intervened several times to adjust the quotas and to enforce provisions for regulating sales, further minimizing the effects of speculation on the copper market. The Copper Institute served as an information clearinghouse for ICC, providing such information as the size of each participant's stocks, sales for future or immediate delivery, and rates of production.[48]

ICC was the most comprehensive market-control arrangement ever implemented in the copper industry. It was unique in that it made every effort to enlist the support of outsiders. Even though the agreement ostensibly excluded U.S. production, the presence of American subsidiaries in the group was itself evidence of support. Similarly, ICC obtained the cooperation of Canadian and Peruvian producers who, although they did not become parties to the agreement, were considered 'friendly outsiders'.[49]

Even though ICC succeeded, to some degree, in restricting copper outputs in the short run, prices were not significantly influenced. Prices did rise early in 1937, however, but fell sharply later that year.[50] In an attempt to avoid encouraging capacity expansions outside the group, ICC's production restrictions were lifted at a price level considered to be 'reasonable'.[51] Nevertheless, as restrictions were lifted, output would soar and prices would tumble. Again, as in the previous cases, the size of the uncontrolled non-membership production prevented effective long-term action. Once more, the production or sale of scrap copper that was not subject to regulation constituted another potential source of competition. The International Copper Cartel ended with the start of the Second World War and its accompanying government intervention.

The copper industry was in disarray following the war. Discussions for renewed market intervention did not come until 1956 when, for the first time, both African and Chilean government representatives, not just company representatives, met to discuss joint curtailment of production in response to price slides that began that year. This was the International Wrought Non-Ferrous Metals Council, the tenth and, perhaps, most successful and sophisticated of all price control schemes involving companies in the history of the copper industry. By the early 1960s, they had managed to cut production by 15 percent in efforts to stabilize prices. As a result, prices fluctuated by only 1.7 percent and 0.1 percent in 1962 and 1963 respectively.[52] In the period from 1964 to 1966, producers rationed sales of copper on the basis of the previous years' supplies in an effort to deter users from buying cheap (at the producer prices) and selling dear (at the LME prices).[53] However, the rationing scheme was very rigid, and as Brown and Butler observed,

> the effects were that fabricators whose output showed the fastest rate of increase were obliged to buy their copper requirements on the open market at high prices, thus pushing their average metal input costs up further than those of fabricators whose business was expanding only slowly and who, hence, needed to buy merely their marginal metal requirements on the open metal market. This gave a direct incentive to the more dynamic fabricators to explore the possibilities for using substitute materials, which was exactly what the producers had hoped to

avoid in their efforts to stabilize copper prices ... This rationing of supplies of metal effectively contributed to the general shortage of copper and gave an added impetus to the upward swing of prices ... *The very existence of two prices for the same commodity is almost certain to guarantee the failure of any attempt to regulate sales over a long period.*[54]

Throughout 1964, the average annual LME price of copper rose by 50 percent, well above the then non-U.S. producer price.[55] With producer rationing, LME prices had ceased to be an accurate indicator of long-term market strength. These prices, therefore, collapsed as the Western world's copper demand, which had fallen by 0.7 percent in 1965, fell again in 1966, by 1.6 percent.[56] As prices collapsed under the pressure of an inflated market, it was time, once again, to abandon the effort to fix (internationally) the price of copper. The price oscillations of the mid-1960s constituted an important background for the formation of the first Third World producers' association, known as the Intergovernmental Council of Copper Exporting Countries (CIPEC) in 1967, made up of Chile, Peru, Zambia, and Zaire.

Although the attempt of the International Wrought Non-Ferrous Metals Council to control the copper market was effective and beneficial over a short period, like all previous schemes it lacked regularized provisions for monitoring the market, regulatory measures to enforce restrictions, and broad membership to eliminate possible sabotage from non-member producers. Hence, according to *Copper Studies*, the historical attempts at copper regulation,

represents more a history of failure than success. No scheme yet propounded has introduced a long-term measure of price stability, at reasonable prices, into the copper industry. Indeed, most collusive agreements have retreated into acrimony and disbandment only to be followed by damaging slides in the copper price.[57]

In this section I have noted that earlier efforts at internationally regulating the copper market involved primarily American and British companies; when membership eventually became international (with the addition of South American and African representatives in the International Wrought Non-Ferrous Metal Council), it included, for the first time, both companies and producer-governments. By 1967, when CIPEC was formed, the industry had accumulated over half a century of producer-intervention attempts (by copper companies) that must have informed CIPEC members. In fact, even before the formation of CIPEC, three of its four founding members, Chile, Zambia, and Zaire, had had prior experience with collaboration, even though it was only confined to short-term market intervention.

As I have noted, in the history of the copper industry, the pursuit of high prices has, in all cases, been detrimental to the interests of the major producers because it has always encouraged the development of substitute materials and increased production outside the producers' organization. One important lesson that may, therefore, have been learned by CIPEC governments is that the usefulness of a producers' association may not necessarily be defined in terms of attaining monopolistic prices.

The Creation of CIPEC

After World War II, corporate concentration and control was very high in the international copper market where CIPEC's four founding members traditionally sold their copper. By 1948, corporate control had been consolidated around the following eight major companies: Kennecott, Anaconda, Phelps-Dodge, International Nickel, Noranda, Anglo-American, Roan Selection Trust, and Union Minière du Haut Katanga.[58] Until the mid-1960s, practically all of the exports of copper in these major Third World copper-exporting countries were produced by these American- and European-owned companies. The two largest copper companies, Kennecott and Anaconda, had built their worldwide operations around powerful, vertically integrated, corporate structures controlling the entire copper production process from the mines in the United States and Chile through the final sales of the end products of copper. The other large firms similarly asserted their influence, though to a somewhat lesser extent, through their ownership of mines, smelters, and refineries, as well as through their worldwide marketing systems. These large firms showed a distinct tendency to erect smelters and refineries in their home countries rather than in Third World areas where the mines themselves were located. For example, while, in 1966, about 50 percent of all mine capacity was located in Third World areas, with over 40 percent of it in Africa and Latin America, only about a third of the smelter capacity and barely 20 percent of the refinery capacity were located there.[59]

The general wave of economic nationalism in the Third World in the mid 1960s was largely in protest against this dominant position of raw materials companies from the advanced countries. CIPEC was created in this nationalistic environment. In the context of the historical attempts to control the international copper industry, CIPEC was unique in that, unlike its predecessors which were companies, the immediate priority of CIPEC members, which are governments, was not to control price *per se*, but to nationalize the properties of foreign mining firms.

This is a point not usually recognized by many who attempt to describe CIPEC as a cartel. The process of nationalization itself was a Herculean enough task for the poor copper exporters; and, as will be noted in this section, it took seven years to nationalize the properties of foreign mining firms in the CIPEC countries to the point where collective action to control prices even became the verbal issue that it still is.

With that point in mind, I shall examine the convergence of economic and political factors that led to the formation of CIPEC in 1967. The copper market was experiencing serious problems in 1966; total world production had fallen by some 2 percent and prices had increased slightly. One of the major reasons for this situation was the political schism between Zambia and Rhodesia following the unilateral declaration of independence by Rhodesia in November

1965, resulting in the interdiction of Zambian copper supply to the world, which was normally dependent upon the Rhodesian railroad for trans-shipment to the port of Beira in Mozambique.[60] In May 1966, the Zambian government ordered Anglo-American Corporation and Roan Selection Trust to stop making payments to the Rhodesian-headquartered railroad company. The government ordered that payments be made to a blocked fund in London instead. The Rhodesian railroad rejected this scheme, and the Zambian government in turn had to look for alternative routes to transport its copper to the ports. While alternative routes were being developed, shipments of Zambian copper almost ceased.[61]

Rhodesia also cut off its usual supply of top-grade metallurgical coal and petroleum, oil, and lubricants (POL) for use in copper production in Zambia.[62] Zambia's copper production and shipments fell by 30 percent as a result, from 65,000 tons in December 1965, to 45,000 tons in December 1966.[63] Rhodesian shipments of POL to Zambia had been halted in January 1966, and by September of that year the government had adopted the policy of sending coal to Zambia only in a direct pound-for-pound exchange for copper shipped out through Rhodesia.[64] Zambia thus found itself in a severe shortage of coal and POL. In place of the rich coal from the Wankie mines in Rhodesia, it was forced to use its own coal from the Nkandabwe coal fields, which was 30 percent less efficient. Even with POL that had to be airlifted into Zambia by the United States and Britain, Zambia's production continued to slip.

The effect of Zambia's supply problems on the world copper market was compounded by the escalation of the Vietnam War during this period. Demand for copper was, therefore, at abnormally high levels. The United States had released a substantial amount of its national stockpile beginning in March 1966 to meet the demands of war. In an attempt to counteract the impending copper shortage, manufacturers had turned to substitute materials like aluminium, plastics and stainless steel.[65] Scrap recovery had increased by 13 percent in the United States at that time. As a reflection of the shortage, the price of copper had increased by 18 percent at LME.[66]

The tension between Rhodesia and Zambia was not the only source of the supply problem that plagued the copper industry in the mid-1960s. After nationalizing Union Minière du Haut Katanga in 1967, the then Congolese government suspended exports for seven weeks.[67] In that same year, strikes in the Chilean and U.S. copper industries almost totally cut back U.S. production in the major mines.[68] These conditions, marked by supply and demand disequilibrium, may have stimulated the major copper-exporting governments to consider forming a consultative organization.

Important political changes in the major copper-exporting countries provided the final impetus for the creation of CIPEC in June 1967. For example, in Chile and Peru, the 'Yankee capitalists' had been 'driven out': and in Zambia and Zaire, the 'European imperialists' had been 'relieved' of their mother roles.

The first contacts for a consultative organization were made by the leaders of the Zambian and Chilean governments.[69] Zambia had received political independence on 23 October 1962, and Kenneth Kaunda had become its first president; in Chile, the Christian Democratic Party under Eduardo Frei had won the election. Soon after Frei's election in September 1964, in a nationwide telecast on 21 December of that year he announced that the Chilean government was entering into a number of lesser joint ventures with CERRO Corporation and Anaconda, and that the government would take over substantial participation of 51 percent in the Braden Copper Company's El Teniente Mines run by Kennecott.[70] The situation in Zambia was somewhat different. Kaunda's Zambianization began primarily as an effort to build a truly Zambian public administration and political system and to place Zambians in better-paid and more responsible positions in administration and the economy.[71] In terms of state power, compared to Frei's Chile, Kaunda's Zambia apparently was not yet in a position to bargain with the large foreign copper firms operating in Zambia. Nevertheless, the dependency of the two economies upon the export of copper which, in both countries, was controlled by foreign-owned companies, contributed a solid foundation for their wanting to form a consultative organization. At the least, both governments would benefit from their respective experiences with copper operations and foreign investors.

The following statement by Prain excellently describes the mentality of the major Third World copper exporters on the eve of the creation of CIPEC:

> The copper producing countries of the Third World are fully conscious of the fact that not only are they the chief suppliers of the metal, outside of the United States, but that they collectively produce about two-thirds of the copper which is internationally traded. They also realize that at least half of the world's presently known and viable copper deposits are spread throughout their territories; they know, too, that the Western world is using up its share of the reserves at a much faster rate than they are and that politically, therefore, they are moving into a position of greater strength, even though the rate of progress of their economies may be relatively slower.[72]

In other words, Third World copper-exporters had become aware of their respective influences as land-owning governments. To consider how such influences could best be consolidated, applied, and maximized, President Kaunda flew to Santiago in November 1966, following an appearance in New York to address the United Nations General Assembly, to talk with President Frei.[73] Kaunda's trip represented his first official visit abroad in his capacity as Zambian president.

The two statesmen noted that their countries together had a strong position in the copper world in terms of their production and share of the international trade. They also noted the potential influence they could have if the production of Peru and Zaire, the two other major Third World copper exporters, were added to theirs. A joint declaration made by Presidents Frei and Kaunda reads as follows:

> The principal economic link between Chile and Zambia is their common condition as large-scale copper producers. Chile and Zambia have strong

positions in the world copper market and, although they produce only 30 percent of the world total, their influence on the supply of copper for the Free World Market can be estimated at approximately 65 percent and 70 percent. If the production of Peru and the Congo [Zaire] is added to those of Chile and Zambia, it appears that these four countries jointly supply three-quarters of world net copper exports.

These characteristics alone of the present world copper supply clearly indicate the immediate possibilities which would be opened by a close relationship between Chile, [Zaire,] Peru, and Zambia.[74]

The two presidents agreed to try to strengthen their economic positions by developing and nurturing closer association among the four governments. According to Prain, some diplomatic probing in Peru and Zaire indicated that the idea of such an association 'was acceptable' and 'invitations were dispatched to each country to send up to ten representatives to a meeting to be held in Lusaka'.[75] After a series of further consultations, the first Intergovernmental Conference of Copper Exporting Countries took place in Lusaka during the first week of June 1967, attended by representatives from Chile, Zambia, Zaire, and Peru. There were observers from Uganda, a small but 'profitable' exporter, and from Botswana, a 'potential' exporter. Obviously excluded from this conference were those countries that were producers as well as important consumers of copper. In other words, the conference was open only to those whose export-economies were based on this one basic product, that is, to the governments of monocultural economies.

It is important to note, however, that the type of unity that these governments sought was, as Kaunda put it, *'not one which would strengthen us to destroy others'*.[76] On the contrary, they were, according to him, only seeking to obtain controlling interests in the management affairs of the mining companies *in order to mesh corporate and national goals*. Thus, despite the uneasiness that the world market had begun to feel in the face of the possibility of a united and positive front being developed by the copper-exporting governments, as Prain put it,

the immediate outcome of the conference was something of an anti-climax. The only real decision was to set up a permanent organization — later to be called Conseil Intergouvernemental des Pays Exportateurs de Cuivre (CIPEC) — to comprise a conference of ministers, a governing board and a copper information bureau. Headquarters were established in Paris and an organization was built up centred on the development of the "information bureau" . . . [*CIPEC was*] *in effect a statistical supply group concerned with . . . information about copper business.*[77]

The immediate impact of the conference, in terms of the expected cartel-like action, was limited. African leaders had emphasized the need for copper-exporting governments to acquire control and ownership over their natural resources. Both South American producers had insisted that the discussions of price policy be excluded from the agenda. Alejandro Halles, the leader of the Chilean delegation to the conference, expressed Chile's position as follows *'We are not at this time worried about the price of copper. The important thing is that our countries are going to take common action to ensure adequate supplies.*'[78]

Accordingly, the preamble of the CIPEC agreement stresses the need to prevent excessive fluctuations in the price of copper and to maintain a fair price of copper for both exporters and consumers in time of war and peace. It also mentions a tendency towards persistent price fluctuations that can be harmful both to the exporters and consumers. The objectives of CIPEC, as stated in the original 1967 agreement, read as follows:

a) to co-ordinate measures designed to foster, through the expansion of the industry, dynamic and continuous growth of real earnings from copper exports, and to ensure a real forecast of such earnings;
b) to promote the harmonization of the decisions and policies of the Member Countries on problems relating to the production of copper;
c) to obtain for the Member Countries better and more complete information and appropriate advice on the production and marketing of copper;
d) in general, to increase resources for the economic and social development of producer countries, *bearing in mind the interest of consumers.*[79]

Obviously, none of these four objectives can be construed as a call for cartelization by the CIPEC governments. Moreover, note the conspicuous absence of even an implicit statement about the maximization of absolute rent as a specific policy objective of the CIPEC agreement. In a revised version of objectives in 1974, CIPEC added the following two clauses:

e) to promote the solidarity of the Member Countries as concerns the problems faced by these countries in the copper industry;
f) to promote the co-ordination of their policies with other organizations of the same type as CIPEC.[80]

However, even after that addition, even CIPEC's spokesmen would not label it a cartel.

In another major addition to the original agreement, a new article with provisions to accommodate a new breed of membership within CIPEC was introduced. Although originally only the four founding members constituted CIPEC, the new charter provided for solicitation for other copper producers to join the organization. Three categories of membership were established: founding members; members with full rights, that is, governments whose copper exports are large and whose interests are analogous to those of the founding members; and associate members, that is, governments having similar interests, but with no voting privileges.[81]

The final aspect of CIPEC's inception to note in this section is its organizational framework. It is composed of the following organs: the Conference of Ministers, the Executive Committee, and the Secretariat.[82] The Conference of Ministers is considered 'the supreme organ' of CIPEC and consists of one minister from each member country who must be the competent authority responsible for CIPEC matters in his country. Although the ordinary session of this organ convenes annually, its extraordinary sessions meet 'when circumstances so require and on the request of not less than half the Member Countries'.[83] The responsibilities of the Conference of Ministers include putting into effect the decisions made, coordinating policies concerning matters falling within CIPEC's competence, classifying subjects to be discussed, according to 'major' or 'minor' importance, and supervising activities of the Executive Committee.[84] Finally, the Conference of Ministers is entitled 'to request from the Executive Committee specific studies concerning the copper industry'.[85]

The Executive Committee consists of 'one or more national representatives of each Member Country, one of them being the Permanent Representative of his country and the others being considered Alternative Representatives and Advisers'.[86] The permanent representatives, who must be nationals of the member countries they represent, are expected to have held responsible positions in their respective countries related to the formulation or implementation of national policy regarding the copper industry. The Executive Committee meets at least every two weeks; the necessary quorum for the meetings to be valid is the presence of two-thirds of the member countries.[87]

The Executive Committee is primarily responsible for

> co-ordinating and proposing to the governments of the Member Countries individual or collective measures relating to the copper market, production processes, the expansion of consumption and any other measures designed to implement the objectives which the Conference of Ministers shall determine and recommend to it.[88]

Furthermore, in addition to approving CIPEC's annual budget and appointing technical committees to study and report on various aspects of the copper industry, the Executive Committee 'shall endeavour to ensure technical and administrative co-operation among Member Countries by formulating specific proposals for this purpose'.[89] Finally, the Executive Committee may, on behalf of CIPEC, 'make whatever consultation and co-operation with other organizations and governments of non-member countries, in accordance with the guidelines established by the Conference of Ministers'.[90] This clause is an important indication of the error in labelling and evaluating CIPEC as a classical cartel.

The Secretariat is composed of a Secretary-General and his staff. The Secretary-General is directly responsible to the Executive Committee, which appoints him, subject to the unanimous approval of the Member Countries. The functions of the Secretary-General, in addition to acting as Secretary to the Conference of Ministers and to the Executive Committee (during its meetings he has the right to speak but not to vote) are also

> to act as the legal representative of the Organization, to see to the preparation of reports, and to appoint the technical and administrative personnel of the Secretariat in accordance with the instructions which he shall receive from the Executive Committee.[91]

The function of the Secretariat is to provide information concerning copper production, consumption, and marketing and to prepare reports on the following:

1. *Demand*
   I: structure and evolution
   II: substitution and new uses of copper
   III: projections;
2. *Supply*
   I: expansion programmes of mines in operation
   II: new production projects
   III: scrap;
3. *Evaluation of the relation between supply and demand*
   I: flow of trade
   II: stock movements;
4. *Marketing*
   I: contract forms
   II: copper prices at different stages of transformation;
5. *Governmental agreements and regulations*
   I: international agreements
   II: tariffs
   III: quotas
   IV: production subsidies
   V: strategic reserves;
6. *Technical advances in mining, processing, utilization of copper;*
7. *Labour, transport, and other economic factors affecting the copper industry;*
8. *All other problems relating to the marketing and sales of copper and its by-products and semi-manufactured products.*[92]

Finally, CIPEC's Secretariat is apparently insulated from the members themselves. Article 16 of the 1977 modification of the CIPEC Agreement states, 'the Secretary-General and staff shall not seek or receive instructions from any government of the Member Country'.[93] In other words, each member government of CIPEC 'must respect the exclusively international character of the responsibilities of the Secretary-General and staff and shall not seek to influence them in the discharge of their responsibilities'.[94]

In concluding this section on the creation of CIPEC, the first Third World producers' association in the copper industry, it is important to remark that when the 1967 meeting in Zambia was announced, most observers thought that concrete proposals would be made reflecting the close cooperation of those attending. More specifically, it was expected that the CIPEC governments would agree on both a copper floor and ceiling price. The issue of immediate action was, however, left out of the meeting. The extent of agreement was limited to the establishment of a permanent body of copper producers. The meeting took no action on either a common price or on production policies. From the standpoint of those who conceive of producers' associations as cartels, the aims of the conference must have seemed very limited. Both the South American and African representatives deliberately decided to exclude discussions of price at that significant meeting.

When CIPEC was formed, its members' priorities were, understandably, to nationalize the properties of the foreign copper companies that dominated their industries. The organization seemed to show a great sensitivity to the health of the copper market and, especially, to the interests of the consuming countries. Therefore the preamble of its agreement insists on the need to maintain a fair price of copper for both exporters and consumers in time of war and peace. Although spokesmen for CIPEC (backed by its written objectives) maintain that the organization is not a cartel, most analysts, however, continue to treat it as one. The following section underlines the conceptual error in treating CIPEC as a cartel.

The Limited Prospects of a Third World Copper Exporters' Cartel

The ability of a producers' association to alter, or regulate, a particular commodity market, that is, to operate as a cartel, depends on both economic and political factors. As noted in Chapter 4, the most important characteristics that would facilitate cartel-like producer collusion are that: the organization controls the supply of the commodity; increases in the price of the commodity do not significantly affect both the demand for the commodity and its supply from sources outside the organization; and there must be sufficient cohesion to keep the organization together. In the light of these conditions, this section will examine the prospects of an organization constituted by the four major Third World copper-exporters operating as a cartel in the international copper industry. More specifically, can CIPEC significantly influence the price of copper through production cutbacks or export restrictions? The question of CIPEC's ability to enforce production cutbacks is pertinent because, as noted in the first section of this chapter, although it is possible in the copper industry to maintain a regional, or even a world, producer price for a short time at a level higher than the free market price, in the longer run, all copper prices will tend to move together, so that the attainment by a group of exporters of control over the price of its output must be achieved by controlling world prices. An increase in the world price of copper over the competitive world market level can only be accomplished by a reduction in supply on the part of the group seeking to influence the world price. CIPEC's ability to operate as a cartel is thus seen as depending not only on the organization's market control, but also on the willingness of its members to cut back on production or sales.

Two measures, percentage of production and percentage of world exports, have often been employed in attempting to describe the market control of a producers' association. As Table 6 and 7 respectively show, the four founding members of CIPEC together, on the average, accounted for about 31 percent of world mine output of copper and about 50 percent of world exports of mine copper between 1973 and 1982. CIPEC's 50 percent share of the world's exports of mine copper, including refined, blister, and concentrates, is, however, not an accurate measure of its control of the world market. This is because national and international markets are linked and because, as will be observed, most of the secondary refined copper produced in the United States, Europe, and Japan, which does not enter into international trade *per se*, still constitutes an important part of the total world supply of copper. For example, although CIPEC governments supplied some 30 percent of the non-Communist world's mine production in 1974, mine production alone represented only 60 percent of the total world supply of copper, with the remainder represented by old and new scrap outputs.[95] In the light of the 40 percent of total world supply represented by old and new scrap outputs, CIPEC governments effectively supplied a much lower percentage of the total supply of copper to the non-Communist world in 1974, than their 50 percent share of world exports suggests at first sight. The picture is the same if we consider the case of refined copper alone. Eighty-three percent of the Western world's supply of refined copper was derived from primary or mine production, so that the CIPEC governments, in effect, supplied only 32 percent of the Western world's consumption of refined copper, including concentrates and blister that were actually refined outside the CIPEC countries.[96]

Against this background, let us consider to what extent CIPEC members would need to cut back their production, or exports, in order to influence the price of copper in both the short and long run. The following formula for determining the elasticity of demand for CIPEC's copper output is useful:

$$E_{Dc} = \frac{1}{m} \times E_{Dw} - \frac{1}{m} \times (1 - m) \times E_{Sr}$$

where E_{Dc} is the elasticity of demand for CIPEC's output
E_{Dw} is the elasticity of world demand for copper,
m is the portion of world demand supplied by CIPEC
E_{Sr} is the elasticity of supply of non-CIPEC sources.[97]

In the short run, if we assume that the CIPEC governments control 33 percent of the world's copper supply, that the elasticity of demand for world copper is minus 0.2, and that the elasticity of supply of non-CIPEC sources is 0.1,[98] then the elasticity of demand for CIPEC's output (E_{Dc}) would be equal to minus 0.8.[99] In other words, to achieve a 10 percent increase in the world price, CIPEC would have to reduce its output by 8 percent. This case would represent the most favourable condition for CIPEC, compared to the least favourable case, with an elasticity of demand for its copper equal to minus 2.3, where the organization would have to reduce its output by 23 percent in order to increase the world price by 10 percent.[100] Such a course of action would be disastrous for the CIPEC governments whose foreign exchange proceeds would fall by over 13 percent as a consequence. In general, in Mikesell's words, it appears very likely that the short-run elasticity of demand for CIPEC copper is in the neighbourhood of unity, which means in effect that they could not increase their export proceeds significantly, if at all, by cutting back on supply.[101]

Similarly, with respect to the longer run, virtually all estimates of demand and of the supply of non-CIPEC producers are near or well above unity.[102]

If we apply the above formula, but now assume that the elasticities of both long-run world demand and long-run supply of non-CIPEC sources are unity, then CIPEC governments would have to reduce their output by 34 percent to increase world prices by 10 percent. According to Mikesell,

> even if all of the developing country copper producers plus Australia joined in a producers' cartel and if the long-run elasticity of the supply of copper from the world outside the producers' cartel were zero, the elasticity of demand for the output of the producers' cartel would be only –1.1.[103]

This means that in order to raise the world price by 10 percent, such a cartel would have to cut back its production by 11 percent so that the export proceeds of its members would actually be reduced.

To summarize the analysis so far, in the short run, for CIPEC to achieve a 10 percent increase in the world price of copper, it would have to cut back its output by 8 percent. In the long run, it would have to cut its production by 34 percent to achieve a 10 percent increase in the world price. Obviously, it would be disastrous for CIPEC members to implement such policies. Generally, the following problems would confront a Third World producers' association in its attempt to act as a cartel:

1. new production of non-member supplies;
2. the existence of secondary supplies;
3. the production of substitute materials; and
4. the existence of materials stockpiles.

With respect to the first problem, CIPEC is faced with the situation in which three superpowers, the United States, Canada, and the Soviet Union together control 42 percent of the world's copper reserves. The United States alone controlled 64 percent of the total reserves of these three countries and 27 percent of the total world reserves. In comparison, the four CIPEC governments accounted for 46 percent of the total reserves.[104] The existence of these important non-CIPEC copper producers suggests that CIPEC's ability to act as a cartel may be inhibited by the possibility that these new suppliers will try to break CIPEC's market control by undercutting its agreed upon prices and frustrating its regulations. This problem is by no means unique to CIPEC. In the oil industry, for example, OPEC's ability to act as a cartel is also potentially threatened by important non-OPEC oil sources located in the North Sea, Mexico, Alaska, the Canadian Arctic, and the Chinese continental shelf. As the history of the oil industry reveals, however, most of these non-OPEC sources, exemplified most notably by the United States, are apparently willing to follow OPEC's pricing policies and, in effect, are becoming *de facto* OPEC members. The relevant question for CIPEC is whether or not the United

Table 6

CIPEC's Share of World Copper Output, 1973–1982
(in thousand ton copper content)

	1973	1974	1975	1976	1977	1978	1979	1980	1981	1982
Mine Production										
Chile	735	902	828	1005	1054	1034	1063	1068	1081	1241
Peru	203	212	181	220	329	376	397	367	328	356
Zaire	489	500	495	444	482	424	400	460	505	495
Zambia	707	698	677	709	656	643	588	596	587	530
Total CIPEC	2133	2312	2181	2378	2521	2477	2448	2491	2501	2622
Total World	7502	7668	7346	7825	7946	7855	7927	7866	8335	n.a.*
CIPEC as Percentage of Total World	28	30	30	30	32	32	31	32	30	n.a.
Unrefined Metal Production										
Chile	590	724	724	856	888	927	949	953	954	1047
Peru	173	177	161	188	321	319	371	349	315	327
Zaire	450	454	463	408	451	391	370	426	468	467
Zambia	683	710	659	706	659	654	595	601	572	598
Total CIPEC	1896	2065	2007	2158	2319	2291	2285	2329	2309	2439
Total World	7717	7879	7532	7940	8134	8071	8101	7920	8316	n.a.
CIPEC as Percentage of Total World	25	26	27	27	29	28	28	29	28	n.a.

Table 6 — continued

	1973	1974	1975	1976	1977	1978	1979	1980	1981	1982
					Refined Production					
Chile	415	538	535	632	676	748	780	811	776	852
Peru	39	39	54	136	188	185	230	231	209	225
Zaire	230	255	226	66	99	103	103	144	151	175
Zambia	639	677	629	695	649	628	564	607	564	596
Total CIPEC	1323	1509	1444	1529	1612	1664	1677	1793	1700	1848
Total World	8521	8904	8345	8790	9084	9212	9348	9363	9656	n.a.
CIPEC as Percentage of Total World	16	17	17	17	18	18	18	19	18	n.a.

Source: *Statistical Bulletin, 1982* (CIPEC, Neuilly Sur Seine, July 1983) pp. 1–3.

* n.a. = not available.

States, Canada, and Russia will expand their production to take advantage of CIPEC's pricing policies. It is impossible to answer this question with any degree of certainty. At any point in time, one can safely say only that the existence of important non-CIPEC copper producers constitutes a potential problem for CIPEC in attempting to operate as a cartel.

This observation is not meant to diminish CIPEC's influence in the copper industry. On the contrary, in terms of statistics, the organization commands some respect. As Mezger has pointed out, in 1973, the countries of the European Economic Commission (EEC), excluding the United States and Canada, together imported approximately 45 percent of their internationally purchased copper from CIPEC countries; in 1972, the figure was 50 percent.[105] In more specific terms, in 1973, Belgium obtained 67 percent of its refined copper and 61 percent of its unrefined copper from Zaire. West Germany imported 37 percent of its refined copper and 33 percent of its unrefined copper from CIPEC countries. Zambia supplied 48 percent of Britain's imports of refined copper. Italy and the Netherlands, which import only refined copper, obtained it principally from Chile, Zaire, and Zambia. Japan imported 60 percent of its copper from CIPEC countries in the form of concentrates.[106] Moreover, copper reserves from the non-CIPEC member countries (as will be observed in Chapter 6) are generally lower in quality than those located in CIPEC countries. This makes the non-CIPEC deposits somewhat less desirable from an investment point of view. Furthermore (as will also be discussed in Chapter 6) there are signs that, especially in the United States, environmental regulations may make increased copper production a very expensive undertaking particularly in the smelting and refining stages. Finally, it has been clear for some time now that the Soviet Union has been having difficulty in raising the necessary capital to develop its large copper reserves. In all, these advantages, from the standpoint of CIPEC, notwithstanding, the existence of important non-member copper producing areas will certainly inhibit CIPEC's operations as a cartel.

The second problem relating to CIPEC's ability to operate as a cartel is the availability of significant secondary supplies of copper. In the copper industry, secondary copper, that is, material recovered from scrap or metallurgical wastes, is often referred to as 'mining above the ground'.[107] Together, these wastes represent a pool of potentially usable material. Their transformation into exploitable reserves depends on technology, investment, infrastructure, quality, and prices. If we assume reserves are thus established, price becomes a major factor influencing the degree to which consuming industries utilize these reserves. Recycling is especially attractive in the industry because copper's secondary product can be a perfect substitute for primary metal obtained from ore. Compared to other minerals industries, the copper industry affords a relatively high recovery rate of copper from wastes because the end uses for refined copper partially produced from scrap are the same as for copper refined from ore, if both types of metal are refined to the same degree. In other words, the market for secondary copper is virtually inseparable from that of primary copper, the relationship between the two appearing on both the supply and

Table 7

CIPEC's Share of World Copper Exports.* 1973–1982
(in thousand ton copper content)

	1973	1974	1975	1976	1977	1978	1979	1980	1981	1982
Chile	657	859	788	982	1008	977	1010	1045	1038	1208
Peru	207	236	149	180	333	356	383	353	322	344
Zaire	476	483	493	421	490	440	366	461	463	513
Zambia	670	682	633	733	655	576	647	617	556	603
Total CIPEC	2010	2260	2063	2316	2486	2349	2406	2476	2379	2668
Total World	4391	4854	4311	4644	4884	4649	4644	5051	4852	5138
CIPEC as Percentage of Total World	46	47	48	50	51	51	52	49	49	52

* Includes ores and concentrates, and unrefined and refined copper.

Source: *Statistical Bulletin, 1982* (CIPEC, Neuilly Sur Seine, July 1983) p. 7.

demand sides.

Gluschkle *et al.* aptly described the importance of secondary copper in the copper industry:

> Recently, there has been a strong resurgence of interest in expanding the recycling of metals in general, especially in the industrialized countries, and this is easy to understand. Recycling helps to reduce consumption of non-renewable resources — a feature particularly attractive to rich countries sensitive to accusations of "reckless resource gobbling". It has, on balance, less harmful effects in the environment than the extraction and utilization of virgin ores. In addition, the recycling of metals can aid in reducing import dependence, since the distribution of recyclable materials strongly favours the industrialized nations. Furthermore, the technology of refining metals from scrap — at least from traditional sources of good-quality scrap — is far simpler than the winning of materials from ores, and the capital requirements for scrap processing are relatively low. *The last two factors contribute to a market structure which is less concentrated and more competitive than that of primary industries. The competitiveness of the scrap market, in turn, constitutes a significant obstacle to attempts at controlling the price of copper.*[108]

There are two main types of secondary copper: new scrap and old scrap. New scrap is the by-product of semi-manufacturing and fabricating operations, and old scrap is the by-product of obsolescence. An important determinant of the availability of new scrap is the level of copper consumption and of activity in the copper fabricating and manufacturing industries.[109] In other words, in general, there is a fairly close relationship between the direct use of scrap (and by inference, new scrap-generation) and copper consumption. Available data indicate that between 1966 and 1976, the ratio between the direct use of new scrap and refined copper consumption in the principal copper-consuming regions, though fluctuating from year to year, remained within relatively narrow margins. On the average, between 1966 and 1976, the direct use of new scrap as a percentage of total copper consumption was about 33 percent in Europe and 40 percent in both Japan and the United States.[110]

The availability of secondary copper from old scrap is related to the size and composition of the stock of copper-using goods, and the price paid for scrap arising from this stock.[111] The size of the stock of copper in use, according to an unpublished CIPEC report, grew fairly steadily on the average, between 1960 and 1974, by about 4.4 percent in the United States, 3.4 percent in the United Kingdom, 3.8 percent in Germany, and 4.5 percent in France. This growth in the size of the stock of copper in use, however, does not alone assure a growth in scrap supplies. What is crucial is the composition of the stock available as old scrap, since there is likely to be a considerable variation in the life span of different copper-using goods. According to Gluschke *et al.*, the average life spans of copper-using products are by no means fixed, but are closely related to current consumption or investment patterns. For example, they argue that a shift in the proportion of national income going to investment may result in a change in the rate of replacement of both investment and consumer goods (the first will rise and the second will fall), and hence in the life span of copper-using products. An increase in house-building may be associated with a rise in demolition rates, thus almost certainly reducing the life span of copper-using products in construction.[112]

The existence and nature of scrap in the industry, nevertheless, threaten the potential operation of a cartel for a Third World producers' association such as CIPEC, especially considering, as has been noted, that there are important non-CIPEC copper producers. Interestingly, much of the copper used more than a century ago is still available for use today.[113] Among recycled non-ferrous metals, copper is first in terms of the largest amount of recovered metal and in terms of the highest proportion of recycled material to its total consumption.[114] According to a CIPEC source, about 61 percent of all types and kinds of scrap available for recycling in the world in 1969 was actually recycled. This includes electric wire and copper tube, magnet wire, cartridge brass, automotive radiators, railroad car boxes, and other brass cast and wrought, low-grade scrap and residues. In the United States, among selected metals, copper had the highest rate of scrap recovery; but this rate fell from 59 percent in 1967, to 52 percent in 1972, and to 47 percent in 1977.[115] In 1976, the United States recovered 63 percent of its secondary copper from prompt industrial waste (new scrap) and 37 percent from old scrap.[116] Between 1966 and 1967, total secondary copper as a proportion of total refined copper consumption was, on the average, 20 percent in western Europe, 12 percent in Japan, and 20 percent in the United States.[117]

In all, the fundamental problem of recycling can, from the standpoint of the cartelization of the copper industry, be understood only in the context of the overall determination of the price of copper. As one study has put it, 'if there is one infallible rule of the market place, it is that a careful price relationship between scrap and virgin metal prevails and in this context the price of scrap follows the direction of the virgin metal price'.[118] According to Mezger,

> A higher rate of recycling would only become possible through higher prices for scrap, which would guarantee the industry profits. Consequently, the recycling problem cannot be considered in absolute terms — that is to say, as the physical process of the recovery of used material — but rather as a problem of costs and prices which is entailed by this process and hence in terms of the likely profits to be made by the relevant industries.[119]

Assuming, therefore, from the point of view of the developed copper-consuming countries, that future cost-price relationships would tend to favour production from scrap over primary copper, one could reasonably expect that if, in the future, the developed economies felt threatened by a cartel-like action by CIPEC, a concerted effort by the consuming countries to recycle copper would be possible. Such a move would, in effect, substantially increase non-CIPEC supplies of copper and diminish CIPEC's market control. In general, then, the existence of secondary materials could substantially inhibit the ability of a Third World copper producers' cartel to create shortages of supply in order to raise prices.

The substitution of materials represents a third problem that would probably threaten the potential market control of a Third World copper exporters' cartel. Copper does have rivals, despite its characteristics that lend it to a wide range of application. Some of copper's useful qualities include its high electrical and thermal conductivity, its ease of working and ability to enter into alloys, its facility for soldering, its suitable mechanical properties such as malleability and tensile strength, its corrosion resistance, its good electro-deposition aspects, and its decorative, artistic, and architectural aptness.[120] Nevertheless, adverse circumstances which can promote the shortage of copper, and the volatility of copper prices have both strengthened the role of substitutes as rivals of copper. Among rivals, iron was perhaps the earliest to appear in history, but copper's most important rival today is aluminium, followed by plastics and stainless steel.[121]

For various technical reasons, however, no rival has totally replaced copper. First, for example, aluminium is an element with an atomic weight of 26.9815. It is lightweight and has a specific gravity of 2.7. Its melting point of 659.7°C is much lower than copper's 1,084°C.[122] Like copper, aluminium is malleable, ductile, and is an excellent conductor of electricity. Aluminium's primary natural source is bauxite. It is lighter than copper and quite strong. Though widely used in transportation and building, its challenge to copper primarily lies in the electrical field, particularly in manufacturing conductors.[123] Although aluminium's conductivity is only approximately 62 percent of copper's, its capacity is not too different, especially on a weight-for-weight basis.[124] A major disadvantage of aluminium, however, is the fact that copper could be produced far more cheaply in terms of energy consumption.

Second, the commercial production of plastics constitutes a spectacular growth industry that could threaten copper, especially in plumbing, in the building industry. One important disadvantage of plastics, *vis-à-vis* copper, is that, per unit weight, plastic raw materials cost more than most common metals.[125] Hence, except perhaps in the building field, plastics' inroads into copper consumption are not likely to be more than small scale.

Third, stainless steel, comprising a wide range of materials based on an iron-chromium combination, can compete with copper throughout the industry. Their prices are roughly the same; however, although stainless steel is harder and more heat-resistant than copper, copper is a better heat conductor.[126] In terms of electrical conductivity, stainless steel is a 'non-starter' compared to copper. Thus, technically, it does not appear that stainless steel would pose a serious threat to a cartel of copper producers in the copper industry.

In general, however, rivals have had some success in replacing the red metal. For example, according to Gluschke *et al.*, as a result of various types of substitution, the amount of copper used in the typical American-built car has been halved in the last 30 years.[127] Aluminium has been used most successfully to replace copper. The following examples suggest the steady substitution for copper by aluminium alone: 1) in the United States, the share of aluminium in the sales of building wire increased from under 4 percent in 1964 to an estimated 21 percent in 1975; 2) in the United States, aluminium's share in cable production increased from about 7 percent in 1966 to nearly 17 percent in 1974; 3) aluminium's share in cable production in the Federal Republic of Germany increased from 6.5 percent to 9.4 percent over a short period of five years, from 1969 to 1975; and 4) in the United States, the share of aluminium, on a conductivity basis in the electrical consumption of copper and aluminium combined, rose from less than 50 percent in 1960 to about 70 percent in 1973.[128]

A fourth market problem potentially facing a Third World producers' cartel can be appreciated in terms of the possibility that major consumers of the material would maintain stockpiles. According to Hveem, the countries that consume raw materials believe that 'stockpiling means building up a reserve before consumption, or further processing, in order to defend normal production against the possibility of supply shortage and/or defend oneself against higher prices due to supply shortage'.[129] From the consumers' point of view, secure availability of raw materials and time are thus the main reasons for stockpiling. Stockpiling is, therefore, a potential threat to the efficiency of a copper exporters' cartel. In the case of the United States, according to Mikesell, 'national stockpiles have been accumulated to support the domestic producing industry or to maintain a specific degree of national self-sufficiency . . . they might be held to combat possible foreign cartel activities designed to force up prices'.[130]

The largest stockpiles in the world copper industry are located in the United States, and are administered by the General Services Administration (GSA). Although U.S. stockpiles are supposedly 'strategic', they have been known to be used to control the price of copper in periods of increasing demand. Hveem explains that

> over long periods, the U.S. stockpiling programme, GSA, has played a major role in influencing markets and in protecting the U.S. against outside influence. Nevertheless, from after the Korean War until the crisis of the early 1970s, there was a *steady reduction* in the level of consumers' or processors' stocks of raw materials in relation to the sales of manufactured output. This trend reflected improvements in management techniques, more reliable and rapid transportation, the expectation that prices would remain stable or decline in real terms, as well as the expectation that the political climate would remain stable and guarantee secure supplies. Then came the crisis of the 1970s — real or imagined — and from 1973 and 1974 on stocks swelled as they had done during the major wars. This was due to "boom-like" buying up by consumers, notably Japan; and to the subsequent recession which made centre manufacturing firms sit on huge volumes of metals that could not be put into production, and which further meant a fall in producers' selling possibilities. This has been particularly noticeable in copper . . .[131]

In general, while the sale or release of stockpiles may have only a short-term impact, they can, nevertheless, significantly affect the international price of copper and diminish the market control of a Third World producers' cartel.

In addition to these previous problems, CIPEC also faces an important threat from the technical viability and economic feasibility of mining the ocean's resources.[132] As was noted in Chapter 3, ocean mining, like the development of scrap and substitute materials, is a good example of the use of technology as a defensive strategy by metropolitan firms. The mining of the sea yields manganese nodules that contain nickel, copper, cobalt, and manganese. It represents one of the last great chances for metropolitan mining companies to obtain virtually absolute control over the world's available mineral resources in order to neutralize any possible threat of Third World governments' landownership.

The impetus to exploit the ocean's resources was provided by the United Nations' Law of the Sea that established a 200-mile zone of economic exploitation. It significantly affected Third World landlord governments, involving the largest exporters of nickel, copper, cobalt, and manganese. One study has estimated that there are, potentially, approximately one to five billion tons of copper resources in nodules, and that the total tonnage of copper contained in nodules in a 2.25-million square kilometre area is, on the average, 58 million tons. Also, it was expected that by 1985, the total tonnage of dry nodules recovered annually could vary from 5 to 10 million tons.[133]

Studies tend to predict that the main effect of the working of manganese nodules would be not on the world's suppliers of copper, but rather on the suppliers of cobalt, nickel, and manganese.[134] What needs to be stressed, however, is that in an industry dominated by metropolitan mining corporations, technological innovations are being manipulated by them as a defensive strategy to uphold their monopolistic positions *vis-à-vis* Third World governments, and to ensure secure supplies of vital resources for their home governments.

A congressman once expressed the U.S. position:

> even though there may not be a tremendous amount of minerals extracted from the seabed for a number of years, the fact that the technology is there gives you an alternative source. In effect, this better negotiating position would have a levelling effect on price and also assure us of some stability of supply.[135]

One analyst wrote that

> the mining of manganese nodules is most unlikely to be a competitive industry. While there are currently more than 25 firms expressing an interest in mining, only a few are likely to mine. The number of mines will probably even be less and some are likely to form consortia or joint ventures for this endeavour.[136]

Mezger has estimated that by 1985, if one assumes (though it is unlikely) that copper consumption in the West would increase by 4 percent per year, the volume of copper consumption in the West that would be accounted for by ocean mining may well increase from 6.7 million tons in 1980, to 10 million tons by 1985, a figure that would be greater than the one million tons of copper that would be produced by Chile, the biggest Third World exporting country.[137] It should, therefore, be expected that rising copper prices, provoked by Third

World copper exporters' production cutbacks, will accelerate interest in ocean mining as an alternative source of copper in the future. Most likely, the future development of ocean mining would significantly weaken CIPEC's ability to operate a cartel in the world copper industry.

One other problem to be considered in this section is the differences in CIPEC members' historical experiences and in the characteristics of their economies, which could inhibit their cohesiveness. Table 8 presents some estimated background data for the four founding members of CIPEC in 1970.

The four CIPEC countries are at historically different stages of political and economic development. Chile and Peru attained independence from the Spanish Empire in the early 1800s, more than 125 years before Zambia and Zaire did. Chile and Peru inherited a powerful domestic class of large landlords. Local businessmen also emerged, especially in trade, some of whom — especially in Chile — had begun to invest in small copper mines even before the turn of the century. Local businessmen also emerged in manufacturing, particularly following the Great Depression of the 1930s. Nevertheless, in both countries the development of large, technologically advanced copper mines was achieved in the 20th Century by a few giant, primarily U.S.-owned, copper companies: Anaconda and Kennecott in Chile, and CERRO de Pasco (more recently, the Southern Peru Copper Company) in Peru.[138] Seidman has nicely summarized the colonial background of Zambia and Zaire and deserves to be quoted at length:

> the initial investments of the big copper companies were made under the umbrella of colonial rule, British in the former case and Belgian in the latter. Taxes on Africans and labour recruitment policies compelled Africans to migrate from remote rural areas to furnish the cheap labour needed to dig the mines. Taxes on company profits were low. Anglo-American Corporation and Roan Selection Trust (which became a subsidiary of American Metal Climax) together with the associated financial and trading institutions, shipped out an estimated half to two-thirds of the investable surpluses produced in the then Northern Rhodesia.
>
> Only after independence, in the 1960s, could African governments attempt to capture the investable surpluses produced by the mines and reallocate them to a diversified range of productive activities. Africanization programmes accelerated the entrance of a few Africans into top ministerial and civil service posts, enabling them to enjoy the high salaries and living standards previously reserved for whites. The bulk of the middle-level jobs, however, continued to be manned by expatriates. A range of government measures facilitated the entry of African entrepreneurs into trade. A handful of Africans began to accumulate wealth and invest in large firms or real estate. Few private individuals had the know-how or capital to enter into industrial production.[139]

One characteristic that is common to CIPEC countries is that although a relatively small proportion of the population is engaged in mining, as Table 8 indicates, the mines still produce an important share of exports and gross domestic product (GDP). On balance, however, copper exports appear to be somewhat less significant in Zaire and Peru (where larger populations and land

Table 8

Some Estimated Background Data for CIPEC Countries: Chile, Peru, Zambia, and Zaire, 1970

	Chile	*Peru*	*Zambia*	*Zaire*
Land area (km²)	741,767	1,285,216	752,000	2,335,409
Population	10,000,000	13,171,800	4,500,000	21,637,876
Urban percent of total	75	52	50	30
Mining output as percent of exports	73	46*	95	67
Percent of GDP	10	5.5	42	26.1 (1969)
Per capita income (dollars)	450	291	299	70–74
World copper position: percent production, 1970 (metric tons)	13.2	4.1	13.4	7.4
Known reserves (millions of tons/copper content)	53.8	18.1	27.2	18.1
Percent reserves (1964): world reserves assessed at 50.5 million tons at same grade as currently produced	21.1	5.9	11.9	9.5
Average grade of ore (percent copper)	1.53	1.14	3.38	4.2
Cost per pound of mining copper: cents per pound	30.88	26.48	30.16	25.32
Range of mining cost: cents per pound	26.30–52.00	25.60–32.00	25.80–35.00	20.10–38.50

Table 8 — continued

	Chile	Peru	Zambia	Zaire
Proportion nationally owned	Major foreign-owned companies expropriated 1971; new investments by foreign corporations encouraged	Peruvian government recovered most of undeveloped copper properties; developed properties mainly owned by foreign firms; Cerro de Pasco mine purchased by government	51 percent equity acquired by government	100 percent equity acquired by government. Foreign consortiums opening new mines with government owning minority of shares
Linkages				
Forward				
Percent refined	40 (1966)	20 (1966)	85 (1970) 79 (1966)	65 (1970) 50 (1966)
Percent fabricated	15	—	—	—
Backward				
Portion of machines, plant, and equipment imported	High	High	Almost all	Almost all
Percent of wage employment	3 (mining) About one-half copper	2 (mining)	14 (mining)	4 (1969)

* Copper = 20 percent

Note: The comparability of the data is necessarily affected by the fluctuations of domestic and international prices, exchange rates, and errors of estimation, so that the data can only be considered comparable in terms of rough orders of magnitude.

Source: Ann Seidman, 'Introduction: Why the Copper Countries?' in Ann Seidman (ed.) *Natural Resources and National Welfare* (Praeger Publishers, New York, 1975) p. 5.

areas have facilitated production of a somewhat more diversified range of exports) than in Chile and Zambia. Copper produced a smaller proportion of the GDP in Chile and Peru (where other sectors of the domestic economy have been somewhat more monetized through the combined efforts of domestic entrepreneurs, government measures, and foreign investment in the last century and a half of formal independence) than in Zambia and Zaire.

These differences in their historical experiences and in their economies, including the differences in the levels of costs affecting them, will make cooperation among these countries difficult. There are also political differences among them. For example, diplomatic relations between Zambia and Chile were, for a while, very unhealthy. Also, however improbable, there have been rumours that Chile wished to leave CIPEC. The point is that the differences of interest among CIPEC countries are enough to exacerbate the weakness of a cartel organized by them. More specifically, even assuming that production cutbacks were possible among members, the differences in interests among them would present problems in their sharing of the costs of such cutbacks. For example, it would be difficult to agree on the terms for determining the base year for a uniform cutback of production. Any base year would most likely be unique for particular countries as a consequence of strikes, transportation difficulties, or other factors affecting the capacity utilization of that year. As Mikesell correctly observed,

> a country whose output has been restricted by say 20 percent as a consequence of special circumstances in the base year is likely to object to a 20 percent cutback on the basis of output during that year. Similarly, a country whose capacity has been increased by 20 percent as a consequence of a new mine which has been completed in the year during which cutbacks are enforced will object to an arrangement which bases the cutbacks on its capacity in the base year.[140]

Moreover, if CIPEC members agree simply to cut back on exports rather than on production, there will be an accumulation of inventories that will surely overhang the market in future years, and their ability to finance inventory accumulation is very limited. In the long run, individual CIPEC members are, in effect, in competition with one another in terms of expanding capacity, and are unlikely to agree on limiting the growth of their productive capacities. Even if they did so, it would almost certainly spur investment in mine capacity in the United States, Canada, South Africa, and other countries that are not likely to join a Third World producers' cartel.

The Uncartel-like Impact of CIPEC's Policy Output

As was noted earlier in this chapter, when it was announced in 1967 that the first inter-governmental conference of copper-exporting governments, which later formed CIPEC, would take place in the first week of June, most observers expected that participants would agree on a floor and ceiling price for copper. Except for the establishment of a permanent body of copper producers, however, no such action was taken at that significant meeting. In fact, not until

1969 was CIPEC's next conference of ministers even convened.

From the point of view of those who expected to see CIPEC operate as a cartel, the organization's earlier years were marked by lack of effective policy action. For example, during CIPEC's earlier years, its members were engaged in a gradual process of institution-building and emphasized information-gathering and statistical studies as the best way to proceed. According to Mingst, an examination of CIPEC documents produced from 1968 to 1972 showed that 'of eighty-three documents of the Governing Board, twenty-nine discussed organizational problems and thirteen were proposals for studies'; in the Executive Committee of the Copper Information Bureau, 'out of one hundred and ninety-nine documents, ninety-eight concerned aspects of administration and fifty were suggested studies'.[141] Even OPEC, with more favourable environmental conditions for immediate cartel action, had to undergo a process of 'inactive' institution-building and also emphasized information-gathering and studies of the oil market. In the case of OPEC, and during a comparable time frame of institutional development (1960–64), although 33 of the 53 resolutions passed concerned administrative matters and twelve authorized studies, only eight could be considered to be policy-oriented.[142] CIPEC's earlier preoccupation with institutional development, like OPEC's, seemed to have pre-empted its supposed concern with policy related to collusive action.

A more important explanation of the absence of positive collusive action during CIPEC's earlier years is that the individual objectives of members of the organization seemed to outweigh any possible benefit from collusive action at that time. Soon after the inception of CIPEC, each of the member governments became engrossed in the different process of acquiring control of their individual copper resources from metropolitan mining firms.[143] Although their new organization must have provided some psychological encouragement in their efforts to nationalize the properties of foreign firms, CIPEC member governments took individual responsibility in its accomplishment. From the perspectives of the individual CIPEC governments, each of which was dependent on the copper industry for a significant proportion of its revenues, this priority of nationalizing their industries was obviously a more economically and politically rational move than the attempt to curtail production and increase prices.

The government of Zaire was the first CIPEC member to nationalize its copper industry. In 1966, six years after Zaire's political independence from Belgium, President Mobutu took over the properties of Belgium's Union Minière du Haut Katanga without specifying how much compensation, if any, was to be paid. That move resulted in a 10 percent reduction in world copper exports and a 70 percent drop in Zaire's foreign exchange earnings.[144] The Belgian company responded by: 1) pulling out its personnel, for whom there were no Zairean substitutes; 2) threatening to bring legal action against the sale of Zairean copper, a move which effectively closed world markets to Zaire's copper; and 3) obtaining assurances from Portugal that the trans-shipment of Zaire's copper through Angola and Mozambique would be prohibited.[145] The economically detrimental impact of Zaire's action notwithstanding, it was justified by Mobutu as a step towards Congolization. Copper exports were suspended until 1967 when negotiations over compensation began, with the World Bank mediating. According to Prain, the process of nationalization in Zaire was long and painful. 'It was undertaken against a background of insurrection, destruction and bloodshed, and six troubled years were to go by before the political and economic situation began to stabilize'.[146]

Upon taking over the properties of Union Minière,[147] the government of Zaire set up a Zairean state corporation, Générale Congolaise des Minerais (GECAMINES), to be responsible for the country's mining. Expatriate technical and management expertise was retained in the country by an agreement with Belgium's Société Générale des Minerais (SGM), which had been responsible for marketing Zaire's copper products.[148] This arrangement left management and marketing control effectively in the hands of the Belgians. On 10 July 1974, the government created the Société Zairoise de Commercialisation des Minerais (SOZACOM) as part of the process of increasing state involvement.[149] It is responsible for marketing the production of all of Zaire's minerals. President Mobutu's Congolization programme, aimed at placing Zaireans in top management positions, continued through the late 1970s.

In Chile, new directions and initiatives with regard to state involvement in the copper industry came from Eduardo Frei and Salvador Allende even before either of them became president. While Frei promoted a Chileanization short of legal expropriation and based on joint-venture companies with governmental participation, Allende sponsored a plan for all-out nationalization of the foreign-owned copper-mining companies.

Frei was elected president in September 1964. By the end of October, he had concluded an agreement with the U.S.-owned CERRO Corporation, according to which a joint-venture company, the Compania Mineria Andina, S.A., was to be formed, in which the Chilean government would hold a 25 percent interest. Frei's negotiations with the U.S.-owned Anaconda Copper Mining Company did not immediately lead to substantial arrangements of the joint-venture type at the time. His negotiations with the other large U.S.-owned, copper-producing company, the Braden Copper Company, a wholly-owned subsidiary of Kennecott Copper Company, proved to be more successful for his Chileanization. The agreement provided that Kennecott's principal property in Chile, the El Teniente Mines, would be acquired by a new joint-venture, the El Teniente Mining Company, Inc., and that the Chilean government would purchase a 51 percent interest at a price of $80 million. Kennecott's Braden Company would hold the remaining 49 percent interest for Kennecott. These agreements were ratified on 25 January 1966, and 24 April 1967.[150]

Under Frei, Chile's copper corporation, CODELCO, was established with full state ownership. It became a holding company for the interests of the Chilean government in joint-ventures that it eventually entered into with the three American copper companies. In his state-of-the-nation message in May 1969, Frei reasserted his firm stand against total nationalization of the U.S.-owned copper companies because, according to him, Chile did not have the financial resources to undertake such an action.[151] He emphasized, however, that Chile wanted a bigger cut of the 'profits' from its copper. Obviously referring to Anaconda, Frei warned, 'we consider it about time that those companies that have strayed away from the Chileanization programme fall back into line'.[152] After further discussions, an agreement with Anaconda was subsequently reached on 26 June 1969, which gave the Chilean government 51 percent interest in Anaconda's Chiquicamata and El Salvador mines.

Prompt criticism against the terms of these agreements soon came from Allende's leftist groups, whose aims were, unlike Frei's, immediate and total nationalization of the American companies. Allende became president of Chile in September 1970. Total nationalization of the three American-owned copper companies went into effect on 16 July 1971.[153] Even though the military junta that overthrew Allende in September 1973 reversed most of the previous policies in favour of the American companies and paid compensation to the companies in cases where such compensation had not been made by one or both of the previous governments, the copper industry was not denationalized *per se*. In the final analysis, the result of Chile's Chileanization was similar to that of Zaire's Congolization: foreign copper companies of both countries were still able to retain management and marketing control.

In Zambia, even though the nationalization spirit had surfaced as early as 1965, the government was not able to organize the programme because of Zambia's foreign relations, which were then complicated by: 1) Southern Rhodesia's Unilateral Declaration of Independence on 11 November 1965; 2) the then unsettled situation in Zaire; and 3) Zambia's strained relations with Portugal.[154] Zambia's President Kaunda could not begin to promote a plan for government participation in his country's foreign-owned copper industry until he had found solutions to these international problems that particularly plagued Zambia's copper industry. It was not until four years after independence that Kaunda, in an address at Mulungushi in late April 1968, first announced a series of measures aimed at giving Zambians greater participation in the economic life of their country.[155] He invited 25 important companies to offer the government a 51 percent participation and introduced a new formula for royalties. At the same time, Kaunda was very careful to explain that foreign investors were still very welcome in Zambia and promised to enact legislation to safeguard approved foreign investments.[156]

On 11 August 1969, Kaunda announced that all rights of ownership or partial ownership of minerals would revert to the state, that new concessions would be granted on the basis of 25-year leases, and that the Zambian state would take over 51 percent of the properties of Britain's Anglo–American Corporation and the U.S.'s American Metal Climax Company.[157] Ostensibly to facilitate the takeover, Kaunda set up, under his personal direction, a Ministry of State Participation. He also assumed the office of Chairman of the Board of Directors of the Zambian Industrial and Mining Corporation, Ltd. (ZIMCO), which functioned as government holding company for the Industrial Development Corporation, Ltd. (MINDECO).[158] Anglo–American and American Metal Climax continued to participate effectively in new enterprises through sales and management contracts with the Zambian government. This arrangement seemed to serve Kaunda's immediate goals of reform by giving the Zambian state access to the local mining industry while attracting foreign management and maintaining prospecting activity and output expansion.

By 1973, it had become clear to Kaunda that the sales and management contracts he had entered into with the copper companies had placed effective control of the enterprises in the hands of the minority shareholders, especially because of their veto power in major management decisions. He therefore announced, in May of that year, that further reforms were to be made, aimed at 'total Zambianization' of his country's copper industry. He set up a government-owned copper marketing company, Metal Marketing Corporation (MEMACO). The Zambian reform can be said to have been completed early in 1975 upon the finalization of compensation agreements involved in the government take-overs.[159]

Peru was the last CIPEC nation to nationalize its copper industry. By January 1974, when the Peruvian nationalizations finally came, the other CIPEC members had become significantly involved in the production of their copper. The Peruvian take-over basically involved CERRO de Pasco, the Peruvian subsidiary of the U.S.-based CERRO Corporation. Upon the overthrow of the government in 1968 by a military junta, headed by General Juan Valasco Alvarado, these companies were warned that the government intended to increase its direct and indirect participation in the production and sale of mineral products. By 1971, the government had gained control of more than 75 percent of its undeveloped copper potential and set up its own marketing agency, Minero-Peru, for marketing all of Peru's copper. By 1974, Peru had nationalized almost all of its major foreign-controlled copper properties.[160]

The argument that CIPEC members individually accomplished the task of nationalization, that is, without collusion in their organization, is supported by the fact that none of these significant changes appeared in CIPEC's agenda. Nevertheless, the rapid succession of events no doubt suggests that CIPEC members were stimulated by their counterparts' actions. In other words, the success of the nationalization move may have had a positive impact on the exporters' perception of their ability to dictate terms to the copper companies. In fact, the nationalization issue did lead to the first semblance of collective action by CIPEC members during 1972 and 1973, provoked by the Chile–Kennecott confrontation.

Before the Chile–Kennecott fracas, CIPEC members had briefly attempted to stabilize the price of copper. The governments of CIPEC had traditionally relied on a three-month forward producer price, but in June 1968, they decided to change to a producer price pegged to the daily spot LME price.[161] The decision was ostensibly designed to assure the organization's direct voice in copper pricing. It was proposed that CIPEC members periodically initiate joint intervention on LME as a means of softening daily price fluctuations. Apparently, it was expected that not only would such actions have a stabilizing effect on the price of copper, but also that they would demonstrate CIPEC's solidarity. However, no such interventionary actions were eventually taken by CIPEC members on LME. This is how one informed observer described the extent of CIPEC's action on LME in the late 1960s:

> Representatives did visit London; small volumes of copper were probably traded under CIPEC supervision. The action proved to be of positive psychological value to members. The act of unilaterally altering price indicators was reinforcing, even though the ramifications of the change were not exploited by the producers in the international market.[162]

In terms of a show of its solidarity, CIPEC's actions in response to Kennecott's strategy against Chile in the early 1970s proved more significant than the organization's proposal jointly to intervene on LME.

Allende's expropriation of Kennecott's remaining 49 percent share of El Teniente in 1971 had seriously affected the company's Chilean operations, which accounted for one-third of its total copper production. The company had responded not only by withdrawing all of its technicians from Chile but also by seeking to place an embargo on payments for Chilean copper delivered in the United States and Europe. The objective of the embargo was to press Kennecott's claim for indemnification on its properties nationalized by Allende in July 1971. Kennecott's actions presented obvious problems for the sale of Chile's copper and threatened the credibility of CIPEC's solidarity. CIPEC responded swiftly in support of Chile's position. In December 1972, at a Conference of Ministers meeting in Santiago, Chile, CIPEC's representatives unanimously adopted a Resolution on the 'Permanent Mechanism of Protection and Solidarity'.[163] Part of the preamble of the resolution noted that:

> the member countries of CIPEC, besides being large-scale producers of copper, are nations whose development possibilities are almost entirely conditioned by the sovereign exploitation and marketing of this natural resource. Hence it is imperatively necessary for them to take concerted action in the face of whatever measures of economic or political coercion may be adopted against any member country and which affect this right . . .. Acts of aggression which impede the sovereignty of States over their natural resources or their right to develop can emanate from other states, illegal regimes, or corporations, especially multinational ones.[164]

'Acts of economic' aggression were defined in the CIPEC resolution under the following categories: 1) action that would dispute the sovereignty of member countries over their natural resources; 2) action that would hamper the development of the production process of CIPEC members; 3) action that would impede the marketing of members' copper; and 4) action that would disrupt the economic life of a CIPEC state.[165]

In the face of any act of economic aggression on a CIPEC member, the Santiago Resolution provides that the responsibility of the permanent mechanism of protection and solidarity would be: 1) 'to defend the right of CIPEC member countries to exercise fully their sovereignty over their natural resources and their right to develop and, consequently, to condemn and oppose any attempt to restrict these rights', and 2) 'to assist the country that is victim of such aggression, in order to settle the situation in the best possible circumstances'.[166] Thirteen 'Concrete Measures on the Face of Economic Aggression' were then specified in the resolution. The most noteworthy one comes under 'Measures for Protecting the Interests of the Country Victim of the Aggression' and requires that quotas formerly sold by a CIPEC member that has suffered acts of economic aggression should not be replaced by other members.[167]

In summary, the 1972 Santiago Conference of Ministers unanimously recommended that members expose Kennecott's economic aggression, suspend all transactions with the company, explore possibilities for alleviating Chile's burden, and agree to refrain from usurping former Chilean markets. But because the market for copper was quite strong up to at least the middle of 1974, there was no real reason for any of the CIPEC members to take over Chile's markets anyway. On the whole, even though CIPEC's symbolic unity had been affirmed in its response to the Kennecott–Chile encounter, as Mingst put it, the strength of CIPEC's commitment went untested.[168]

The essence of the Santiago resolution was demonstrated on another occasion (during the closure of the Zambian–Rhodesian border in 1973) when CIPEC condemned Rhodesia's action and promised Zambia 'financial, economic, and diplomatic action'. Nobody really expected much further action from CIPEC on that occasion, but the Zambians did welcome its show of support.[169]

What is important to note about the Santiago resolution is that it did not specify for CIPEC members any enforcement mechanism. Furthermore, no threats were made against CIPEC members who would not observe the provisions of the resolution. This tactic is atypical of cartels; it was also noticeable in CIPEC's first attempt to coordinate pricing and production policy in 1974.

The international copper market was chaotic from 1972 to 1974. One reason was that supply shortages had been caused by a 1973 strike in Chile's El Teniente mine, and by chronic Zambian–Rhodesian transportation bottlenecks. Moreover, demand was increasing due to heavy buying by both Japan and the People's Republic of China. Furthermore, the floating exchange rates in the international monetary system helped exacerbate the basic instability of the copper market by accentuating speculation on LME.[170] By April 1974, the price of copper, at $1.52 per pound, had reached the highest level in modern history. By late September of that year, however, the price had fallen by 65 percent to about 60 cents per pound.[171]

Japan's reaction to the price decline exacerbated the problems faced by CIPEC members in the situation. In an attempt to avoid supply shortages associated with the earlier high price of copper, the Japanese had purchased large quantities. When the price began to drop, the Japanese resorted to dumping their over-stockpiled copper on the world market and to cancelling longstanding orders from copper-exporters, actions that further lowered the price of copper. CIPEC confronted the matter with diplomacy. Its Executive

Director was said to have sent a letter to the Japanese government on behalf of CIPEC's four founding members recalling CIPEC governments' traditional policy of cooperation with the importing governments, and he, therefore,

> expressed his astonishment at the contradictions between the spirit of the long-term supply agreements signed by the exporters at Japan's request so as to cover the needs of the Japanese economy, and a re-export policy [by Japan] which tended to bring down systematically the world prices which were basic to these long-term agreements.[172]

CIPEC's Executive Director moreover emphasized in his letter to the Japanese government that by maintaining such a policy 'in order to confront short-term difficulties, the Japanese government might endanger its long-term relations with the exporter-countries'.[173] An exchange of views between the Japanese government representatives and those of CIPEC followed soon after, and finally led to an official visit to Japan by CIPEC's Executive Director. Following that meeting, the Japanese government's Ministry of International Trade and Industry (MITI) announced, on 30 September 1974, a 50 percent reduction in Japan's export shipments of refined copper, and a temporary ban on sales to LME.[174] CIPEC's diplomatic persuasion, couched in terms of the mutual interests of both copper exporters and consumers, resulted in a decline in copper supply available in the international market, and psychologically encouraged CIPEC members to initiate their first attempt to formulate a policy of production cutbacks.

CIPEC's first agreement jointly to regulate copper production was thus the result of the price declines of late 1974. Because the demand for copper is primarily influenced by the economic cycle in Western industrialized states, the slowdown in Western economic activity at the time had a depressing effect on the price of copper. In view of the downward trend in world economic conditions, and of the fact that CIPEC members could not take effective action to change demand conditions, CIPEC's best option to influence price was to attempt to alter supply. On 19 November, at an extraordinary Conference of Ministers' meeting in Lima, CIPEC announced agreement on a quota system for shipments of all forms of copper. The quotas comprised initially a 10 percent reduction in exports during the following six months; in April 1975, the system was increased to a 15 percent cutback on both production and exports.[175] The goal was to stabilize prices by holding copper off the world market. Symbolically, the cutback measures were important. It was the first time, since CIPEC's inception in 1967, that its members had agreed on a joint market action.

CIPEC's cutback effort was, however, to be short-lived. As one study put it,

> the export quota system was a disappointment — not so much because it was probably too limited to really put a dent in the 1975 oversupply of copper, but because of all the advance publicity promising that CIPEC would announce a move of much greater magnitude ... CIPEC officers huddled "informally" with a number of non-member "observers" in the two weeks immediately preceding the opening of the Lima meeting, leading the press to believe that an earthshaking announcement was imminent.[176]

In fact, it was estimated that CIPEC's copper output for the first half of 1975 was only 8 percent below the comparable figure for 1974.[177] Moreover, the measures adopted by CIPEC were generally unenforceable, given the conflicting output and pricing objectives of its members. For example, although the government of Chile, because of its disputes with international copper companies, its labour unrest, and other disruptions during Allende's time, was willing to support any CIPEC proposal to curb production, the situation in other CIPEC countries precluded subsidizing Chile's production problems by cutting production. Peru's government also had problems with its copper industry similar to Chile's. Because Peru was a relatively new and low-cost copper-exporter, however, its government was the least disposed of CIPEC's members towards production cuts or slowing expansion. The government of Zambia, a high-cost producer, which often opposed Chile's government in the early 1970s (preferring to support the copper companies) was a proponent of price ceilings and floors rather than of production adjustments. Because Zambia's copper production was increasing, its government officials sought to maintain high rates of exports through price manipulation. Zaire's copper industry, like that of Zambia, was expanding. While the government of Zaire has generally shown a positive attitude towards CIPEC, it has, however, been relatively passive in most decisions.[178] CIPEC's decision to discontinue the cutback policy after mid-1976 was thus inescapable, especially in terms of internal problems. Because the policy to cut back production was not compatible with the individual interests of all the CIPEC members, it was ineffectual.

It had become apparent to CIPEC's members that their organization could not unilaterally implement cartel-like action in the copper industry. Their efforts since then have, therefore, centred on developing a dialogue with copper consumers as a means of stabilizing the price of copper. CIPEC sought to encourage such dialogue through the United Nations Conference on Trade and Development's (UNCTAD) Integrated Programme for Commodities (IPC).[179] In May 1976, at the UNCTAD IV meeting held in Nairobi, Kenya, a resolution on an Integrated Programme for Commodities was adopted, which gave rise to a series of negotiations for the establishment of international community price stabilization agreements between consumers and exporters. The objective of IPC apparently included 'the avoidance of excessive price fluctuations', improved terms of trade for developing countries, and the promotion of 'equilibrium between supply and demand within expanding world commodity trade'.[180] IPC calls for the establishment of international commodity stocking arrangements for ten 'core' commodities, including cocoa, coffee, rubber, sisal, tea, and tin, together with seven other commodities — bananas, bauxite, beef and veal, iron ore, rice, wheat, and wool — for which measures other than buffer stocks may be employed. In addition, the UNCTAD resolution provides for the negotiation of a 'common fund' for financing the stabilization arrangements.[181]

With respect to copper, an Intergovernmental Group of Experts on Copper began meeting at the UNCTAD headquarters in Geneva in November 1976 to prepare the ground for what was hoped would be the actual negotiations of an international buffer stock agreement. According to Mikesell, during the course of the discussion, as it became clear that CIPEC's members wanted some form of supply management in the international copper industry and would not be satisfied with a buffer stock operation alone, the representatives of the copper-consuming developed countries pointed to the legal difficulties in supply-management involving copper producers in developed countries.[182] It is clear that it is most unlikely that the governments of developed countries (such as the United States), which are both large producers and consumers of copper, would agree to impose output or sales limitations on their own producers. According to a CIPEC official, a mood of pessimism remains concerning the possibility of any real consensus on the part of those involved in the UNCTAD negotiations. In his words,

> Dialogue is one thing, but dialogue leading to constructive action is another. The talks within UNCTAD aimed at stabilization have tended to bog down in discussions over the best machinery for stabilization.
>
> Also, the machinery for stabilizing the copper price has tended to get mixed with the machinery for stabilizing the prices of the seventeen other commodities being discussed under the Integrated Programme. In the end, it seems highly unlikely that sufficient unanimity will be achieved under the Programme to allow effective measures to be taken for copper in the near future.[183]

In short, the results of the UNCTAD talks initiated by CIPEC itself have been, from the point of view of CIPEC's spokesmen, 'effectively — or ineffectively — zero'.[184]

CIPEC governments, cognizant of the possibilities of substitute materials for copper and of the possibility of a fall in the growth rate in copper consumption, are also involved in efforts to promote the use of copper.[185] But efforts to promote the use of copper are not new. While, in the United States, the Copper Development Association (CDA) had been promoting the consumption of copper for a long time, such promotion is relatively less active in Europe and Japan, the most important markets for CIPEC producers. In 1961, a Copper Promotion Producers Committee (CPPC) had been formed by copper producers in London; CPPC became the International Council for Copper Development (CIDEC) in 1965. Its mission was 'to raise the necessary producer funds to support existing development centres in major copper-consuming countries or if and when necessary, to set up such centres'.[186] Although CIDEC was completely financed by copper producers, with CIPEC providing approxi-mately 80 percent of its budget, it could not, however, adapt its organization to the new structure of the copper industry in the Third World countries and therefore had to cease operations in 1976.[187] By May of that year, CIPEC's Conference of Ministers was studying means by which the promotion of copper consumption could be continued. By November, they had decided to grant existing copper promotion centres an emergency aid of $250,000, a figure which was later raised to $375,000.[188] CIPEC's overall objective in this respect is, according to one of its officials, 'to find ways and means to avoid unwarranted substitution which, once it occurs, even if unjustified, is often irreversible'.[189] According to him, the most urgent step for CIPEC is substantially to increase aid to the various existing copper promotion centres.[190]

CIPEC registered a second significant achievement in diplomatic persuasion in 1978, in its response to a petition by 12 of the major U.S. copper producers on the 23 February 1978, requesting protection against copper imports into the United States.[191] The twelve producers accounted for about 93 percent of U.S. mining production capacity and 88 percent of its refined production. The final decision rested on U.S. President Carter, then in office. The U.S. producers were requesting that copper imports, irrespective of their source, should be subject to a quota of 300,000 short tons per year, a measure that, it was figured, would have limited U.S. imports of copper to no more than 198,000 tons till the end of 1979.[192] The adoption of such a measure would have presented problems for traditional copper exporters, that is, the CIPEC countries. According to a CIPEC paper, 'the Organization as a whole, and more particularly the member country governments, waged a war of defence, through individual action at the diplomatic level and a collective effort coordinated through the President of CIPEC'.[193] President Carter rejected the U.S. producers' petition on 20 October 1978. One of his reasons was that a U.S. import relief programme 'would have undermined the competitiveness of copper fabricating industries and would have a severe impact on a number of developing countries heavily dependent on copper exports for foreign exchange earnings . . .'[194]

In the previous section of this chapter some market control problems that are germane to the world copper industry were identified. In concluding the present section on CIPEC's policy output, it would be useful to note briefly the extent, if any, to which CIPEC's actions were geared to solving its market control problems. In that respect, its diplomatic action on Japan and the United States can be seen as a solution, though essentially an *ad hoc* one, to the problem arising from the existence of non-CIPEC copper suppliers. More significant in this respect was CIPEC's 1974 resolution, which invited new members to join the organization. Accordingly, new members have been admitted, including Indonesia as a full member, and Australia, Papua New Guinea, Mauritania, and Yugoslavia as associate members. Moreover, Iran, Mexico, Poland, and the Philippines are frequently mentioned as possible candidates for CIPEC membership. Although it seems reasonable to expect that CIPEC will continue to attempt to increase its membership in order to increase its share of world production and exports and, therefore, to heighten the legitimacy of the organization as a representative of the world's copper producers, such a move will not necessarily result in cartel-like action by its members unless they can reach a consensus on their attainable objectives. Furthermore, the greater the number of members in such an organization, the more difficult it will be to arrive at such a consensus. With respect to CIPEC's market control problems caused by the availability of secondary copper, substitute materials, and stockpiles, CIPEC's actions have been limited to studies and the promotion of copper consumption in the industrialized countries. In 1974, in anticipation of CIPEC's announcement of the ineffectual quota system, rumours circulated that a transfer of funds between CIPEC and OPEC for a copper stockpile was imminent. Though copper prices recovered slightly as a result of this speculation, there was actually no transfer of funds from OPEC for a permanent joint action.[195]

On the whole, CIPEC's efforts and contacts notwithstanding, the organization did not seem interested in formulating and implementing a systematic price and production policy geared to facilitating its operations as a cartel. CIPEC has been in existence for over 15 years now. Its original image as an organization not only interested in, but capable of, unilaterally causing important changes in the copper industry has gradually deteriorated to that of a forum that, at best, provides access for discussions between copper exporters and consumers. CIPEC's most visible activity today is its involvement in the interminable negotiations at UNCTAD that are apparently seeking to stabilize the ever-fluctuating price of copper. But not very much has emerged from the UNCTAD accord as yet. An overall assessment of the impact of CIPEC's policy output so far reveals that the organization is not interested in operating as a cartel in the copper industry.

Summary and Conclusion

The precondition for the exaction of absolute rent by Third World landlord governments in today's world capitalist minerals sphere is their successful operation of minerals cartels. This chapter has discussed the limited prospects of the CIPEC governments to cartelize the copper industry.

Observers had thought that CIPEC was formed to force copper consumers to pay higher prices. It would appear, however, that there is hardly sufficient incentive for CIPEC governments closely to coordinate their pricing and output policies. This tendency is consistent with the earlier history of the international copper industry. So far, CIPEC governments have not been able significantly to increase their copper revenues, as absolute rent, through cartelization.

This situation is related to the fact that the international copper industry is run by a large oligopoly, with about 20 members, at least 12 of which are important mining MNCs. The rapidly fluctuating price of copper dictated by these MNCs cannot be called a 'producers', that is, monopoly, price. If the price of copper does rise significantly in the future, it would probably be not as a consequence of the effectiveness of CIPEC as a mineral cartel, but as a result of the cooperation of these metropolitan copper MNCs and their home governments.

The point is that the CIPEC governments are heavily dependent on the copper MNCs in a number of crucial areas, including the exploitation of new mines, the provision of technology and management, and the use of world-wide sales networks. Even if the potential for cartelization existed within CIPEC, the high level of dependency of its member governments on foreign copper MNCs is likely to prevent an independent price policy within the organization. CIPEC governments' independence in the crucial areas of the internationalized process of copper production will not only facilitate their effective control over prices, but will also encourage effective consultation among them.

As a Third World producers' association, OPEC has not only had a longer, but also a more successful history of collaboration than CIPEC. On balance, the propensity for capturing maximum absolute rent will be higher in the case of OPEC and the oil-exporting governments than in the case of CIPEC and the copper-exporting governments.

In the first place, with respect to cartelization, the great potential strength of OPEC is that at least one of its members, that is, the government of Saudi Arabia, is in a good position, if only theoretically, to cut production if necessary in order to support high prices. And while OPEC governments generally have higher foreign exchange reserves, the CIPEC governments are not nearly so rich.

OPEC governments also account for a higher percentage share of the international export market for their resource than do CIPEC members. Although OPEC accounts for some two-thirds of the non-Communist world's petroleum production, CIPEC accounts for only one-third of the non-Communist world's copper production.

Furthermore, the demand for, and the competitive supply of, petroleum adjust only slowly to changes in price. Secondary copper, on the other hand, responds quickly to price changes.

Finally, the technology to develop a substitute for petroleum, compared to that to develop one for copper, has not yet been perfected. From the standpoint of minerals-consuming countries, a petroleum substitute is more costly than one for copper. Hence, they appear more willing to pay higher prices for their increasing petroleum needs than for their copper needs. There is, therefore, a higher propensity for capturing larger absolute rents in OPEC than in CIPEC.

Despite OPEC's relatively unique advantages from the standpoint of capturing absolute rent, only recently has the organization temporarily succeeded in capturing significant shares of this surplus profit from oil. It is, therefore, reasonable to suggest that CIPEC's record with respect to capturing absolute rent will be worse than OPEC's.

This is not to argue that CIPEC is entirely useless as an organization of copper-exporting Third World governments. On the contrary, the untouted role of the organization as an information-gathering mechanism and as a depository of statistical studies must not be disregarded. The increasing tendency to acquire and to exchange such relevant copper industry information among CIPEC governments will facilitate their individual abilities to make intelligent minerals-related decisions. Also, following CIPEC's inception, the process of nationalization in the member countries, though largely unsuccessful in the long run, may temporarily have enabled the CIPEC governments to increase their shares of differential rents, if not of absolute rents. Finally, CIPEC's dialogue for price stabilization at UNCTAD, including its promotion of the use of copper, must be appreciated as a necessary and desperate attempt by a fledgling — though no longer new — organization of Third World landlord governments to survive in the difficult copper industry.

Notes

1. CIPEC is the French acronym for the Conseil Intergouvernemental des Pays Exportateurs de Cuivre (Intergovernmental Council of Copper Exporting Countries).

2. Adelaide Walters, 'The International Copper Cartel', *Southern Economic Journal* 11, no. 2, October 1944, p. 133.

3. Alex Skelton, 'Copper' in William Yandell Elliot *et al.*, *International Control in the Non-Ferrous Metals* (The Macmillan Company, New York, 1937) p. 363.

4. The instability of copper prices has been due not only to the inability of the copper industry to meet sudden surges in demand, but also to the inadequate response of copper production to the underlying changes in the durable goods business cycle, protectionist economic policies, and random disturbances. Pronounced price peaks have tended to occur in times of war (often dampened by government intervention) and booming industrial growth.

5. A good account of earlier attempts to control the copper market can be found in Skelton's chapter on 'Copper' in Elliot *et al.*, *International Control in Non-Ferrous Metals*, chap. 8. See also Walters, 'The International Copper Cartel'; 'Copper Price Controls; 1840–1965', *Copper Studies* 1, no. 2, 21 February 1967, pp. 3–9; Ervin Hexner, *International Cartels* (The University of Northern Carolina Press, Chapel Hill, 1946) pp. 223–8, and especially appendix viii-D; and Orris C. Herfindahl, *Copper Costs and Prices: 1870–1957* (The Johns Hopkins University Press, Baltimore, 1959) chap. 4–7.

6. 'Copper Price Controls', p 3.

7. Skelton, 'Copper', p. 393.

8. 'Copper Price Controls', p. 4.

9. Skelton, 'Copper', p. 393.

10. 'Copper Price Controls', p. 34.

11. Skelton, 'Copper', p. 395.

12. *Ibid.*

13. *Ibid.*

14. *Ibid.*, p. 396.

15. 'Copper Price Controls', p. 4.

16. *Ibid.*

17. Skelton, 'Copper', p. 397.

18. 'Copper Price Controls', p. 4.

19. *Ibid.*

20. *Ibid.*, pp. 4–7.

21. Skelton, 'Copper', p. 399.

22. *Ibid.*

23. *Ibid.*, pp. 408–9.

24. 'Copper Price Controls', p. 7.

25. See Hexner, *International Cartels*, p. 224.

26. *Ibid.*

27. Skelton, 'Copper', p. 422.

28. *Ibid.*, p. 425.

29. *Ibid.*, p. 421.

30. Walters, 'The International Copper Cartel', p. 134.

31. Skelton, 'Copper', p. 417.

32. *Ibid.*, p. 420. In fact, if CEA had operated some ten years after it did, the development of Canadian and African mines would have drastically altered this scenario of its success.

33. Walters, 'The International Copper Cartel', p. 134.

34. 'Copper Price Controls', p. 7.

35. Walters, 'The International Copper Cartel', p. 134.

36. 'Copper Price Controls', p. 7.

37. *Ibid.*

38. *Ibid.*

39. *Ibid.*

40. Walters, 'The International Copper Cartel', p. 135. See also Herfindahl, *Copper Costs and Prices*, pp. 108–9.

41. See Walters, 'The International Copper Cartel', pp. 135–6.

42. *Ibid.*, p. 135.

43. *Ibid.*, p. 136.

44. For a full text of this agreement, see Hexner, *International Cartels*, Appendix viii-D, pp. 436–42.

45. *Ibid.*, pp. 225–6.

46. *Ibid.*, p. 436.

47. Walters, 'The International Copper Cartel', p. 140.

48. *Ibid.*, pp. 141–2.

49. *Ibid.*, p. 139.

50. 'Copper Price Controls', p. 7.

51. *Ibid.*

52. *Ibid.*, p. 8.

53. See Martin S. Brown and John Butler, *The Production, Marketing, and Consumption of Copper and Aluminium* (Frederick A. Praeger Publishers, New York, 1968) p. 133.

54. *Ibid.*; my emphasis.

55. 'Copper Price Controls', p. 8.

56. *Ibid.*

57. *Ibid.*

58. The 'Big Three' (Kennecott, Anaconda, and Phelps-Dodge) accounted for more than 80 percent of U.S. production, and the 'Big Seven' accounted for 70 percent of free-world production. Associated with this high degree of concentration was, as Tanzer points out, a relatively high rate of profit. For example, during 1946 to 1956, the average profit rate on investment was: for Phelps-Dodge, 17 percent; for Kennecott, 16 percent; and for Anaconda, 7 percent (the latter's relatively low profit rate was a result of its costly U.S. mines). See Michael Tanzer, *The Race for Resources: Continuing Struggles Over Minerals and Fuels* (Monthly Review Press, New York, 1980) pp. 126–7.

59. See Ann Seidman, 'Introduction: Why the Copper Countries?' in Ann Seidman (ed.) *Natural Resources and National Welfare: The Case of Copper* (Praeger Publishers, Inc., New York, 1975) p. 8.

60. On this, see 'Zambia Opens New Roads to Market', *Metals Week* 38, no. 19, 8 May 1967, pp. 8–10.

61. In place of the usual 1,450-mile Rhodesian route to the port of Beira in Mozambique, Zambia's alternative routes included: the 1,450-mile rail route via the Benguela railway to the port of Lobito in Angola; the 1,250-mile truck route to the

port of Dar-es-Salaam in Tanzania; an 850-mile airlift to Dar-es-Salaam; a 1,000-mile rail-truck-rail route to Beira, Mozambique. None of these routes was totally satisfactory, however.

62. 'Zambia Opens New Roads to Market', p. 8.
63. *Ibid.*, p. 9.
64. *Ibid.*
65. Karen A. Mingst, 'Cooperation or Illusion: An Examination of the Intergovernmental Council of Copper Exporting Countries', *International Organization* 30, no. 2, Spring 1976, p. 271.
66. Vincent A. Ferraro, 'The Political Dynamics of International Resource Cartels: Case Studies of Petroleum and Copper' (PhD dissertation, Massachusetts Institute of Technology, 1976) p. 291.
67. See 'Copper: In Constant Crisis', *Metals Week* 38, no. 9, 27 February 1967, p. 19. The problem stemmed from the Congolese government's insistence that Union Minière's headquarters be located in the then Congo. The government had to block all Union Minière's shipments of copper from the Congo when the company refused to make its headquarters in the Congo and shortly thereafter seized the company's properties. The flow of Congolese copper that was about 8 percent of the free world supply was blocked from late December 1966, until the third week of February 1967.
68. Mingst, 'Cooperation or Illusion', p. 271.
69. See Wolf Radmann, 'Intergovernmental Cooperation: The Case of Foreign Investment in Zambia and Chile', *PanAfrican Journal* 5, no. 2, Summer 1973, pp. 201–21; and his 'CIPEC — The Copper Exporting Countries', *Intereconomics*, no. 8, August 1973, pp. 245–9.
70. Radmann, 'CIPEC', p. 245.
71. *Ibid.*
72. Ronald Prain, *Copper: The Anatomy of an Industry* (Mining Journal Books, Ltd., London, 1975) p. 248.
73. *Ibid.*
74. As quoted in Jean d'Hainaut, 'A Brief Glimpse of CIPEC', CIPEC Document No. INFO/251/79, March 1979, p. 4.
75. Prain, *Copper*, p. 250; my emphasis.
76. As quoted in *ibid.*
77. *Ibid.*, p. 251; my emphasis.
78. 'Four-National Conference Leaves Bad Taste', *Metals Week* 38, no. 24, 12 June 1967, p. 5; my emphasis.
79. See CIPEC, *Annual Report, 1974* (Paris, June 1975) Appendix III, p. 82. The the emphasis is mine.
80. *Ibid.* While the former of these two new objectives probably reflected CIPEC's first attempt at collective action, i.e., the adoption of measures to stop the threatened embargo against Chile by Kennecott in reprisal for Chile's expropriation of Kennecott's copper properties in 1977, the latter goal referred to CIPEC's increasing contacts with OPEC during 1973 and 1974, in efforts to discuss common problems for jointly funded projects, as well as to contacts established with the then newly created International Bauxite Association. See Mingst, 'Cooperation or Illusion', p. 274.
81. CIPEC, *Annual Report*, 1974, pp. 82–3. This new membership provision may have been a reflection of the recognition by CIPEC's founding members that CIPEC's shaky international impact may be corrected if the organization could

control a higher percentage of the copper market by attracting and including new members. In 1967, CIPEC, consisting of just the four founding members, represented only 36 percent of the total world mine production and 52 percent of copper exports of all market economies. Indonesia is now a full member of CIPEC; Australia, Mauritania, Papua New Guinea, and Yugoslavia are associate members. The discussion of CIPEC in this chapter will, however, be limited to the original four founding members.

82. See CIPEC, *Conference of Ministers, Modification of the CIPEC Agreement*, CM/102/77 (CIPEC, Paris, 22 June 1977) pp. 4–10.

83. *Ibid.*, p. 4.

84. *Ibid.*, p. 5.

85. *Ibid.*

86. *Ibid.*

87. *Ibid.*, p. 6.

88. *Ibid.*, p. 7.

89. *Ibid.*, p. 6.

90. *Ibid.*, p. 8.

91. *Ibid.*

92. *Ibid.*, p. 9.

93. *Ibid.*, p. 10.

94. *Ibid.*

95. Raymond F. Mikesell, *The World Copper Industry: Structure and Economic Analysis* (The Johns Hopkins University Press, Baltimore, 1979) p. 208.

96. *Ibid.*

97. This formula was given by Kenji Takeuchi in his 'CIPEC and the Copper Export Earnings of Member Countries', *The Developing Economies*, 10, no. 1, March 1972, pp. 14–16.

98. There is a wide variation in econometric estimates of the relevant elasticities of demand for, and supply of, copper. See, for example, F.N. Fisher *et al.*, 'An Econometric Model of the World Copper Industry', *Bell Journal of Economics and Management Science* 3, no. 2, Autumn 1972, pp. 587; and *ibid.*, p. 22. In view of these estimates, it is reasonable to assume, following Mikesell, a range of –0.2 to –0.5 for the elasticity of total non-Communist world demand, and a range of 0.2 and 0.4 for the short-term elasticity of copper supply from non-CIPEC countries for purposes of determining the short-run elasticity of demand for CIPEC's copper output. See Mikesell, *The World Copper Industry,* p. 210.

99. Mikesell, *The World Copper Industry*.

100. *Ibid.*, p. 211.

101. *Ibid.*

102. *Ibid.*

103. *Ibid.*

104. Alexander Sutulov, *Minerals in World Affairs* (The University of Utah Printing Press, Salt Lake City, 1973) p. 170.

105. Dorothea Mezger, *Copper in the World Economy* (Monthly Review Press, New York, 1981) p. 51.

106. *Ibid.*

107. See Wolfgang Gluschke *et al.*, *Copper: The Next Fifteen Years* (D. Reidel Publishing Co., Boston, 1979) chap. 7; Mikesell, *The World Copper Industry*, pp. 76–7 and 339–49; Mezger, *Copper in the World Economy*, pp. 36–7; and N. Iwase, 'Recycling and Substitution', in S. Sideri and S. Johns (eds.), *Mining for*

Development in the Third World (Pergamon Press, New York, 1980) pp. 266–74.

108. Gluschke *et al.*, *Copper: The Next Fifteen Years*, p. 85; my emphasis.

109. *Ibid.*, p. 86. Quality and price play a role.

110. *Ibid.*, p. 87.

111. *Ibid.*

112. *Ibid.*, pp. 86–7.

113. See Ferdinand Banks, *The World Copper Market* (Ballinger Publishing Co., Cambridge, Mass., 1974) p. 3.

114. Iwase, 'Recycling and Substitution', p. 271.

115. *Ibid.*

116. *Ibid.*, p. 272.

117. Gluschke *et al.*, *Copper: The Next Fifteen Years*, p. 94.

118. Quoted in Mezger, *The World Copper Industry*, p. 37.

119. *Ibid.*

120. Robert Bowen and Ananda Gunatilaka, *Copper: Its Geology and Economics* (John Wiley and Sons, New York, 1977) p. 306.

121. *Ibid.* There are other rivals of copper such as titanium, sodium, lead, cadmium, and niobium, to name a few, which are even less perfect substitutes than aluminium, plastics, and stainless steel. See Gluschke *et al.*, *Copper: The Next Fifteen Years*, p. 37.

122. Bowen and Gunatilaka, *Copper: Its Geology and Economics,* p. 306.

123. Bowen and Gunatilaka, *ibid.*, estimate that about 10 percent of the annual production of some 12 million tons of aluminium goes to manufacturing conductors.

124. *Ibid.*

125. *Ibid.*, p. 307.

126. *Ibid.*

127. Gluschke *et al.*, *Copper: The Next Fifteen Years*, p. 37.

128. *Ibid.*

129. Helge Hveem, *The Political Economy of Third World Producer Associations* (Universitetsforlaget, Oslo, 1977) p. 102.

130. Mikesell, *The World Copper Industry*, p. 301.

131. Hveem, *The Political Economy of Third World Producer Associations,* pp. 102–3; emphasis in original.

132. For an introduction to this subject, see the following: Danny M. Leipziger and J.L. Mudge, *Seabed Mineral Resources and the Economic Interests of Developing Countries* (Ballinger Publishing Co., Cambridge, Mass., 1976); Bowen and Gunatilaka, *Copper: Its Geology and Economics*, chap. 8; Gluschke *et al.*, *Copper: The Next Fifteen Years,* Appendix A; Mikesell, *The World Copper Industry,* pp. 349–56; Mezger, *Copper in the World Economy*, pp. 85–92 and 160–4; Nina Cornell, 'Manganese Nodule Mining and Economic Rent', *Natural Resources Journal* 14, no. 4, October 1974, pp. 519–31; Chennat Gopalakrishnan, 'Multinational Corporations, Nation States and Ocean Resource Management', *American Journal of Economics and Sociology* 38, no. 3, July 1979, pp. 253–60; Tomotaka Ishime, 'The Law of the Sea and Ocean Resources', *American Journal of Economics and Sociology* 37, no. 2, April 1978, pp. 129–44; V.E. McKelvey, 'Seabed Minerals and the Law of the Sea', *Science* 209, 25 July 1980, pp. 464–72; and Tanzer, *The Race for Resources*, chap. 15.

133. Gluschke *et al.*, *Copper: The Next Fifteen Years,* pp. 122–3.

134. See *ibid.*, p. 123.

135. As quoted in Tanzer, *The Race for Resources*, p. 199.
136. Cornell, 'Manganese Nodule Mining and Economic Rent', p. 3.
137. Mezger, *Copper in the World Economy*, p. 91.
138. See Seidman, 'Introduction: Why the Copper Countries?', p. 4.
139. *Ibid.*, pp. 4–7.
140. Mikesell, *The World Copper Industry*, p. 213.
141. Mingst, 'Cooperation or Illusion', p. 275.
142. *Ibid.*, pp. 275–6.
143. For an introduction to earlier nationalizations in CIPEC countries, see Prain, *Copper*, chaps. 16 and 17; Wolf Radmann, 'The Nationalization of Zaire's Copper: From Union Minière to Gecamines', *Africa Today* 25, no. 4, October–December 1978, pp. 25–48; Radmann, 'Intergovernmental Cooperation'; Mark Bostock and Charles Harvey (eds.) *Economic Independence and Zambian Copper: A Case Study of Foreign Investment* (Praeger Publishers, New York, 1972) chaps. 5–7; Norman Girvan, *Corporate Imperialism: Conflict and Expropriation* (M.E. Sharpe, Inc., New York, 1976) chap. 2; and M.L.O. Faber and J.G. Potter, *Towards Economic Independence: Papers on the Nationalisation of the Copper Industry in Zambia* (Cambridge University Press, Cambridge, 1971).
144. Ferraro, 'The Political Dynamics of International Resource Cartels', p. 296.
145. *Ibid.*
146. Prain, *Copper*, p. 224.
147. Zaire's compensation agreement of 24 September 1969 with Belgium's Union Minière had provided for less financial compensation to the company than it had originally asked for. See Radmann, 'The Nationalization of Zaire's Copper', p. 40, and Kenneth W. Clarifield *et al.*, *Eight Mineral Cartels: The New Challenge to Industrialized Nations* (McGraw-Hill, New York, 1975) p. 92.
148. CIPEC, *Quarterly Review*, July–September 1976, p. 51.
149. Radmann, 'Intergovernmental Cooperation', p. 203.
150. *Ibid.*, p. 205.
151. *Ibid.*, pp. 205–6.
152. *Ibid.*, p. 207.
153. *Ibid.*, p. 208.
154. *Ibid.*
155. *Ibid.*, p. 209. For the essence of Kaunda's Mulungushi speech, see Bostock and Harvey (eds.) *Economic Independence and Zambian Copper*, pp. 121–4. An excerpt of the speech is in Faber and Potter, *Towards Economic Independence*, p. 81.
156. Radmann, 'Intergovernmental Cooperation', p. 210. This announcement was made in another of Kaunda's popular 'nationalist' speeches, the Matero Speech, given at a meeting of his United National Independence Party at Matero Hall in Lusaka. See Faber and Potter, *Towards Economic Independence*, pp. 92–5, for a summary.
157. Radmann, 'Intergovernmental Cooperation', p. 211.
158. *Ibid.*, p. 212.
159. Compensation amounted to about $118 million for RST and $176 million for Anglo-American Corporation. Mezger, *Copper in the World Economy*, p. 149.
160. Compensation to Cerro de Pasco amounted to $67 million. *Ibid.*, p. 151.
161. This change was said to have been championed by Chile. See Mingst, 'Cooperation or Illusion', p. 279.
162. *Ibid.*, pp. 279–80.
163. See CIPEC, *Annual Report*, 1974, pp. 94–9.

164. *Ibid.*, p. 94.

165. *Ibid.*, pp. 96–7.

166. *Ibid.*, p. 96.

167. *Ibid.*, p. 98.

168. Mingst, 'Cooperation or Illusion', p. 279.

169. Ferraro, 'The Political Dynamics of International Cartels', p. 307.

170. Mingst, 'Cooperation or Illusion', p. 283.

171. Ferraro, 'The Political Dynamics of International Cartels', pp. 308–9.

172. CIPEC, *Annual Report, 1974*, p. 48.

173. *Ibid.*

174. *Ibid.*

175. Mingst, 'Cooperation or Illusion', p. 286.

176. Clarifield *et al.*, *Eight Mineral Cartels*, pp. 95–6. As Mezger correctly observed, one example of the ineffectiveness of the CIPEC cartel and its *de facto* subordination to the 'corporate system' is the reaction of LME to the notice given by CIPEC countries regarding their intention to curtail production and export of copper. According to her, 'on the LME, which supposedly reacts like a seismograph to such changes, the price of copper fell even further. The price did not begin to rise again until the spring of 1975, after consultations with the copper conglomerates.' Mezger, *Copper in the World Economy*, p. 119.

177. Ferraro, 'The Political Dynamics of International Resource Cartels', p. 309.

178. Mingst, 'Cooperation or Illusion', p. 282.

179. d'Hainaut, 'A Brief Glimpse of CIPEC', p. 10.

180. Mikesell, *The World Copper Industry*, p. 189.

181. *Ibid.*

182. *Ibid.*

183. d'Hainaut, 'A Brief Glimpse of CIPEC', p. 11.

184. *Ibid.*, p. 12.

185. *Ibid.*

186. *Ibid.*, pp. 12–13. CIDEC is the acronym of the organization's name in French: Conseil International pour le Développement de Cuivre.

187. *Ibid.*, p. 13.

188. *Ibid.*

189. *Ibid.*, p. 12.

190. *Ibid.*, p. 14.

191. *Ibid.*, pp. 8–9.

192. *Ibid.*, p. 9.

193. *Ibid.*

194. *Ibid.*

195. Mingst, 'Cooperation or Illusion', p. 286.

5. Differential Rent in the World Copper Industry

Introduction

Substantial surplus profits exist in the world mining sphere that, according to Marx's scheme of income distribution between landlord and capitalist, could today accrue to Third World landlord governments as differential rents. But because of structural constraints in the international political economy, these governments fail to capture these rents in full.

As a rule, copper occurs in relatively limited quantities and is distributed unevenly over the globe, with sizeable differences in costs of producing it. Costs of production differ depending on whether capitalist operators control the better or poorer quality deposits in the world. Copper is produced under both these high- and low-cost conditions precisely in order to satisfy completely the increasing demand for it as a commodity. Herein lies the explanation of the formation of differential rent, an important surplus profit in the world copper sector.

More specifically, differential rent exists in the world copper industry because, compared with conditions of copper production in the advanced copper-consuming countries, operating costs in CIPEC copper-exporting countries are lower (since their ore grades are higher, their labour costs lower, and their general investment climate more favourable). In other words, in the context of the world copper industry, the productivity of labour performed in the Third World's rich mines is higher than that which determines the world market value of copper, that is, the productivity of labour performed in the advanced countries' relatively marginal mines.

At any one time, the large metropolitan copper MNCs that dominate the world copper sector are likely to be evaluating several investment opportunities in different foreign areas. Where they will eventually invest will depend on a number of considerations. High ore grade, low labour costs, and favourable investment climate are the most important factors from their standpoint of seeking access to potentially high profits. Therefore, the individual competitive position of these large copper MNCs lies in their ability to control the rich copper deposits in CIPEC countries where these higher profit opportunities exist.

Given the above scenario and following the classical Marxian rent mechanism, if one assumes free competition among the metropolitan copper MNCs, the differential rent arising from the more favourable productivity of CIPEC governments' mines can be captured by them in full, since these governments own the world's richest copper mines. CIPEC governments, however, like most Third World landlord governments, effectively experience monopoly, not competition, in the supply of production, technology, and equipment controlled by the few metropolitan mining firms that dominate the working of their rich mines. Under the circumstances, these copper MNCs are likely to be receiving above-average profits, that is, to the extent that they can capture, through high charges for management and technology, some of the surplus profits that would have accrued to CIPEC governments as differential rents.

In this chapter, focusing on U.S. data as an example,[1] the significant cost differential between the domestic copper industry of an advanced copper-consuming country and the copper industries of CIPEC countries, as an indication of the basis of differential rent in the world copper industry, is first identified. Then the basis of this cost differential is discussed in the following section. These include ore grade, labour cost and government policies with respect to pollution control and land-use management.

Having demonstrated that the internationalized production of CIPEC governments' rich copper deposits involves substantial surplus profits, data that show that the profitability of the U.S. domestic copper industry is poor compared to the lucrative profit rates that are applicable in CIPEC countries are then discussed. The next section elucidates the limited appropriation of differential rents by the CIPEC governments. In the absence of adequate financial data to provide a quantitatively meaningful analysis of the limited appropriation of differential rent,[2] this section discusses a number of other kinds of available data that strongly suggest that CIPEC governments are not capturing the full differential rents from world copper mining. These data reflect the super-profits in CIPEC countries, their generous tax provisions, the high charges by metropolitan copper MNCs for management and technology in CIPEC countries, and the generally extra-favourable investment conditions provided by CIPEC governments' policies with respect to foreign mining investors.

Conceptually, from the standpoint of CIPEC governments, the problem is that they seem to have failed to satisfy the very basic precondition for capturing differential rents in full, that is, independently and completely controlling and operating their rich copper mines. Therefore, the prospects of their producer power will depend on their individual abilities independently to provide the crucial facilities and expertise required in the internationalized process of copper production. This conclusion is reasonable since the supply of these resources is dominated by a few large and very powerful metropolitan copper MNCs who have supplied them to CIPEC governments, if at all, only at monopolistic prices.

Operating Cost Differential

By a number of measures, the performance of the U.S. copper industry indicates an industry in distress. The numerous problems facing it within the context of the changing structure of the world market have affected its performance over most of the past decade. Production costs in the United States are, for example, about 10 cents per pound higher than the world average.[3] In the context of relatively slowly growing demand, the increasing disparity between the cost of producing copper in the United States and elsewhere is the ultimate cause of poor profitability and, therefore, of the growing U.S. dependence on foreign copper sources.

Production costs in CIPEC countries can be significantly higher than the world average, which is roughly estimated to be lower than production costs in the United States by some 10 cents per pound. Table 9 shows estimated operating costs for the world's major copper-producing areas. According to this U.S. Bureau of Mines source, while between 1970 and 1979, the weighted average operating cost of the largest U.S. copper producers was about 70 cents per pound, the figure was roughly 43 cents per pound during the same period with respect to producers in CIPEC countries.

Many precautions must be noted in attempting to interpret the cost estimates contained in Table 9.[4] For example, the strong competition faced by the U.S. domestic copper industry over the past few years has forced the closing, at least temporarily, of several marginal and relatively inefficient operations. This phenomenon, which did reflect a sharp increase in the productivity of the U.S. domestic copper industry, must similarly have reflected, in the country's statistics, an overall reduction in average costs of production which may be misleading. The lack of full coverage of the U.S. copper industry is a related problem. Moreover, because 'cost' in the Third World includes management and technology costs as well as padded employment costs, the available data may not reflect the actual difference between costs of copper production in the United States and in CIPEC countries. Even when one takes the generally tentative nature of the available data into account, it still appears that production costs in CIPEC countries can be over 20 cents per pound below U.S. costs.

Another perspective of the problems that have confronted the U.S. copper industry in the past decade is provided by Figure 2, which demonstrates the relationship between copper costs and price trends in the United States. Again, although these data are tentative, the figure shows how rising costs in the industry were accompanied by falling prices over much of the 1970s. These simultaneous trends, which appear to have continued, cannot help but reduce the U.S. domestic copper industry's rate of return. As the spread between copper prices and costs continues to narrow in the United States, pressure to reduce costs by the major U.S. copper firms will persist. More explicitly, as the conditions in the United States continue to make it the marginal mine in the context of the world copper industry, the persistent pressure to reduce costs implies that control of the lower-cost conditions available in foreign areas, in particular in CIPEC countries, will increasingly be the priority of U.S. copper companies.

Cost differentials between the copper projects of the United States and those of CIPEC countries explain the basis of differential rent in the world copper industry. American copper firms that are able to control the low-cost conditions offered in CIPEC countries will be able to receive super profits, that is, profit rates above the diminishing rate of return obtainable under the high-cost conditions in the United States. This super profit represents part of the differential rent that could accrue in full to individual CIPEC countries if they effectively own and control their copper deposits.

Factors Accounting for Cost Differential

There are a number of economic, technical, and policy-related factors that have contributed to the cost differential between U.S. and foreign copper producers. These factors include ore grade, labour costs, government regulation of the environment, and land-use management.

Ore Grade

Ore grade, the quality of the mineral, is the principal determinant of production costs.[5] The quality of the ore can be described in many ways, including location, size, and thickness of the ore body, the amount of overburden to be removed, and the kind and amount of by-products and impurities to be recovered or removed. However, the most important ore quality parameter is the percentage of copper contained in the ore, that is, ore grade. The average ore grade in the United States has been declining compared to foreign deposits.

The average grade of U.S. copper ores is presently around 0.62 percent copper.[6] Ore grade is an important factor affecting production costs because it determines the amount of crude ore that must be mined and concentrated to yield a measurable unit of copper metal. Based on an average recovery rate of 81 percent, one ton of copper mined in the U.S. yields, on the average, about ten pounds of copper. With respect to labour costs, ore with a recoverable content of 1 percent will, for example, require only about half the labour required to produce a pound of metal with an ore-grading of 0.5 percent, unless of course it is offset by technological improvements.

Table 10 shows the long-term relationship between the average yield of copper ore mined in the United States and the corresponding producers' price (used as an estimate of the long-run trend in the cost of producing copper) of the metal. The table indicates that the average yield (and the corresponding grade) of copper ore mined in the United States has been declining steadily during most of this century, from 1.88 percent in 1919, to 0.49 percent in 1979. Principally because of advancing technological innovation, however, the price of copper in constant dollar terms actually declined from one dollar per pound in 1910, to 57 cents per pound in 1930; price then generally remained in the 60

Table 9

Estimates of Operating Costs for Major World Copper-producing Areas
(cents per pound. 1977 constant dollars)

Country and Company	1970	1971	1972	1973	1974	1975	1976	1977	1978	1979
United States:										
Atlantic Richfield–Anaconda	NA	NA	68	68	82	82	72	68	NA	NA
ASARCO Inc.	83	NA	NA	75	86	68	71	67	58	68
Cyprus Mines (Standard Oil of Indiana)	NA	NA	57	63	70	61	65	60	NA	NA
Inspiration Consolidated Copper Co.	62	63	59	67	79	80	78	84	NA	NA
Kennecott Corp.	64	NA	NA	51	NA	67	NA	62	64	62
Louisiana Land–Copper Range Co.	70	76	74	72	87	81	76	86	NA	NA
Newmont Mining Corp.	66	NA	48	48	52	55	62	64	57	63
Phelps-Dodge Corp.	70	NA	43	41	48	66	61	61	53	58
Canada:										
Inco Ltd.	64	NA	NA	68	NA	NA	NA	51	47	54
Lornex Mining Corp.	NA	NA	NA	65	57	42	38	40	44	31
Noranda Mines Ltd.	77	NA	58	82	81	61	60	55	53	50
Sherritt Gordon Mines Ltd.	NA	NA	NA	38	41	36	38	40	NA	NA
Chile: Codelco	NA	NA	NA	NA	NA	NA	44	45	39	36
Peru: Southern Peru Copper Corp.	33	NA	38	44	55	68	56	44	47	42
Zaire: Gecamines	42	39	41	45	54	43	37	41	NA	NA

Table 9 — continued

Country and Company	1970	1971	1972	1973	1974	1975	1976	1977	1978	1979
Zambia:										
Nchanga Consolidated Copper Mines	NA	NA	NA	54	60	65	61	51	NA	NA
Roan Consolidated Mines Ltd.	NA	NA	61	57	59	65	61	59	NA	NA
South Africa, Republic of:										
Palabora Mining Co. Ltd.	31	29	31	31	36	37	48	49	NA	NA
Australia: MIM Holdings Ltd.	83	80	74	69	69	60	56	62	NA	NA
Papua New Guinea:										
Bougainville Copper Ltd.	NAp	NAp	NAp	46	61	47	50	51	19	23
Philippines:										
Atlas Consolidated Mining & Development Corp.	34	NA	NA	41	NA	54	58	58	52	56

NA = Not available
NAp = Not applicable; production commenced in 1973

Source: Louis J. Sousa. *The U.S. Copper Industry: Problems, Issues, and Outlook* (Bureau of Mines, Washington. D.C.. 1981) p. 24.

Figure 2
Average U.S. Costs in Comparison with Average Prices, 1973–1979

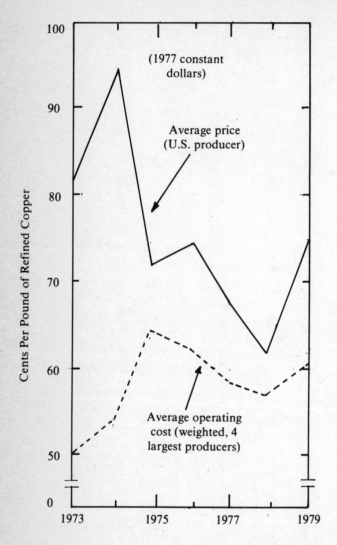

Source: Louis J. Sousa, *The U.S. Copper Industry: Problems, Issues, and Outlook* (U.S. Bureau of Mines, Washington, D.C., 1981) p. 25.

Table 10

United States Copper Yield and Prices, 1910–1979

Year	Average Copper Yield		Tons of Ore to Yield Per Ton of Copper	Average Producers' Price Cents/Pound	
	Percentage	*Pound/Ton of Ore*		*Current Dollars*	*1979 Constant Dollars*
1910	1.88	37.6	53.2	12.9	100.0
1920	1.63	32.6	61.3	17.5	63.4
1930	1.43	28.6	69.9	13.1	57.0
1940	1.20	24.0	83.3	11.4	59.1
1950	.89	17.8	112.4	21.5	64.8
1960	.73	14.6	137.0	32.2	78.9
1970	.59	11.8	169.5	58.2	108.0
1979	.49	9.8	204.1	93.3	93.3

Source: Louis J. Sousa, *The U.S. Copper Industry: Problems, Issues, and Outlook* (Bureau of Mines, Washington, D.C., 1981) p. 27.

cents per pound range over the next 20 years, despite the fact that the average yield declined by 38 percent.[7]

Table 11 shows that the average grade of copper ore mined in the United States is approximately 30 percent less than the world average of 1.03 percent. In the principal exporting countries of CIPEC — Zaire, Zambia, Chile, and Peru — copper ores are considerably higher in copper content than the average ores in the United States. Even though the average grade of copper mined in the United States is similar to, or higher than, the grade of ores produced in Canada, the Philippines, and Papua New Guinea, these producers, unlike the U.S. producers, benefit from the recovery of substantial quantities of nickel, molybdenum, or gold co-products and by-products, a recovery that helps to offset the costs incurred in mining their low-grade copper ores.[8]

In comparison to costs in the rest of the world, the low average grade of U.S. copper ores has been a major factor contributing to the relatively high costs encountered by U.S. domestic copper producers. As reflected by the metal yields, however, there has been very little fluctuation in average U.S. ore grades over the past few years.[9] In fact, the average yield in 1979 exceeded that of 1975 by 0.02 percent.[10] The apparent reversal in the long-term trend in declining ore grades is believed to be mainly a result of the temporary closing of several marginal mines in the United States and the tendency to mine selectively more highly graded material to remain competitive. That ore grade in the United States has remained fairly constant for the last few years suggests that other aspects of production costs have contributed to the growing disparity between U.S. companies and their foreign counterparts.

Labour Cost

Labour is the largest component of total operating costs in the domestic copper industry of the United States. It is estimated to account for about one-third of the total cost of production. Labour costs are, thus, a second major factor which must be noted as capable of threatening the competitiveness of the U.S.` domestic copper industry, in the context of the world copper market.

In 1977, total wages paid in the U.S. copper industry amounted to $526.9 million. That year, total payroll costs were $744.3 million. In that same year, U.S. production of primary refined copper was just under 3 million pounds. Payroll costs thus averaged about 25 cents per pound of copper produced in 1977 in the United States.[11]

Wages accounted for 70 percent of the average payroll costs of 25 cents per pound of copper produced in the United States in 1977. In 1980, labour was estimated to have cost the U.S. domestic copper industry between 24 and 29 cents per pound; total operating costs were estimated at 80 cents per pound, including depreciation and allowance for by-product credits.[12]

Labour costs are determined by productivity, that is, hourly wage rates and output per worker-year. On this score, although U.S. copper mines are among the most productive in the world (because they utilize advanced technology), hourly wages in this country are also among the highest in the world. As a result, labour costs in particular in the United States may be as much as 10 cents per pound higher than those in some CIPEC countries.[13]

Table 12 provides a comparison of labour costs per ton of copper mined in the United States and some other producing countries. The data show that the United States has the second highest labour cost in the world, per ton of copper mined. The only higher labour cost producer is Canada. Among CIPEC countries, Zambia's comparatively high labour costs stem primarily from very low productivity, as well as from high turnover among the Zambian and expatriate labour force.[14]

Table 11

Average Grade of Copper Reserves in Major Producing Countries (1976)[a]

Country	Average Grade
Chile	1.11
Zaire	3.90
Zambia	3.06
Peru	1.07
United States	.71[b]
Canada	.70
Europe[c]	.73
Centrally Planned Economies[d]	1.57
Australia	2.58
Republic of South Africa	.71
Philippines	.54
Papua New Guinea	.47
World Average[e]	1.03

[a] Producing mines
[b] This figure is higher than Sousa's estimate of 0.62 percent
[c] Excluding centrally planned economies, but including Yugoslavia
[d] Bulgaria, Hungary, Poland, Romania, Russia
[e] Excluding China

Source: Derived from Wolfgang Gluschke, Joseph Shaw and Benison Varon, *Copper: The Next Fifteen Years* (D. Reidel Publishing Company, Boston, 1979) p. 51.

Even if one allows for possible errors in the available data, labour costs in most CIPEC countries would be far below those in the United States. The relatively high productivity of U.S. miners, stemming from the use of sophisticated technology, would appear, on the whole, to have been more than offset by the extremely low wages paid to most foreign workers. The low labour cost countries of CIPEC, in particular, account for a substantial percentage of both U.S. imports and world production. The available evidence suggests that labour costs are a significant disadvantage to the competitiveness of U.S.

Table 12

Employment, Productivity, and Earnings of Copper Industry Workers in the United States and Selected Countries

Country	Production Workers[a] (Thousands)	1978 Output Per Production Workers[b] (Tons of Copper)	Annual Earnings Per Production Workers[c] (1978 Dollars)	Production Workers' Earnings Per Ton (Copper Content[d])
United States	22.9	65	17,600	271
Canada	16[e]	45	16,100	358
Zambia	43[f]	16	3,300	206
Peru	11	37	3,300	89
Philippines	19	15	800	53
Chile	30	38	1,100	29

[a] U.S. — *Employment and Earning Report, BLS;* Canada — *1977 Canadian Minerals Yearbook;* Others: 1979 *E&MJ International Directory of Mining and Mineral Processing Operations.* Employment for foreign countries estimated by multiplying the all-employees figures by the U.S. ratio of production workers to all employees (9.76).

[b] 1978 copper content of ore produced divided by number of production workers.

[c] Data reported by BLS in U.S. Dollars: U.S. — 1978; Canada — 1977; Zambia — 1974; Peru — 1977; Chile — 1975. Figure for Philippines reported by International Labour Organization and converted to U.S. dollars using average 1978 exchange rate of 7.37 pesos per dollar. All data converted to 1978 U.S. dollars using BLS Producers Price Index for Nonferrous Metals and rounded to nearest $100. Figure for Zambia estimated using 94 percent of the rate for Zambians of $2,927, and 6 percent of the rate for non-Zambians of $9,703.

[d] Annual earnings divided by output per worker.

[e] Includes workers producing co-products.

[f] E&MJ, November 1979. Cobalt is a co-product.

Source: Louis J. Sousa, *The U.S. Copper Industry: Problems, Issues, and Outlook* (Bureau of Mines, Washington, D.C., 1981) p. 32.

domestic copper firms, especially in comparison with firms operating in the Third World, in particular in CIPEC countries, where very low wages are paid.

Moreover, there has been a generally poor record of productivity improvement, based on recoverable metals, in the U.S. copper industry over the past two decades.[15] Also, continuing declines in average ore grades are expected. These trends, including the possibility of more underground mining, point to increases in the real cost of labour in the United States in the future.

Unless extensive cost-cutting programmes are instituted by U.S. domestic copper companies, they are likely to face stiffer profitability-disadvantages in the world market as the relatively highly productive U.S. mining technology is adopted in foreign copper-producing countries with low labour costs. If the world demand for copper grows slowly over the next two decades, the world market will likely remain intensely competitive, from the standpoint of the profitability of U.S. producers with low grade ores and higher labour costs.

In the competitive world copper market, rising wage demands and diminishing ore grades in the United States will tend either to eliminate domestic jobs, or transfer production overseas. The second tendency is obviously in operation. U.S. copper imports are growing and U.S. MNCs, affiliates of the domestic copper firms, are continuing to stay in CIPEC countries, despite the so-called political and economic risks otherwise associated with these areas.

Government Policies on Pollution Control and Land-Use Management

Structural changes in the world copper market in the last several years have made the effects of government policies on the copper industry in the United States particularly significant. A third factor accounting for the cost differential between U.S. domestic and foreign copper producers, which I want to identify in this section,[16] is related to the effects of environmental, health, and safety regulations, and public land-use policies of the U.S. government on the operating costs of its domestic copper industry. In comparison with the relatively stringent policies of the U.S. government on these issues, the virtually promotional policies of foreign governments in CIPEC countries have further placed the U.S. copper industry at a comparative disadvantage in the world copper market.

Environmental, safety, and health regulations: For about a decade and a half now, the U.S. federal government has increasingly regulated all phases of the copper production cycle, from mining to fabrication, in order to curb air pollution, protect ground and surface water, stabilize mining and waste disposal areas, minimize land disturbance, and protect worker health and safety. The principal government regulations affecting the U.S. copper industry include the Clean Air Act and Amendments, the Water Pollution Control Act and Amendments, the Solid Waste Disposal Regulations, and the Health and Safety Regulations.[17]

The costs of meeting air-quality standards have had serious adverse effects on the U.S. copper industry, forcing it to invest significantly more of its capital in pollution control than do other major basic resource extraction industries such as steel and aluminium. Although specific estimates of the pollution-control-related capital and operating expenditures of the U.S. domestic copper industry differ, there is broad agreement that these expenditures are measured in billions of dollars.

According to a survey in the *Wall Street Journal*, conducted in December 1978, four leading U.S. copper companies had spent about $1.4 billion in attempting to comply with pollution control regulations. Kennecott had spent $411 million; Phelps-Dodge, $330 million; ASARCO, $239 million; and Inspiration, $123 million.[18] Anaconda's pollution control expenditures were estimated at $260 million by another source.[19] In 1981, *Forbes* reported estimates of $2 billion in environmental expenditures in the previous 12 years for air pollution equipment alone in the U.S. copper industry.[20]

Published estimates show that Kennecott's expenditures for pollution control have exceeded those of all other U.S. copper producers. In particular, a major portion of this investment, an estimated $280 million, has been spent in rebuilding the largest copper smelter in the country — the 250,000 ton-per-year plant in Garfield, Utah. Although the new production facilities were designed to minimize operating costs, the remodelling was known to be in response to clean air standards, and yielded no increase in copper capacity. The renovated smelter captures about 86 percent of the sulphur contained in the plant's feed material, compared with 55 percent before reconstruction. In particular, the 86 percent recovery of sulphur was in compliance with standards promulgated by the U.S. Environmental Protection Agency (EPA), before commencement of the reconstruction effort. However, EPA proposed, and eventually adopted, a much more stringent standard — requiring the equivalent of 96.5 percent sulphur-recovery — while construction was in progress.[21]

Phelps-Dodge, the second largest copper producer in the United States, has, as noted earlier, reportedly spent over $330 million to comply with air pollution regulations. Recently, the company has been known to be negotiating with EPA over proposals to modernize its Morenci and Ajo smelters at an estimated cost of $200 million.[22] Phelps-Dodge must now operate these smelters intermittently to comply with sulphur dioxide emission limits. The company is said to have stated that it is not economically feasible to install a sulphuric acid plant at another of its smelters, located at Douglas, Arizona. Douglas may have to close down for environmental reasons at some point in the 1980s.[23]

The approximately $260 million spent by Anaconda, another major U.S. copper producer, on a variety of pollution control schemes since 1970, includes an estimated $65 million at the firm's only smelter in Anaconda, Montana. Faced with stringent federal and state environmental and safety requirements, which Anaconda claimed would have cost $400 million to meet, the company closed its smelter and the associated refinery in Great Falls, Montana, in September 1980.[24] The closure of the two plants reduced U.S. copper smelter and refinery capacity by 8 and 9 percent, respectively.[25]

The Vice-President and Director of the Environmental Affairs of the Magma Copper Company, a subsidiary of Newmont Mining, has provided a detailed description of the effects of government regulations on the earnings and operations of the company. This description is interesting to note because it represents typical problems facing other U.S. copper firms. The regulatory impacts included:

1. an 8.1 percent reduction in copper production in 1978; 24,272 tons of copper valued at $35.4 million, owing to intermittent curtailment of smelter operations to meet ambient air standards;

2. an estimated $46 million in capital expenditure;

3. a total of 346 inspector (MSHA, OSHA, state)[26] worker-days spent at company facilities in 1978;

4. an addition of 155 full-time positions, which represents 3 percent of the total employees of 5,500, since 1974 as the direct result of regulation; and

5. a cumulative and identifiable cost of regulation estimated in the range of ten to fifteen cents per pound of copper: an estimated annual cost of $35 million to $50 million.[27]

In general, the costs to the U.S. domestic copper industry of complying with various pollution control standards have increased significantly since the early 1970s when the first ambient-air-quality standards were introduced in the country. Another useful perspective of the cost-disadvantage of the U.S. domestic copper industry owing to stringent environmental regulations can be gained by comparing its pollution-related capital expenditures with those of other U.S. domestic industries. (See Table 13.)

The table lists a number of U.S. domestic industries with the largest capital expenditures for pollution control between 1973 and 1979. Compared with the 5 percent average for all U.S. industries between 1973 and 1979, the table shows that copper industry capital expenditures on pollution control represented about 41 percent of the industry's total capital expenditures between 1973 and 1977.

Increases in regulatory costs have been a major factor contributing to the cost differential between the U.S. domestic copper industry and foreign copper-producing areas. It would also be useful to appreciate the potential impact of the cost increases that will certainly be involved in the future in order to meet proposed sulphur dioxide emissions limits.

According to the U.S. Bureau of Mines, environmental regulation can affect the U.S. copper industry in two ways: 1) direct costs of compliance, that is, capital expenditures and operating and maintenance expenses; and 2) indirect compliance costs owing to forced periodic shut downs or restrictions on capital expansion. Particular regulatory requirements will affect certain sectors of the industry to a much higher degree than others. For example, according to an estimate of the U.S. Commerce Department, compliance costs for sulphur dioxide emission control standards at primary smelters will probably comprise over half the total cost of regulation to the entire industry from 1978 to 1987.[28]

In contrast to the high cost of pollution control within the U.S. domestic copper industry, the available information suggests that there generally has been less concern for the environmental effects of copper production in most other major copper-producing areas. High costs of pollution control are, therefore, not a serious problem confronting copper firms operating in areas outside the United States.

Most international trade in copper originates in Third World countries, and mostly those within CIPEC, where mining is usually regarded as a key factor on which to base the pursuit of higher levels of economic growth. The economies of CIPEC countries are all heavily dependent on earnings from the sale of copper. Their governments will, understandably, be reluctant to undertake any actions that might jeopardize the operations of their copper projects, and hence limit their earnings potential.

In fact, outside Europe, Japan, and North America, most of the major minerals-exporting governments do not impose strict environmental regulations on their smelting industries. Producers in CIPEC countries, which are

Table 13

Pollution Control Capital Expenditures for Major U.S. Domestic Industries, 1973–1979

Industry	Total Capital Expenditures ($ million)	Total Pollution Control Capital Expenditures ($ million)	Pollution Control Capital Expenditures as a Percentage of Total Capital Expenditure
Electric Utilities	144,395	14,174	10
Petroleum	81,736	7,748	9
Chemical	45,489	4,063	9
Paper	22,423	2,864	13
Non-ferrous Metals	15,643	2,829	13
Primary copper[a]	1, 691	697	41
Steel	17,649	2,742	16
Other industries	584,168	10,055	2
Total, All Industries	*913,194*	*45,172*	*5*

[a]1973–1975, plus 1977. Complete data not available for other years. Compiled from various sources. Included in data for non-ferrous metals.

Source: Louis J. Sousa, *The U.S.Copper Industry: Problems, Issues, and Outlook* (Bureau of Mines, Washington, D.C., 1981) p. 55.

major exporters of copper to the United States, have significant cost advantages, with respect to lenient pollution control requirements.

Except for the Canadian government, the largest exporters of refined copper to the United States are the governments of CIPEC countries. Among these countries, only the Canadian government has imposed some requirements for sulphur capture solely to reduce pollution. Even this effort, however, seems to have been made with considerable flexibility. The average capacity-weighted sulphur-capture rate for Canadian copper smelters is about 18 percent;[29] this is significantly less than the 86 to 97 percent range for the United States. It appears that the Canadian government will provide enough flexibility to take into consideration such factors as the location of particular smelters and the cost-effectiveness of additional controls.[30] As a U.S. Bureau of Mines study has stated it,

> the Canadian approach involves considerable cooperation and voluntary effort by the concerned companies. The targeted abatement levels that have been established are not strictly a matter of complying with predetermined emission limits. Rather, they have been developed in a cooperative manner and represent a control level mutually agreed upon as practical and attainable.[31]

In Zambia, there are no legal requirements for sulphur-capture from the three existing copper smelters. The two smelters run by Roan Consolidated Mines have no capture, while the smelter run by Nchanga Consolidated Copper Mines captures about 40 percent, mainly because of a good market for the resulting sulphuric acid, not for environmental reasons.[32]

Chile provides a good example of the way CIPEC governments treat the environmental problems associated with copper production. No body of laws controlling environmental pollution exists in Chile, although some smelters may be subject to local environmental regulation. According to a U.S. Bureau of Mines source, U.S. Embassy officials located in Chile have reported that the government seems willing to permit operating companies to modify their production systems gradually as part of investment for modernizing plant and equipment. In the United States, firms are required to modify constructed plants and equipment to meet current standards, but in Chile existing plants are allowed to continue operating on the basis of norms prevailing at the time of construction.[33]

Despite a shortage of sulphuric acid in Latin America as a whole, most smelters in this region do not have acid plants. The largest Chilean smelter, Chuquicamata, with a capacity of 400,000 tons per year, has no sulphur-capture whatsoever; neither does the Ilo smelter in Peru, with a capacity of 315,000 tons per year. The Disputada's Chagres smelter in Chile captures about 60 percent of its sulphur emissions and, like the Zambian case, mainly in order to sell sulphuric acid at a good profit in a good market.

In general, producers in CIPEC countries, the major copper-exporters to the United States, have, for the most part, not been burdened with stringent environmental requirements for control of air pollution. Often, sulphur-capture is done for the easy profits it affords the mining operator, not for environmental reasons.

Land-use policies: In addition to environmental regulations, another source of the cost-disadvantage of the U.S. domestic copper industry is the impact of land-use policies. Because the federal government is the owner of much of the land with the best potential for copper in the United States, its land-use policies can influence the future availability of copper in this country.

Although federal policy once encouraged mineral development on public lands, this position gradually shifted during the 20th Century until public lands policy came to emphasize land retention and management in the public interest. In the last 20 years, since the passage of the Wilderness Act and other laws calling for areas of land to be set aside for wilderness purposes, some 300 million to 350 million acres, or about 40 or 50 percent of federal lands, became unavailable or restricted from mining.[34]

In addition, proposed wilderness areas managed by the U.S. Forest Service (primitive areas) became subject to many of the same restrictions as wilderness areas established under the Wilderness Act. Other large areas of public land administered by the Forest Service (roadless areas) and the Bureau of Land Management (wilderness review areas) were also identified for possible inclusion in the wilderness system.

The number of minerals patents issued in the United States had, accordingly, been declining steadily, from 117 a year from 1960 to 1964, to 37 by 1979.[35] It would appear that minerals development is assigned a low priority by land managers in the United States.

The Alaska Native Claims Settlement Act (ANCSA) of 1971 was responsible for the single largest withdrawal of public lands from minerals development that was ever enacted in the United States. As a result, over 250 million acres — about one-third of all federal lands — were at least temporarily withdrawn from copper, and other metal-mining, entrepreneurs. Under its provisions, Alaska's public lands were to be allocated to three major dispositions, including the state of Alaska, native Alaskans, and a large pool of land from which national forests and parks, monuments, wildlife refuges, and wild and scenic rivers could be selected.[36]

Public comments in response to land-use issues indicated that the most common difficulty encountered by the U.S. minerals industry when dealing with federal land agencies is their slowness to respond to requests and to make decisions related to permits for access to public lands for exploitation and development. According to the U.S. Bureau of Mines, industry officials indicate that it is not uncommon to wait two years or more to obtain a prospecting permit, and that delays, solely as a result of regulation, increased project completion time by as much as 42 percent.[37] Such delays, from the standpoint of the copper companies, add to costs and can obstruct mining on federal lands.

In the United States, the cumulative effect of delays, and the increased chances that production will be denied and investment lost, have tended to discourage investment in new mining projects. Important difficulties facing the U.S. copper industry thus include uncertainty, regulatory delay, and lack of security for investment because of the unknown decision of the government as to production rights and terms.

Despite the generally restrictive effect of federal land policies on mining in the United States, the country's copper supplies do not yet appear to have been significantly affected. In fact, domestic sources are, according to the U.S. Bureau of Mines, still able to provide between 80 and 90 percent of the country's copper needs on an annual basis.[38]

However, because of the long lead time between discovery and commercial production from a particular deposit, restrictive land policies could well have a delayed impact and could, eventually, affect the quantity of domestic copper production and U.S. self-sufficiency in copper. As U.S. copper ore grades decline, public land-use policies could eventually lead to a situation in which several of the richer domestic copper deposits are inaccessible and undeveloped. As this occurs, the opportunity cost of leaving these deposits undeveloped would continue to rise. If, as many copper analysts expect, a major price increase does occur over the next several years, the cost of restrictive land policies would be further exacerbated. If such a price increase is accompanied by a shortage of copper supplies, then the true cost of these policies would become even more apparent.

The long lead time required to develop a new copper deposit would prevent less restrictive land policies from quickly correcting cyclical copper shortages, or contributing to lower price levels. Even if shortages and major price increases do not occur, the 'locking up' of many potential copper deposits, which restrictive land-use policies imply, means that the costs of producing domestic copper will probably continue to increase in the United States as the ore grade in deposits presently being mined continues to decline. Because the copper market is international, U.S. domestic copper prices will, however, not be able to rise much above the prevailing world price, that is, that fixed at LME. The result will be increasing marginality of U.S. copper production conditions, *vis-à-vis* foreign conditions, in the context of the world copper market. The resultant tendency for the United States to rely on foreign sources to supply its copper requirements implies that the control of these low-cost foreign sources will increasingly become a priority for U.S. copper MNCs.

Poor Profitability in United States Domestic Copper Industry

Although there are many measures that may be used to assess the financial performance of a firm or industry, profitability is probably the indicator most widely used. The two most widely accepted measures of profitability include rate of return on shareholders' equity and rate of return on average total invested capital.

The cost-disadvantages of the U.S. domestic copper industry *vis-à-vis* those of CIPEC countries are reflected in the former's relatively poor profitability trend. Available data show that annual rates of return on shareholders' equity, and on invested capital for the fourteen largest U.S. *domestic* copper-producing companies from 1969 to 1978 were below normal.

For example, Table 14 compares the industry's recent average rate of return on equity with that of all U.S. manufacturing firms. Note that the figures, from a U.S. Bureau of Mines source, refer to the profitability of U.S. domestic operations and not to the profitability of U.S. companies' worldwide operations. According to the table, from 1969 to 1978, the principal U.S. primary copper producers averaged a rate of return on equity of only 9.8 percent, in comparison with a 13.4 percent figure for all U.S. domestic manufacturing firms. Figure 3 (based on Table 14), more closely demonstrates the deterioration in profitability that has characterized the U.S. domestic copper industry in relation to other U.S. domestic industries.

Table 14

Comparison of Estimated Rates of Return on Shareholders' Equity (U.S. Copper and Manufacturing Firms, 1969–1978) (in percentages)

Year	14 U.S. Copper Producers	U.S. Manufacturing
1969	14.0	12.4
1970	12.4	10.1
1971	1.8	10.8
1972	8.9	12.1
1973	12.7	14.8
1974	16.1	15.4
1975	5.1	12.3
1976	7.4	15.0
1977	9.8	14.9
1978	9.7	15.9
10-year average	9.8	13.4

Source: Louis J. Sousa, *The U.S. Copper Industry: Problems, Issues, and Outlook* (Bureau of Mines, Washington, D.C., 1981) p. 17.

The need to cut costs because of the declining profitability in the U.S. domestic copper industry means that U.S. companies will, increasingly, find foreign, especially CIPEC, conditions attractive for investment. That the cost-differentials between U.S. and foreign copper projects have been transformed into higher profits for the copper MNCs' foreign operations is revealed by figures in Table 15 which shows profit rates on U.S. mining investments in Canada, Latin America and the Caribbean, and South Africa.

According to the table, annual rates of profit in Canada, as averaged over five-year intervals, between 1953 and 1977, fluctuated between 5 and 10 percent and averaged 7.4 percent. In Latin America and the Caribbean, profit rates fluctuated between 10 and 20 percent, and averaged almost twice the Canadian level. The figures for South Africa show profit rates varying from 20 to 43 percent and averaging 31 percent per annum, that is, twice the Latin American and Caribbean levels.

The South African profit rate is, according to a director of a U.S. mining

Figure 3

Comparison of Estimated Rates of Return on Shareholders' Equity (U.S. Copper and Manufacturing Firms, 1969–1978).

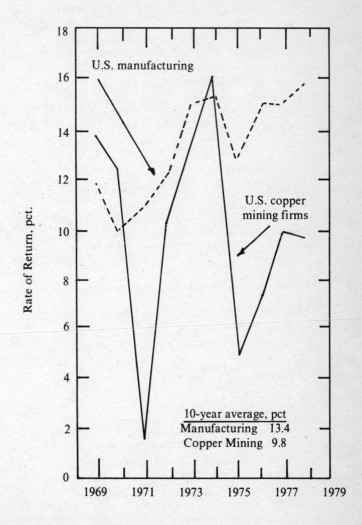

Source; Louis J. Sousa, *The U.S. Copper Industry: Problems, Issues, and Outlook* (Bureau of Mines, Washington, D.C., 1981) p. 18.

operation there, so high that 'it makes a U.S. mining company's mouth water'.[39] This brief statement describes very adequately the lucrativeness of the 'efficient' economic application of racist labour laws in that country.

With respect to U.S. copper MNCs' profitability, the situation is not significantly different in Zambia and Zaire. Even though, strictly in terms of racist labour laws in South Africa, one could expect corporate profit rates to be slightly lower in Zambia and Zaire than the 31 percent per annum figure in South Africa, the point to be emphasized is that profit rates in Zambia and Zaire are still significantly higher than those in the United States and Canada.

Although data are available only for Zambia to buttress the previous point, it is reasonable to assume that corporate profit rates in mining in Zaire are comparable to those in Zambia. Table 16 shows that in Zambia, between 1960 and 1969, MNC rates of profit in copper mining were, on the average, 25.8 percent for NCCM and 20 percent for RST (now RCM). Between 1972 and 1976, profit rates in the NCCM group varied between 18.8 percent and 26.5 percent, while those of the RCM group varied between 17.2 and 26.1 percent.[40]

Table 15

Rate of Return on Total Book Value, United States Firms' Direct Foreign Investment in Mining and Smelting (in percentages)

Years	Canada	Latin America and Caribbean	South Africa
1953–1957	8.3	10.4	25.7
1958–1962	5.9	14.5	20.8
1963–1967	9.9	19.9	43.3
1968–1972	5.3	12.8	31.6
1973–1977	7.5	11.7	n.a.
Average for 1953–1977	*7.4*	*13.9*	*30.4*

Source: Michael Tanzer, *The Race for Resources* (Monthly Review Press, N.Y., 1980) p. 49.

The available data suggest that average profit rates for U.S. copper MNCs in the CIPEC countries are roughly 14 percent for Latin America and 25 percent for Africa. Compare these estimates with the 9.8 percent average rate of return on shareholders' equity that was estimated for the U.S. domestic copper industry between 1969 and 1978, as shown in Table 14. It then becomes clear that U.S. copper MNCs that control the production of CIPEC governments' rich copper mines can earn above-average, or super, profits, including the differential rent that would otherwise have accrued to the CIPEC governments if they effectively controlled and operated their copper mines.

Figure 4 provides a further picture of the comparative disadvantages, in

Figure 4

Profitability of United States Copper MNCs Operating in CIPEC Countries
Versus Profitability of United States Domestic Copper Firms

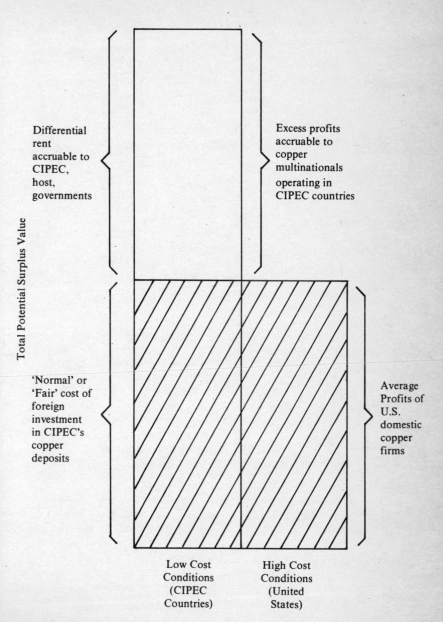

terms of profitability, of U.S. domestic copper firms operating under the high-cost U.S. conditions, *vis-à-vis* U.S. copper MNCs operating in CIPEC countries' low-cost conditions. The formation of differential rent in the world copper industry is a result of the higher than average individual rate of profit in CIPEC countries.

Table 16

MNC Rates of Profit[a] in Zambian Copper Mining, 1960–1969

Year	Nchanga Consolidated Copper Mines Ltd. (NCCM)[b]		Roan Selection Trust Ltd. (RST)[c]	
	Gross (Percentage)	*Net (Percentage)*	*Gross (Percentage)*	*Net (Percentage)*
1960	56.7	36.1	34.4	23.7
1961	51.4	31.7	23.0	15.2
1962	50.0	31.0	20.8	13.0
1963	41.8	25.9	21.8	13.5
1964	48.3	26.7	27.5	12.9
1965	43.1	21.4	31.3	17.5
1966	44.5	23.7	36.2	19.2
1967	34.7	18.0	32.9	18.5
1968	41.4	25.5	48.8	29.7
1969	26.5	18.1	55.1	35.1
Average	*43.8*	*25.8*	*33.1*	*19.8*

[a] Gross Profits are defined as profits before income tax and depreciation charges; net profits as profits after income tax but before depreciations. Gross and net rates were obtained by expressing these sums as percentages of net assets employed during the year. Royalties and export taxes were treated as costs, together with replacements.
[b] Year ending 31 March.
[c] Year ending 30 June.

Source: Calculated from Philip Daniel, *Africanisation, Nationalisation and Inequality: Mining Labour and the Copperbelt in Zambian Development* (Cambridge University Press, London, 1979) p. 78.

According to the classical Marxian rent mechanism, the difference arising from different productivities, that is, between the individual and the social, or average, value (which is the source of surplus profit), would disappear from time to time from one capitalist operator only later to accrue to another as a result of competition to improve technology and labour organization. The exception is, however, with respect to capitalist production in the extractive sphere where, for example, in copper production, the equalization of different productivities is hampered by natural forces. A lasting difference, therefore, appears in the return beyond the temporary extra profit that previously existed in the extractive sphere, which provides the basis for differential rent.

More precisely, the surplus profit that arises from the difference between the low production costs of U.S. firms operating under the more favourable conditions in CIPEC countries and the high costs obtainable under U.S. conditions explains the basis of Marxian differential rent in the world copper industry. Although this surplus value could accrue to CIPEC governments because they are the owners of the rich copper mines, as Figure 4 shows, it can also be captured by the U.S. copper MNCs, as above-average, or super, profits.

There is hardly any firm basis for estimating the magnitude of the potential differential rent that would accrue to CIPEC governments from the cost-differentials at their advantage. Radetzki, former chief economist at CIPEC, has noted the 'great uncertainties' with respect to relevant data for estimating rent. He has, however, attempted to estimate CIPEC governments' *additional* (differential) rent[41] returns by assuming that their 6.2 percent average growth rate in copper production, which was applicable in the 1950s, was maintained through 1974. (The growth rate of the group's output actually fell, from 6.2 percent in the 1950s, to 2.7 percent between 1960 and 1974.) According to him, the differential rent accruing to individual CIPEC governments each year was derived by deducting estimates of production costs from estimates of incremental revenues. To neutralize the effects of inflation, the rent estimates were deflated by the U.S. wholesale price index. The present value, in 1960 dollars, of CIPEC governments' rent receipts was computed with a 10 percent rate of discount. The exercise led Radetzki to conclude that the present value of each CIPEC government's potential differential rent receipts would have been increased by about $300 million in 1960 dollars, or by about $500 million in 1974 dollars, if their production had grown at 6.2 percent per annum in the 14-year period from 1960 to 1974.

Note that Radetzki's estimates represent only incremental, not total, potential differential rent, which must be higher, following his assumptions. Also, Radetzki himself stresses that his exercise was based on 'broad generalizations' and warns that his estimates may, therefore, grossly underestimate the 'potential gains'.

Indeed, it is difficult to determine the magnitude of potential differential rent that the cost-differentials favouring CIPEC governments represent. It is correct to say, though, that it is large enough to constitute an important developmental input for these Third World governments of monocultural economies.

The figures in Table 17 further demonstrate the magnitude of the differential rent accruable to CIPEC governments. The figures are rough estimates of CIPEC governments' potential differential rent; they assume my earlier estimated 20 cents per pound cost-differential in their favour between 1967 and 1981. According to the table, between 1967 and 1981, CIPEC governments' potential differential rent averaged about $753 million per year. The corresponding figure between 1967 and 1976 was $578 million per year. But in the five years between 1977 and 1981, the CIPEC governments' total potential differential rent averaged $1,222 million per year.

The available data suggest that the differential rents that could accrue to CIPEC governments have not been insignificant over the years. In the next section, I will show that there is ample evidence that these governments are not capturing all, or even a significant portion, of these surplus profits involved in the capitalist exploitation of their rich copper mines.

On the Limited Appropriation of Differential Rent by CIPEC Governments

The world copper industry is dominated by large metropolitan copper MNCs. Theoretically, the primary objective of CIPEC landlord governments would be to tax, or obtain through ownership and management of their copper projects, the full potential differential rent from their rich copper mines. Potential differential rent is, for the copper industry, the difference between the total sales proceeds from CIPEC governments' copper and the total cost of producing that copper, including the payment of the average profit to the mining entrepreneur.

Table 17

Estimates of CIPEC Governments' Potential Differential Rent, 1967–1981

Year	Volume of Copper Produced (in million pounds)	Total Potential Differential Rent (in $ millions)
1967	2364	473
1968	2456	491
1969	2728	545
1970	2676	525
1971	2672	534
1972	2964	592
1973	2964	592
1974	3408	682
1975	3274	655
1976	3434	687
1977	6230	1246
1978	6140	1228
1979	6010	1202
1980	6054	1211
1981	6112	1222
Average	*3966*	*753*

Source: Copper production figures from CIPEC's *Statistical Bulletin* (CIPEC, Neuilly Sur Seine, June 1976 and June 1982).

This concept of rent offers a very useful theoretical framework for more efficiently evaluating the success or failure of Third World producer power. For example, the success or failure of individual CIPEC governments, as Third World landlord governments, to introduce equity into their relations with foreign copper MNCs (that is, the attainment or non-attainment of the so-called new international economic order) can be conceptualized in terms of their ability or inability individually to maximize, over time, a definable value, or surplus, known as differential rent, which is theoretically the landlord's income.

To verify whether this surplus value has been maximized by a particular CIPEC, or any landlord, government, one would compare, over time, the magnitude of the total actual revenue garnered by the government from a particular project with the magnitude of total potential differential rent. The following formula would be useful for such an exercise:

Total Potential Differential Rent = Total Copper Revenue –
Total Cost – (Average Rate of Profit × Total Capital Outlay).

According to this measure, a CIPEC government is maximizing its producer power if, over time, the ratio of actual revenue to potential differential rent approaches unity. On the other hand, if this ratio approaches zero, one can say that the government is not maximizing its landlord power.

In the absence of adequate financial data to provide a quantitatively meaningful analysis of the limited appropriation of differential rent by CIPEC governments, this section will, instead, stress other kinds of available data that strongly suggest that CIPEC governments are not capturing the full differential rent from their rich copper deposits. Indeed, it is only the fact of this tendency — that CIPEC governments are not capturing the *full* differential rent that could accrue to them and not the exact proportion of the rent that has actually been captured by them, that needs to be established to emphasize the relevant issue in this study: Third World producer power is not a real threat to the super-profitability of metropolitan mining MNCs.

Super Profits

The single most important piece of available data that clearly demonstrates the limited appropriation of differential rent by CIPEC governments is the record of the comparatively higher average rate of profit in CIPEC countries for U.S., and other, copper MNCs operating there. In summary, the available data suggest some 25 percent rate of profit for Africa, and about 14 percent rate of profit for Latin America. These figures are in contrast to the 9.8 percent average rate of return on total book value applicable to U.S. domestic copper firms.

The best way for a Third World landlord government to ensure that it will capture the full differential rent from mining is for it effectively to control and operate its mines. Metropolitan copper MNCs, however, especially those from the United States, dominate the operations of the copper mines in CIPEC countries and control the global network for the sale of their products. The higher profitability from CIPEC governments' rich mines which are enjoyed by metropolitan copper MNCs in these countries, translates into above-average, or super, profits. It is certainly composed of a significant portion of the differential rents that could have accrued to CIPEC governments.

CIPEC governments have not attained the most basic precondition for capturing differential rents in full, that is, independently owning and operating their copper mines. In general, they need to assume full management of their projects and to acquire access to pertinent technical knowledge and markets. No CIPEC country has, however, fully satisfied all of these requirements, that is, without dependent links with foreign copper MNCs. Although their governments have tried to gain some influence over the exploitation of their mines by both partial and total nationalizations, neither of these efforts has succeeded in gaining for them the full benefits, or differential rent, from their mining projects.

Generous Taxation

Because CIPEC governments do not have authentic control over their minerals projects, their options to capture differential rents are limited to various forms of minerals taxation, much of which, as was noted in Chapter 3, are only indirectly, if at all, designed to capture differential rents for Third World landlord governments. Another good indicator of the limited appropriation of differential rent by CIPEC governments is, thus, the comparatively generous tax incentives that they offer to the metropolitan copper MNCs that work their mines.

Although it would be useful to compare the effects of different government tax policies on the copper industry of various countries, such an exercise is potentially difficult for a number of reasons, including the lack of relevant data. First, tax laws are often general and do not distinguish among specific industries. Second, because of the complexity of tax laws and the limited availability of information, most analyses will be limited to certain tax provisions. Third, because specific tax incentives identified in an analysis may not be representative of a country's overall structure, international comparisons can be misleading. Fourth, difficulties in comparative analysis also arise because of differences between free enterprise countries (for example, the United States) and those where government control of the mining industry and/or mineral deposits is the rule. In a predominantly free enterprise system like the United States, taxes are a cost to firms and thus affect their profits. The extent to which the profit motive is equally, or even comparably, operable in some supplier-nations, such as those within CIPEC, is uncertain. As an article in *Forbes* pointed out about CIPEC, 'having nationalized their copper industries, the member countries run them, not as businesses, but as sources of jobs, patronage and foreign exchange.'[42]

Table 18 summarizes in matrix form selected tax law provisions for five countries: the United States, Canada, Chile, Zambia, and Peru. The information is taken from a U.S. Bureau of Mines source. Note that, according to Sousa, its author, the information should be interpreted with caution because the actual tax provisions are much more complex than is indicated in the table. 'For example', Sousa wrote,

> there may exist limitations to, or qualifications for, the use of the specific provisions. Also, the data may be less than complete because secondary rather than primary sources of information were used. Another limitation is that only income tax provisions are shown here, but it is necessary to analyze the total tax structure to obtain a definitive assessment. For example, Peru has a value-added tax, but mining is exempt. Finally, state and provincial taxes are not included, although . . . they are quite important in the United States and Canada.[43]

Despite these qualifications, the information in Table 18 gives a rough indication of the tax policies of the few countries included, and, thus, serves as a basis for comparison.

A tax system may be divided into two components, the rate and the base. In Table 18, tax rates are shown in the first column and adjustments to the base are shown in the remaining columns. The 46 percent corporate tax rate for the United States and Canada does not seem too high compared with the rates shown for Chile, Peru, and Zambia. Notice that the 46 percent standard rate in Canada is reduced to 36 percent because of the 10 percent abatement to allow for Provincial income taxation. In Chile, the standard rate of 55 percent is reduced to 49.5 percent for ten years to attract foreign investors. Because of adjustments to a country's tax base, it would be misleading to consider only the tax rate in any international comparison of taxation systems.

Zambia's tax law provides for the complete expensing of capital expenditures, and Canada's does likewise for new mines and major expansions of existing ones. Only Chile's tax system, with regard to exploration and development costs, appears to be more unfavourable than that of the United States. Although the U.S. tax law does provide for the current financing of exploration and development costs, as do the laws of most of the other countries, the exploration expenditures must be recaptured once production commences.

From the limited information available, it appears that taxation may be adversely affecting the competitiveness of the U.S. copper industry. This is especially true in comparison with policies in CIPEC countries where the copper industry is generally a major part of the national economy. Although the U.S. corporate tax rate is not relatively high, other tax provisions, which are important to the copper industry and which reduce the tax base, appear to be less significant in this country than in other major copper-producing countries.

According to Sousa, Vogely, another mineral industry analyst, said with regard to U.S. tax policy, that 'it is simply not in the nature of our political system to develop sector-oriented policies and we tend to pass policies that do not relate directly to these interest groups'.[44] Also, according to Sousa, although adherence by the United States to basic tax principles 'is perhaps the best way to formulate tax policy when concern is about the

Table 18
Comparison of Selected Income Tax Law Provisions Affecting the Copper Industry of Major Producing Countries, 1981

Country	Corporate Tax Rate	Capital Recovery	Exploration and Development Costs	Regional Development	Discretionary	Other
Canada	46 percent (reduced to 36 percent due to abatement).	30 percent annually, but up to 100 percent for new mines and expansions.	Currently deductible.	Highest investment tax credit for certain regions.	None.	Resource allowance. Earned depletion allowance. Investment tax credit.
Chile	55 percent 49.5 percent for 10 years for foreign investors.	Accelerated system. Authority to give copper producers special treatment.	Deducted over life of mine.	Tax reduction for companies in less developed provinces.	Foreign investment contract. Depreciation for new copper investments.	Special tax for small mining companies.
Peru	Graduated to 55 percent. Special rates for SPCC.[a]	20 percent annually	Exploration costs currently deductible.	Tax reduction for companies in specified area.	None.	None.
United States	Graduated to 46 percent.	Accelerated methods available.	Currently deductible but exploration costs must be recaptured.	None.	None.	Percentage depletion allowance. Investment tax credit.
Zambia	50 percent plus mineral tax of 51 percent (deductible in computing income tax).	100 percent.	Currently deductible.	Incentive to locate in rural areas.	Tax relief for export and development activity.	Tax holidays.

[a]Southern Peru Copper Corp.
Source: Louis J. Sousa, *The U.S. Copper Industry: Problems, Issues, and Outlook* (Bureau of Mines, Washington, D.C., 1981) p. 63.

competitiveness between and among industries within the United States ... it may be questionable when dealing with the competitiveness of the same industry among nations.'[45] The relatively more generous tax provisions offered by CIPEC governments to the United States and to other metropolitan copper MNCs that dominate the operations of their mines clearly indicate that these governments are not capturing the full differential rents involved. Actually, if taxation, conceptually considered as the important means of capturing differential rents, is the same or less in CIPEC countries (compared to the United States), it will capture *none* of these surplus profits for CIPEC governments.

High Charges for Management and Technology

In response to the growing involvement by governments in minerals projects in the Third World, metropolitan mining MNCs are now increasingly utilizing management contracts in their dealings with landlord governments. Another good indication that CIPEC governments are not capturing the full differential rent today is the prevalent high fee for supplying management and technology which oligopolistic copper MNCs charge.

Metropolitan copper MNCs demand very high compensations in the form of mark-ups on their contracting fees. It is very likely that, in many cases, fees offered by a CIPEC host government will be considered inadequate by the company involved, since there are no generally accepted criteria with respect to mining under contract, and since the companies have monopoly over technology and sophisticated management expertise.

According to an unpublished CIPEC study, the common features of management contracts include the following:

1. *Fees*, which are usually on a cost-plus basis for management and technical consultancy, that is, a straight reimbursement of cost as claimed by the contractor, which is normally listed out on a category basis;

2. *Personnel*, which are costed on the basis of a multiple of salary; for example, a U.K. consulting firm operating in South America might typically be costed in dollar terms at eight times the consultant's salary in sterling. The 'plus' element in the contract is normally 10 percent;

3. *Subsidiary fees*, which are not normally charged except for engineering consultancy; they may be charged for on a commission basis;

4. *Purchasing contracts*, which may be on a commission basis, but cost-plus is more usual;

5. *Recruitment fees*, which are normally cost-plus;

6. *Availability fees*, which used to be a fairly standard feature, but are now few or excluded;

7. *Sales contracts*, which usually involve revenue-related fees;

8. *Projects work*, which are usually charged on a proportionate fee basis; and

9. *Hybrid fees*, which comprise: 1) a fixed fee for normal day-to-day monitoring and routine supervisory work; and 2) cost, cost-plus, or budgeted

fees for special work, consultancy, etc.

Following the nationalization of Union Minière's interests in Zaire in 1967, the company's parent, SGM, continued to provide a full range of management, technical, and marketing services under contract to the state corporation, GECAMINES. The fees for these services involved cost-plus elements, for example, on technical consultancy services, and percentage commission elements, for example, on metals sales. The contracts, said the CIPEC study, were undoubtedly 'very rewarding' financially for SGM, with fees varying between 15 and 20 million dollars annually. These fees almost certainly contained elements of the differential rent accruable to Zaire.

In Zambia, the nationalization agreements for 51 percent, signed at the end of 1969, included terms similar to those in Zaire's agreements, under which associate companies of the principal minority shareholders, AAC and RST, in the new operating companies, NCCM and RCM, respectively, would provide a wide range of services under contract. The contracts were similar for both companies. They were valid for 12 years at NCCM and ten years at RCM. Fees for the main contracts in Zambia were as follows:

1. *Management:* 1) 0.75 percent of gross sales; and 2) 2 percent of consolidated profits after charging all revenue expenditure and outgoings, and after provision for replacements and minerals tax but before all other income taxes and before deduction of reserves;

2. *Sales:* 0.75 percent of gross sales (except cobalt, at 2.5 percent);

3. *Engineering Design:* cost together with 3 percent of cost of capital goods and equipment;

4. *Purchasing:* reimbursement of declared cost; and

5. *Recruitment:* cost together with 15 percent of first year's total emoluments of each recruit.

In all, according to the CIPEC study, these fees provided 'substantial' revenues for the contracting companies concerned. For NCCM, for the first 15 months of the contracts, from January 1970 to March 1971, these fees were estimated to amount to $16.3 million. Of this amount, management fees alone represented 55 percent and sales fees accounted for 30 percent. This total of $16 million excludes certain other revenues payable by host governments under contract. Moreover, the profits of the contracting firms were high because the costs involved in producing many of the services provided under the contracts are borne only partly by the contracting MNC.

The above fees are an example of the kind of generous terms a contracting MNC can obtain in CIPEC countries under favourable circumstances. They significantly drain differential rent that could accrue to CIPEC governments. For example, in the case of Zaire, in 1967, total copper production amounted to some 644 million pounds. If one assumes my estimated 20 cents per pound cost-differential in favour of CIPEC countries, then the country's total potential differential rent was roughly $128 million that year. Given the $20 million that was roughly estimated for management fees that year, this one means of rent-drainage represented 16 percent of Zaire's total potential differential rent! The corresponding figure in 1970 was 14 percent.

In 1970 in Zambia, with a total production of about 1,378 million pounds of copper, total potential differential rent amounted to $275 million. The roughly estimated management fee of $16 million in Zambia that year represented 6 percent of this rent. The result was the same in 1976.

If we consider that the total fees estimated in these two countries exclude other possible fees paid under contract, we can say from the above figures that management fees constituted a significant proportion of total potential differential rents in these countries. Moreover, high charges for management and technology, as a means of draining differential rents, are mostly applicable to the state-owned mining sector. Since nationalizations in CIPEC countries, state-owned copper corporations abound that depend on metropolitan MNCs for the supply of management and technology. In summary, high charges for the supply of management and technology mean that metropolitan copper MNCs can drain differential rents from CIPEC countries.

Extra-favourable Investment Climate

The world copper industry is dominated by oligopolistic copper MNCs from the metropolis. In the final analysis, the size of the differential rent that can be captured by CIPEC governments will depend on the individual strengths of their overall policies affecting these foreign mining investors. CIPEC governments, who lack the necessary capital and technology independently to exploit their rich mines, attract these resources by generally offering the metropolitan MNCs that control them extra-favourable investment incentives, including differential rents. A summary of CIPEC governments' minerals policies towards foreign investors, provided in an unpublished CIPEC study, reveals this tendency.

In Chile, mineral rights are vested in the government. The government retains ownership of deposits while seeking to attract foreign companies, who will be entitled to a share of output sufficient to cover capital costs and ensure 'fair profits'.

Chile has a 'company tax' levied at a rate of 35 percent on net profits. However, special concessions are available for new companies if the initial investment is made under 'prescribed conditions'. Another form of taxation, known as 'Cowi', operates in Chile. It is a general tax assessed at 5 percent of gross corporate profits. This tax is, however, often reduced in proportion to the company's contribution to workers' housing, or to one of the state housing corporations. There is also a withholding tax, levied at a rate of 37.5 percent on distributed profits transferred abroad.

Finally, the Chilean peso is now convertible, but there are controls on currency transfers. In principle, however, current profits and the proceeds of disinvestment can be transferred abroad, in full.

In Peru, even though the government had sought, since 1968, to tighten regulations concerning foreign firms, the present rulers are pursuing a liberal and 'flexible' policy towards foreign investors. The government is committed to Peruvianization of all major foreign companies in the minerals sector. This ultimate objective is to be achieved by the gradual distribution of equity to Peruvians through profit-sharing schemes.

Mining companies in Peru are subject to a scaled tax on corporate income, varying from a flat 20 percent rate on income up to 10,000 soles, to a 40 percent rate on incomes reaching 100,000 soles. A surtax is levied on that part of corporate income considered to be in excess of that figure.

An annual concession fee of 2.50 soles per hectare is payable on all mining rights. When a particular concession is exploited, an annual fee of 3 soles per hectare is assessed. Mining companies are also required to pay an annual land tax at a rate of between 7.50 and 90 soles per hectare.

Another tax, known as 'capacity tax', of 2 soles per year is also charged mining companies for each ton of rated capacity. Ostensibly to discourage the 'locking-up' of ore in the ground, this tax is quadrupled for a company that after five years does not reach a stipulated minimum output.

To comply with the Peruvian government's regulations concerning profit-sharing and worker-participation, mining companies are expected to distribute 4 percent of their pre-tax profits to a workers' association (to enable them eventually to acquire up to 50 percent of company equity), and to pay 1 percent of pre-tax profits to the government's mining research department.

The long-term aim of mineral policy in Peru is to Peruvianize all foreign companies in the minerals sector. The Peruvian sol is convertible, and the proceeds of capital disinvestment can be repatriated as can current profits, since they are subject to a withholding tax.

In Zaire, mineral rights are vested in the state. Taxes on mining companies include an export tax payable on revenue from overseas sales, at the rate of 40 percent. An additional export duty is payable at varying rates when copper prices are 'high'. In certain circumstances, a tax at between 7 and 10 percent on gross sales may be payable. Corporate income tax is levied on the balance of income at varying rates, up to a theoretical maximum of 40 percent.

'Special arrangements' are, however, often negotiated for new ventures. For example, La Société Minière du Tenke-Fungurume (SMTF) was known to have enjoyed a five-year tax exemption from start-up. SMTF is one of the two mining companies formed by a five-company consortium of American, British, Japanese, and French interests in a contract with the Zairean government to explore and exploit mines in the country's Tenke and Fungurume regions of eastern and south-eastern Shaba.

In Zaire, mineral companies are also required to set up a reserve fund, described as 'the reserve for the restoration of the ore deposit', to finance further exploration and mine development. This fund which is, in effect, a depletion fund, must be spent within four years of being established.

Zaire also has the royalty system. Mining companies are required to remit a portion of mine output to the state, the actual output being subject to negotiation. Set fees are charged for exploration rights (10 zaires per year per hectare) and for standard thirty-year mining concessions (one likuta per year per hectare).

There is no general regulation on foreign shareholders in Zaire. Foreign share holdings, therefore, vary according to individual cases, from 0 percent (GECAMINES) to 85 percent (SODIMIZA).

With regard to exchange control, capital brought into Zaire and profits arising from its use may be remitted abroad, in full, subject to approval, which is often automatic, from the Central Bank, except during a new venture's initial tax holiday. With regard to export-sales, the state marketing corporation nominally handles all non-ferrous metal export deliveries.

Finally, in Zambia, mineral rights are also vested in the state, and concessions are issued in the form of prospecting, exploration, and mining licences. Taxes include corporate income tax, calculated at 45 percent of taxable income. There is also a mineral tax, payable normally on gross profits at rates varying from 10 percent for precious metals to 51 percent for copper. Mineral tax is allowable from income tax; thus the combined rate of mineral tax and income tax on profits for copper mining is 73.05 percent. Mineral tax is recoverable if a mining company's gross returns on equity fall below an average of 12 percent over a three-year period.

There are also 100 percent 'investment allowances' in Zambia for all capital expenditure claimed by mining companies other than those in the NCCM and RCM groups. These two big mining companies can write off capital expenditure against tax at varying rates, according to the assets purchased. Investment allowances can be carried forward without limit.

Zambia also has a withholding tax on dividends, interests, royalties, consultancy, and management fees. This tax is payable at a rate of 15 percent and allowable against personal income tax only for resident recipients of dividends. Other special concessions in Zambia include the possibility of offsetting all expenditure on prospecting and exploration against income tax on profits from non-mining activities, including exemptions for small mines and cooperatives.

Zambia's state mining corporation, MINDECO, has a statutory option to acquire up to 51 percent of shareholders' equity in a new mine. This option can be compulsorily exercised up to six months from the date of issuance of a mining licence. There is no additional limit on the extent of foreign ownership of equity in a mining company. Zambia's state marketing corporation, MEMACO, is nominally responsible for all export-sales of non-ferrous metals.

Foreign funds can be brought into Zambia without restriction, and the proceeds can be automatically repatriated, though subject to the approval of the Bank of Zambia. Profit remittance by non-Zambian-controlled companies (with 51 percent or more of the equity held outside the country) are subject to exchange control. Remittance is limited to 50 percent of post-tax profits, or 10 percent of paid-up capital, whichever is lower. Permission from the Bank of Zambia is required for the transfer of fees to non-resident directors, and, indeed, for any foreign currency payment.

My primary objective in describing these policies is not to assess the extent to which they can increase or reduce CIPEC governments' rent appropriation, but to underline the common characteristic that these policies share, namely, that they are definitely not designed to capture differential rents in full, if at all. Notice the complete lack of any reference to the problem of rent in all of them. What the minerals policies of CIPEC governments do accomplish is that by offering all sorts of loopholes and special concessions, they effectively accommodate the high-profitability interest of foreign mining investors.

The problem, from the standpoint of CIPEC governments, is that they want to expand their copper operations, but they are very heavily dependent on metropolitan mining MNCs for the necessary capital and technology. Moreover, as was pointed out in the previous chapter, it is possible that CIPEC governments are effectively in competition with each other to attract these foreign investors.

CIPEC governments are forced to offer incentives to draw the capital and technology that are monopolized by mining MNCs. Under these circumstances, MNCs do not have to surrender the differential rents to CIPEC host governments.

Obviously, the extent of rent-appropriation by CIPEC governments is likely to vary from country to country and over time. What is important to stress is that CIPEC governments share a common problem, that is, their technological dependence on foreign copper MNCs, which affords these firms the opportunity to siphon huge portions of the differential rents from CIPEC governments' lucrative copper projects.

Finally, the point that CIPEC governments offer extra-favourable investment conditions to foreign copper operators, in terms of sharing the differential rents involved with them, is further supported by the continued presence of the MNCs in CIPEC countries, even after nationalizations in these countries, and despite the so-called risk supposedly associated with Third World nationalism. There are a few empirical data to support the argument that copper MNCs are now returning, in full force, to CIPEC countries and that they have, therefore, continued to receive above-average profits after the initial wave of nationalizations in the 1960s and 1970s. For example, in Zaire, projects for expansion involving foreign capital amounted to 200,000 tons of mining capacity in 1980, whereas expansion plans in the state sector aimed at no more than 120,000 tons. Also, in Peru, in addition to ongoing negotiations with a German firm for a turnkey plant in Cerro Verde II, negotiations for the development of the Tantaya Deposit by a consortium of Canadian, French, and Japanese interests are well advanced.[46] And, according to Fortin, the clearest example of the wooing of foreign copper operators by a CIPEC government is certainly in Chile where 'the state company is being held back in its investment by the government while major concessions are being handed out to foreign capital for exploration and exploitation of new deposits or expansion of existing ones.'[47]

The Chilean government's economic model of full integration into the world capitalist economy illustrates that CIPEC governments, like most other Third World minerals-exporting governments, are today paying less attention to the nationalist rhetoric that once dominated their earlier positions in the natural resources debates. Given this tendency, the governments of Chile, Peru, Zaire, and Zambia, the important Third World copper-exporters, will probably continue not to be the only claimants to the differential rents from the capitalist exploitation of their rich copper mines.

Summary and Conclusion

This chapter has been concerned with extending Marx's concept of differential rent to the world copper industry, and with suggesting that this surplus profit is not appropriated, in full, by CIPEC landlord governments. The chapter has shown that differential rent exists in the world copper industry because the copper mines in the advanced countries, with the United States as the focus, have lower ore grades, possess higher labour costs, and yield poorer rates of profit, compared to those in CIPEC countries. The comparative advantages that thus stand in favour of CIPEC countries can, according to Marx's scheme, be appropriated by their governments in full as differential mining rent.

Complete and definitive financial information for quantitatively analysing CIPEC governments' limited rent appropriation is not available now. As I have shown, however, other, good empirical data are available that strongly suggest that these governments are not capturing differential rents in full.

CIPEC governments do not have effective control over their copper projects. They are, rather, very heavily dependent on metropolitan copper MNCs in a number of areas, including the opening up of new mines, the availability of technology and management expertise, and the use of worldwide marketing networks. It seems that CIPEC governments' dependence provides the dominant copper MNCs the opportunity to siphon, as super profits, handsome shares of the differential rents involved in mining CIPEC governments' rich copper deposits.

Independence in the crucial areas of world copper mining is a pre-condition for CIPEC governments' effective control over their copper projects in the future. Thus, their prospects for realizing their full potential (landlord's) benefit, or the differential rent, from their future copper projects are not very bright, in view of the overwhelming structural constraints working against their peripheralized and mono-cultural economies within the world capitalist market.

Notes

1. It has almost become common practice in scholarly analyses to use the United States as an example of the typical advanced country. In this chapter, my use of the U.S. copper industry as an example of the marginal production condition that is characteristic of the advanced copper-consuming countries should be obvious to the reader. Nevertheless, a brief explanation of my choice is in order here.

First, although each of the advanced copper-consuming countries is an essential component of the imperialist centre, the United States has, since World War II, become the largest and most dominant imperialist power in the centre. Second, as the largest producer and consumer of copper in the world, the United States occupies a key position in the world copper industry. The country accounts for somewhat less than one-fifth of total world copper production, capacity, and reserves, and a slightly greater proportion of the world's consumption of copper. Third, in addition to contributing a basic link in the country's industrial infrastructure, the U.S. copper industry also provides an important strategic metal used not only in ordnance, but also as components of military command and control, transportation, and advanced weaponry systems. Fourth, the United States is the home of most of the few and highly integrated copper MNCs that dominate the world copper industry. Fifth, data on the U.S. copper industry were more readily available. Above all, U.S. conditions, in comparison with those of other advanced copper-consuming countries, actually represent 'the marginal mine' in the context of the world copper industry.

2. To conduct such an exercise, one would need complete financial data on total copper revenue, total costs, total capital outlay, and the average rate of profit for many years, with respect to each of the four CIPEC countries in question. However, government and corporate officials treat such information, especially regarding costs, as secret. A number of copper industry experts have been known to make remarks similar to those made in a personal letter to me from a World Bank official regarding 'the difficulties of doing an empirical analysis of economic rent' in the copper industry. The letter read, *inter alia*, 'I am afraid that I cannot help you in providing information on costs that is obtained from Bank borrowing countries on a confidential basis. In any case, such information is scarce.'

Although some rough calculations can be made from relevant, though notoriously unreliable, corporate annual reports, only those of Zambia were available to me. Even then, they were for only Roan Consolidated Mines (RCM) and for a very limited number of years, from 1975 to 1979. Moreover, the limited data from RCM's annual reports represent only part of the financial information with respect to copper production in Zambia. Most of the country's copper is actually produced by Nchanga Consolidated Mines (NCCM) and RCM. Furthermore, it is impossible to determine a realistic 'capital outlay' from the available annual reports. The figures quoted represent investments for the year and may, therefore, underestimate capital outlay for rent purposes. To use the cumulative capital outlay, however, even if the figures were available, would definitely suggest that no differential rents exist in the CIPEC countries, which would be absurd. A meaningful quantitative analysis of rent appropriation by the CIPEC governments is, therefore, impossible at this stage.

3. See Louis J. Sousa, *The U.S. Copper Industry: Problems, Issues, and Outlook* (U.S. Bureau of Mines, Washington, D.C., 1981) p.3. Most of the data in the following sections of this chapter are drawn from this important U.S. Bureau of Mines source.

4. The available data for measuring the costs of production in the copper industry are largely tentative and should be interpreted with caution. Some of the problems include the use of a variety of accounting conventions. For example, in Zambia no depreciation provisions are taken, whereas replaced equipment is included as an operating cost. There can also be a difficulty because some accounts cannot separate depreciation, depletion, or amortization. Also, countries and industries vary with respect to royalty rates and degrees of vertical integration. Moreover, different technologies can be used at the same mine. For example, at some mines

copper is produced via open-pit as well as underground mining, or as a sulphide concentrate or via leaching and precipitations. Sousa, *The U.S. Copper Industry*, p. 24.

5. Both the physical quantity and quality of copper reserves are important determinants of the relative costs of production. In the past, it was the huge quantities of U.S. domestic copper reserves that provided the basis for its representing the world's largest copper industry. However, the long-term declining trend in the average grade of U.S. copper reserves has tended to increase the cost of producing copper in the United States in relation to the rest of the world. Despite an expected continuation in the declining grade of U.S. copper reserves, the size of the remaining reserve base is such that a good portion of U.S. copper ore needs could, if necessary, be met from domestic sources, at least through the end of this century. In the final analysis, the major problem from the standpoint of the United States and its domestic copper industry arises not so much in the context of shortages of physical reserves, but in the context of the pressure to reduce high operating costs, principally caused by the relatively low grade of copper ore mined in the country.

6. Sousa, *The U.S. Copper Industry*, p. 27.

7. *Ibid.* Both advancing technology and greater economies of scale were important factors that acted to offset the upward cost pressure created by declining ore grades and metal yields. See Marian Radetzki, 'Metal Mineral Resource Exhaustion and the Threat to Material Progress: The Case of Copper'. *World Development* 3, nos. 2, 3, February–March 1975, pp. 135–136.

However, according to Sousa, by the late 1950s, the marginal rate at which technological innovation could continue to reduce real price was apparently beginning to slow as the real price of copper began to increase, reaching an average, in constant dollars, of 78.9 cents per pound in 1960. Since then, according to him, 'the long-term price trend has continued to rise, though the market irregularities of the last several years appear to have temporarily interrupted the upward movement'. (*Ibid.*)

8. Sousa, *The U.S. Copper Industry*, p. 27.

9. The average yield of U.S. copper ores from 1973 to 1979 were, in percentages: 0.53 for 1973; 0.49 for 1974; 0.47 for 1975; 0.51 for 1976; 0.52 for 1977; 0.51 for 1978; and 0.49 for 1979. *Ibid.*, p. 28.

10. *Ibid.*

11. *Ibid.*, p. 31.

12. Since 1970, hourly earnings in U.S. copper mining have increased at an average rate of 10.1 percent. As in most other mining and metals industries in the country, hourly earnings in the copper industry have increased more rapidly than earnings in the overall manufacturing sector. In the decade from 1970 to 1979, in contrast to the 10.1 percent average increase in U.S. copper workers' hourly earnings, the corresponding rate of increase for the typical worker in the manufacturing sector was only 7.6 percent.

Hourly earnings in 1970 amounted to $3.93 and to $9.53 in 1979. The corresponding figures for copper smelting and refining were $3.67 and $9.20. For all manufacturing, the figures were $3.25 and $6.69. With respect to the total private non-agricultural sector of the U.S. economy, hourly earnings amounted to $3.23 in 1970 and $6.16 in 1979. *Ibid.*

13. *Ibid.*

14. This is according to a U.S. Bureau of Mines source, which also warns that the available data on labour costs have varying degrees of reliability. For example,

Canada, the only higher labour cost producer after the United States, also produces substantial quantities of co-product nickel, the value of which could not be factored into the cost data. *Ibid.*, p. 33.

15. *Ibid.*

16. The factors identified here do not represent an exhaustive treatment of the cost problems facing the U.S. domestic copper industry. For example, one other problem area, less relevant to my present discussion, is the high cost of energy. According to a U.S. Bureau of Mines source, energy has been the most rapidly rising cost factor in the U.S. copper industry over most of the past decade. Also, rising prices have greatly increased the significance of energy costs in relation to the total costs of producing copper in the United States. By 1980, energy costs had risen to between 12 and 17 cents per pound. However, the U.S. domestic copper industry has probably not been as severely affected by increased energy prices as Chile, Peru, and Japan. See Sousa, pp. 32–35.

17. According to the U.S. Bureau of Mines, the Clean Air Act is the most costly of these various regulations to the U.S. copper industry. For a discussion of these regulations, see Sousa, pp. 49–51.

18. J.C. Simpson, 'Clearing the Air: Anti-Pollution Costs Drive Copper Firms into Debt, Make Them Take Over Targets', *Wall Street Journal*, 28 December 1978, p. 26.

19. A.D. Rovig and R. Doran, 'Copper: A Decade of Change and Its Meaning for the Future', *Mining Congress Journal* 66, no. 12, December 1980, pp. 36–40.

20. According to Everest Consulting Associates, Inc., and CRU Consultants, Inc., *The International Competitiveness of the U.S. Non-Ferrous Smelting Industry and the Clean Air Act* (ECA, Inc., and CRU, Inc., New York, 1982) p. 2.24.

21. 'Utah Copper and the $280 Million Investment in Clean Air', *Engineering and Mining Journal* 179, no. 4, April 1979, p. 72.

22. 'Phelps Dodge to Modify Smelters', *Mining Journal* 196, no. 7592, 20 February 1981, p. 129.

23. See 'U.S. Production Review II', *Copper Studies* 7, no. 4, October 1980, pp. 1–8.

24. Sources outside the firm, however, indicated that other non-environmental factors also contributed to the firm's decision to close the plants. In particular, according to a U.S. Bureau of Mines source, EPA has stated that only $120 million to $160 million of Anaconda's total estimate was directly attributable to compliance with the Clean Air Act, and that about half of the total was related to improvements in plant processes. EPA further commented, according to the source, that Anaconda had not considered applying for a Nonferrous Smelter Order, an alternative that would have extended Anaconda's compliance deadline to 1988. Sousa, *The U.S. Copper Industry*, p. 52.

25. 'Anaconda Mulls World Class Smelter', *American Metal Market* 88, no. 233, 20 November 1980, p. 1, and 'Company Town Struggles to Survive Alone', *Washington Post*, 22 February 1981, pp. G1, G3.

26. MSHA stands for Mine, Safety, and Health Administration; and OSHA stands for Occupational, Safety, and Health Administration.

27. Magma's 1978 net income was $13.6 billion. See D. Ridinger, 'Cost of Regulations to the Mining Industry', *Mining Congress Journal* 66, no. 2, February 1980, pp. 42–44.

28. Sousa, *The U.S. Copper Industry*, p. 58.

29. Everest and CRU, *The International Competitiveness of the U.S. Non-Ferrous*

Smelting Industry, p. 10.7.

30. *Ibid.*

31. Sousa, *The U.S. Copper Industry*, p. 56.

32. Everest and CRU, *The International Competitiveness of U.S. Non-Ferrous Smelting Industry*, p. 10.8.

33. *Ibid.*

34. Sousa, *The U.S. Copper Industry*, p. 4.

35. *Ibid.*, p. 61.

36. *Ibid.*, p. 60.

37. *Ibid.*, p. 61.

38. *Ibid.*

39. Quoted in Robert Pollin, 'The Multinational Mineral Industry in Crisis', *Monthly Review* 31, no. 11, April 1980, p. 28.

40. Philip Daniel, *Africanisation, Nationalisation, and Inequality: Mining Labour and the Copperbelt in Zambian Development* (Cambridge University Press, London, 1979) p. 79.

41. See Marian Radetzki, 'Long-Term Copper Production Options of the Developing Countries', *Natural Resources Forum 1*, no. 1, 1977, pp. 145–55. This article provides only a summary of the actual study in which Radetzki carried out the exercise. The study, entitled 'Would CIPEC Have Gained From Faster Expansion in the Years 1960–74?' is an unpublished note, which, according to him, was to be incorporated in his *Development Through Minerals Exports: A Study of the Copper Exporting Developing Countries and the Role of Copper in Their Development Endeavors*, prepared at the Institute for International Economic Studies, University of Stockholm.

Note that Radetzki uses the term 'rent', not 'differential rent', but defines his usage as 'the difference between the sales proceeds of copper and all costs for its production, including a "going" return to the capital used'. Differential Rent, according to him, 'can thus be considered a "surplus" profit resulting from the richness of the resources exploited'. Correct!

42. 'Why CIPEC's no OPEC', *Forbes*, June 1977, p. 59.

43. Sousa, *The U.S. Copper Industry*, p. 62.

44. *Ibid.*, p. 63.

45. *Ibid.*

46. See Carlos Fortin, 'Changing Roles for MNCs in the Evolving World Mineral Economy', in S. Sideri and S. Johns (eds.) *Mining for Development in the Third World: Multinational Corporations, State Enterprises and the International Economy* (Pergamon Press, New York, 1980) p. 343.

47. *Ibid.*

6. Conclusion

This study has extended Marx's theory of agricultural rent to contemporary world mining. More specifically, one important objective of the study was to provide a more meaningful methodological approach to the issue of the distribution of wealth from the capitalist exploitation of the world's rich mines.

Towards an Alternative Approach to Analysing Government–Foreign Investor Relations

Marx's rent theory, that is, the alternative approach presented in this study, is a response to the inadequacies of the bargaining model which has hitherto predominated in the literature on the relationship between Third World landlord governments and metropolitan mining firms. To reiterate briefly, besides lacking in theoretical content, an important problem with the bargaining model is that it presents the so-called bargaining power of Third World governments as irreversible in their relations with foreign mining operators. This problem exists because, in general, the model does not appreciate the relationship between the developed and under-developed countries in the context of the systematically exploitative operations of the world capitalist division of labour, that was structured to the disadvantage of the latter.

Unlike the bargaining model, this study was, therefore, designed on the premise that the global economy is a political system in which the advanced and underdeveloped countries can be seen as classes, the former monopolizing the primary means of production (that is, capital and technology), and the latter, being mono-cultural, suffering exploitation because of their relatively insignificant ownership of the means of production. In contemporary capitalist society, it is capital and technology, especially the latter, that in production mediate between man and nature. In other words, it is by means of these factors that the modern capitalist harnesses nature in satisfying society's wants. Accordingly, the global production system may be divided into those countries that relate to nature as owners of capital and technology (that is, industrialized or developed countries) and those that relate to it as non-owners of these resources (that is, mono-cultural, underdeveloped, primary producers, or suppliers of raw materials). This division, typical of national capitalist society, roughly represents the class division of the global production system.[1] From this perspective, in this study, metropolitan mining MNCs are identified as the class representatives of the advanced countries, and Third World landlord governments as the class representatives of underdeveloped countries.

In the ensuing struggle between these two class representatives over the wealth from minerals production, the obvious weakness of the underdeveloped countries, whose landlord governments are now obliged to 'bargain' for charity and to make do with a pittance, is most striking. The weakness of Third World landlord governments *reflects their countries'* relative lack of the modern instruments of labour, compared to mining MNCs and their metropolitan home governments. It is precisely because of their relative lack of these instruments that Third World landlord governments are unable, in today's world, to exploit any potential 'bargaining' power they might have as an effective weapon in their struggle with metropolitan mining MNCs. To produce their valuable minerals, Third World landlord governments generally depend on the capital and technology monopolized by these firms. Under the circumstances, contrary to the bargaining model, in the relationship between the two dominant class representatives involved in the world mining business, the 'bargaining' power of Third World landlord governments is, therefore, not only reversible but also quite limited. In other words, contrary to the bargaining model, Third World landlord governments of mono-cultural economies are unlikely to be able to overcome the poverty characteristic of their economies, much less to threaten the potential super profits of metropolitan mining MNCs. In the final analysis, and in view of the depth of the economic and technological dependence of Third World governments, the effect of the global struggle between the two is rather precisely the establishment of a patron-client type of situation where landlord governments organize the super profitable access of metropolitan mining MNCs to the Third World's rich natural resources.

There is obviously a need for an alternative, and analytic, approach to the study of government–foreign investor relations in world mining. In this regard, the exposition of Marx's rent theory is very useful. As this study has shown, the theory is important for explaining the persistent underdevelopment characteristic of mono-cultural export economies. In particular, as presented in this study, the theory provides a more meaningful methodological approach than does the dominant bargaining model for analysing government–foreign investor relations in the world minerals industries.

While the application of Marx's rent theory to contemporary world mining is relevant and important, only two scholars, Massarrat and Nore, have attempted to tackle this task. From the standpoint of analytical rigour, the present study, compared to these existing works on rent, goes far beyond their rather preliminary and hazy conceptualizations. Furthermore, while the existing works narrowly focus on the oil industry, the extension of Marx's rent theory in this study has embraced the entire minerals issue, and has systematically analysed empirical data on both the oil and copper industries.

205

Moreover, existing studies on rent, typical of most Marxist works, uncritically apply Marx's rent theory, whereas this study has shown that the theory needs some fundamental modifications to remain valid in today's world.

This study, unlike existing literature on Marx's rent theory, has, therefore, adopted a critical perspective, underlining three important conditions that had informed Marx's rent theory, but that are not applicable in the contemporary world mining business. In summary, first, Marx had assumed that competitive capitalism would enable the landowner simply to appropriate differential rent I. It is monopoly, however, not competition that prevails in contemporary world capitalism. Second, Marx's notion of the greater power of landlords *vis-à-vis* capitalist-entrepreneurs, which would enable the former to impose short and frequently-changed leases and allow them to appropriate differential rent II, is inapplicable in today's world mining business where Third World landlord governments typically provide concession terms lasting for over one century. Third, modern landed property does not have a concerted and absolute monopoly over the world's natural resources, a situation that would enable landlord governments to create absolute rents in today's world. Marx had witnessed, however, an English landed gentry that he thought had a greater monopoly, based on landownership, *vis-à-vis* their capitalist opponents.

Summary of the Major Arguments

In capitalism, the landlord's income has an inverse relation to the capitalist's super profits. In other words, if that part of surplus value known as rent is appropriated by the landlord, the capitalist entrepreneur's excess profits will be reduced. As a rule, the larger the landlord's rent, the lower would be the capitalist entrepreneur's above-average, or super, profits. The lower the capitalist entrepreneur's super profits, the lower would be his rate of accumulation.

Rents, the excess profits inherent in world mining today, are relevant to accumulation, both in the centre and in the periphery of the world capitalist economy. The Third World landlord governments of mono-cultural economies are in dire need of, and depend on, these surplus profits to pursue their peripheral accumulation. However, if all these profits are captured by these governments, then accumulation will probably not take place at what would be considered a 'rapid' or 'maximum' rate in the metropolitan countries. This would be so because all that the metropolitan mining MNCs would, in effect, get by working the Third World's rich mines would be the normal, or average, rate of profit only.

The essence of today's so-called mineral crisis is the struggle between the principal class representatives involved in the world mining business — metropolitan mining MNCs and Third World landlord governments — over who will acquire the larger portions of the enormous surplus value, or rents, inherent in the international and capitalist exploitation of the world's important minerals deposits. This study has argued that, in this struggle, the power of the former far surpasses that of the latter.

The Marxian rent approach, adopted here, recognizes two kinds of surplus profits — absolute rent and differential rent — in the capitalist exploitation of natural resources. The approach is useful because it allows us to appreciate the pattern that the distribution of the enormous wealth inherent in the world mining business should, theoretically, assume in today's world political economy.

First, with respect to the first form of wealth, if Third World landlord governments occupied an absolute monopoly position in today's world mining business, *vis-à-vis* metropolitan minerals-consuming governments and their mining MNCs, these landlord governments would be in a position to exact a monopoly charge, or absolute rent, on the increasing global demand for their 'scarce' minerals. However, this study has shown that the governments of OPEC and CIPEC do not occupy such an absolute monopoly position today. Moreover, the fact of their ideological and economic heterogeneity would not allow them to organize effective, that is, concerted and long-term, minerals cartels, which represent the basic prerequisite for exacting Marxian absolute rent by Third World landlord governments today.

Under these circumstances, and in view of the enormous influence of mining MNCs and their metropolitan minerals-importing governments in the world minerals sphere, whatever surplus profits or absolute rents that arise from the growing global demand for minerals are not the prerogative of only the Third World landlord governments to capture. Today, such surplus profits are, in fact, shared among the metropolitan minerals-importing governments, their mining MNCs, and Third World landlord governments. The governments receive their shares in the form of taxes, while the mining MNCs receive theirs as above-average profits, that is, super profits.

OPEC, the forerunner of Third World producers' associations, has had a longer and more successful history of collaboration than CIPEC. For a number of reasons noted in this study, the propensity for exacting monopoly charges on the metropolitan consumers of natural resources in the future is higher for OPEC and the oil-exporting governments than for CIPEC and the copper-exporting governments.

On the whole, the exaction of absolute rents by Third World landlord governments, through their producers' associations, is as yet an uncertain proposition, partly because of their relative ignorance about the workings of the international minerals industries. Therefore, the unpublicized role of Third World producers' associations as information-gathering and statistics-assembling institutions can be systematically exploited by individual member governments to acquire relevant minerals industry knowledge, and to master how to run their rich mines independently, for their own benefit. Viewed from this perspective, Third World producers' associations may, ultimately, positively influence the appropriation of absolute rents by their member governments.

The Marxian rent approach also allows us to appreciate the proper pattern that the distribution of a second kind of surplus wealth, in addition to absolute rent, could be taking in today's world. If competition among metropolitan mining MNCs were allowed absolute free play, and Third World landlord governments authentically owned and controlled the crucial facilities and expertise needed in the internationalized process of minerals production today, these governments would be in a good position to capture the full excess profits, or differential rents, arising from the comparative advantages of their rich mines. This book has, however, pointed out that Third World landlord governments, who lack authentic ownership of, and control over, their minerals industries, are very heavily dependent on a few large and very powerful metropolitan mining MNCs to operate them, process the minerals, and sell the products. Under these circumstances, significant portions of the differential rents that could accrue to Third World landlord governments can be concealed in, and drained through, the artificial and high prices charged by MNCs for the so-called transfer of technology, and for the management fees, involved in the dependent position of landlord governments.

Because of the historical dominance of metropolitan mining MNCs over the dependent minerals-exporting governments, these governments have experienced two basic types of roles in the history of the international mining business.[2] First, the governments of some countries are essentially passive tax-collectors, having turned over the risk of minerals exploration and full control of such exploration and development to private foreign companies, often in exchange for a share of their profits from the sales of the minerals, which remain in the control of the foreign companies. This can be called the tax-collector role of the host government. Second, some governments essentially become partners with private foreign companies, on the understanding that the companies put up the funds for exploration, and that the output is shared on some agreed basis between the companies and the governments when minerals are found. This approach can be called the production-sharing role of the host government. What these two approaches have in common is that, lacking the rent mentality, they are not geared to capturing differential rents. On the contrary, they are designed to accommodate foreign minerals operators' high profitability precisely by sharing differential rents with them.

An alternative to the passive tax-collecting and production-sharing roles is conceivable. Increasing interest should be shown for it as it involves the Third World government itself in bearing the risk of exploration, retaining full control over exploitation and development and, therefore, receiving 100 percent of the benefits, that is, differential rents, resulting from its mineral projects. This arrangement can be called the 100-percent-control role of the landlord government.[3] In principle, from the standpoint of minerals-related development, this approach will provide the best chances for Third World landlord governments to maximize differential rent.

On balance, it would seem that the role of passive government tax collector is more or less rapidly dying out in the Third World, and is being replaced by the production-sharing approach. In a few 'radical' or 'anti-imperialist' areas, there is at least an interest, if only expressed in rhetoric, in replacing the production-sharing approach with the 100-percent-control role itself (for example, Libya, Algeria).

In view of this situation, one can argue that the passive tax-collector approach was a product of colonialism, that the production-sharing approach is a product of neo-colonialism, and that the 100-percent-government-control approach is a product of an interest in achieving an authentic economic *uhuru* from metropolitan mining MNCs in the Third World, the difficulty of the task notwithstanding.[4]

The point is that although, until the 1960s, the passive government tax collector was the dominant role in the Third World, the countries that continue to accept this arrangement will tend to be extremely weak ones that are still virtually colonies. An example is Liberia. Also, although the production-sharing arrangement which was popularized in Indonesia in the 1960s seemed progressive in form at the time, it was, in substance, often similar to the passive tax-collector role. This was so because although the government received some of the oil itself, rather than only money profits as in the tax-collector role, it often simply sold back its share of the oil to the companies and ended up in the same position.[5] This is also the situation in Nigeria today. In fact, the misnomer, 'production-sharing' is deliberately deceiving. Because of the arrangements involved in production-sharing, it should more properly be labelled 'rent-sharing'.

There are a number of reasons why one would expect some Third World governments to want to move to the 100-percent-state-control role in the future. The most important and fundamental reason is the increasing spread of knowledge concerning the operations of the international minerals industries, including, in particular, the beginning of the erosion of certain myths prevailing in the minerals industries. The problem, however, is that being highly profitable to the metropolitan mining companies, these myths are perpetuated by them, as well as by some international agencies, to discourage Third World governments from entering the lucrative minerals industries, in particular, the exploration phase.

Briefly, these myths are, according to Tanzer, that only the large international minerals companies possess the technology and capital necessary to carry out minerals exploration and development, and can afford the risk of failure. With respect to the myth that only the large mining companies control vital exploration technology, Tanzer maintains that, in the case of oil, 'the facts are that' today most oil exploration efforts, both onshore and offshore, are not carried out by the large oil MNCs, like Exxon and Mobil, but by smaller specialized drilling firms, who will sell their services to anyone 'usually for a flat fee', that is, not for a share of differential rents. According to him,

> while it is true that in the underdeveloped countries these drilling firms work to a large extent for the big oil companies, this is so because the governments of these underdeveloped countries usually leave the control of exploration to the oil companies under the production-sharing arrangements. *What is more relevant, however, is that any government which is willing to pay the going market rate for these drilling operations can obtain them without recourse to the big oil companies,*

and without giving up a share of production or profits [rents] (. . . this is also true of pre-drilling exploration, such as geological and seismological surveys, which in the case of Puerto Rico were carried out by the government's hiring Western Geophysical Company, and not by a big oil company).[6]

With respect to the prevailing myth that only the large oil MNCs have the capital necessary for exploration and development, to quote Tanzer at length again,

this falsehood exists because of a failure to recognize that *while very large amounts of capital are required for finding and developing an oil field, only a small part of these funds (perhaps 5 percent or less) is needed for the truly risky function of exploration. The large bulk of the capital required is for development of an oil field once* [it is] found, and this is not a risky job. Moreover, given the great value of oil in the world today, oil in the ground is an extremely bankable asset, and the necessary development capital can easily be raised by loans, on quite favourable terms. [If the international economic system operated on a fair, competitive basis,] such loans . . . can be obtained from international agencies, commercial banks, equipment suppliers, or countries and oil companies that are anxious to secure future supplies of crude oil.[7]

Yet another myth is that only the mining MNCs can afford the risk of minerals exploration. This falsehood exists, according to Tanzer, because of excessive concentration on the potential cost of exploration, with hardly any attention being paid to the potential benefits to the government. Again, consider his argument on this point, in the case of oil and Puerto Rico:

whether or not a risk is worthwhile, or affordable, as the oil companies know so well, depends not only on the costs but also on the possible benefits, and what resources can be diverted from other uses to take the gamble. If, by way of a not-so-hypothetical example, $10 million has to be spent on exploration, and the chance of finding a one-billion-barrel field worth 1,000 times the oil exploration investment is one out of two, surely no rational person would say the country cannot afford the risk. After all, any country — no matter how small — has some resources available which it could shift to such an exploration "gamble". In the case of Puerto Rico, which though a small country has a Gross National Product far greater than many larger underdeveloped countries, is it not worth the gamble of less than one-tenth of one percent of the government's annual budget to finance a venture which could give the country a huge boost in its economic development?

Further, it should be pointed out that exploration is not an all-or-nothing thing, but a series of steps seeking information, which can be cut short if the initial information indicates that prospects are dim. Thus, if four wells cost $10 million, but the first two give very bad results, then *you can cut your losses by ending exploration, and hence your actual risk capital will turn out to be much less than the maximum.*

Finally, on the question of what Puerto Rico can "afford", *one must also ask whether the country can afford to give up control of a large share of its oil resources to a giant multinational company which has many interests all over the world. This is particularly important because in today's world, oil is a scarce resource whose value is often far greater than its market price. This may be particularly true for a country which might hope to use oil [or other minerals] as a basis for further industrialization . . .*[8]

Tanzer's arguments, strongly support the feasibility of the proposition that Third World governments of mono-cultural economies should completely control and operate their mines as a precondition for maximizing differential rent.

Now, in view of the increasing dissemination of knowledge concerning the workings of the world minerals industries, and of the beginning of the erosion of these myths, why have many Third World governments not moved beyond the existing production-sharing arrangements? A fundamental reason is, according to Tanzer,

> the historically very strong opposition of the international [mining] companies backed by their powerful home governments and international lending agencies like the International Monetary Fund and the World Bank, to state companies entering into the [mining] companies' highly profitable business.[9]

In other words, the minerals-exporting governments' prospects for maximizing differential rents, through completely controlling and running their mines, are limited by the prevailing power structure of the global capitalist economy. More fundamentally, it would appear that in the particular context of the global capitalist division of labour and in the interest of capital accumulation in the metropolis, the primary role of Third World landlord governments is not that of rent-maximizing, non-capitalist landlords, as the classical Marxian exposition of rent theory implies, but that of peripheral capitalist minerals-suppliers.

Future Research Scheme

Despite the extensiveness of the research in the present study, there obviously still remain a number of implications or extensions of the subject with which I have not dealt, either because of the very limited resources at my disposal, or because it was practically impossible, organizationally, to incorporate such implications or extensions at this stage. In the remainder of this concluding chapter, it is proposed to identify some research exercises that can follow from the present study, but which I have not embraced explicitly.

Application of Rent Concept to Negotiations in International Organizations

The rent concept is an important instrument for exposing the myth propagated by the bargaining model that the negotiations going on in international organizations today will lead to significant structural reforms in the world system and to the attainment of a new international order by Third World countries. More explicitly, since I have, I hope, demonstrated in this study, a clear and comprehensive understanding of the operations of Marx's rent theory in contemporary political economy, it would be interesting to apply this notion of rent to the conscious negotiations that have been going on over the past 20 years in some natural resource-related international organizations, such as UNCTAD, North-South, OPEC, CIPEC, the Law of the Sea Conference, etc. The research would then no longer be concerned with how to think of rent, but with how to investigate the extent to which those involved in negotiations in the international mining business have been conscious of the rent concept, which is so central to the world minerals problem. This task could be accomplished by studying statements, proposals, policy actions, etc., emanating from such negotiations. I believe that, ironically, there has been a clear lack of appreciation of the rent concept even in these conscious minerals-related international negotiations that have been going on since the beginning of economic nationalism in the Third World. From this perspective, and to the extent that rent maximization is a valid measure of a landlord government's attainment of the so-called new international economic order, the systematic pursuit of this order, not to mention its attainment, has, contrary to the bargaining model, not even begun within international organizations.

Quantitative Analysis of the Limited Appropriation of Rents by Third World Landlord Governments

To the extent that rent maximization by a landowner is a valid measure of an equitable relationship between the landowner and capitalist entrepreneur, it would also be useful to provide a quantitative analysis of the approximate extent of rent appropriation by individual landlord governments over time. The accomplishment of this task in the future will depend on the possibility that the problem of unavailability of data (described earlier) does not persist. Such an analysis would obviously enhance some of the arguments advanced in the present study about the limited appropriation of rents by Third World landlord governments in today's world.

Class Analysis

The capitalist exploitation of natural resources gives rise to a number of possible contradictions between social classes. The present study has concentrated mainly on the important contradiction between international capital and modern landed property, respectively represented by metropolitan mining firms and Third World landlord governments. However, at least two other types of class struggle can arise from minerals production, which must be appreciated in addition to the contradiction dealt with in this study between international capital and modern landed property.

There is, in the first place, a fundamental need to analyse the class struggle between the exploited mining workers and the ruling class coalition in Third World minerals-exporting countries. This task is particularly important because, after all, Marx's theory underlines the fact that the surplus value that eventually gets appropriated as rents or surplus profits by either the landowner or the capitalist is, in the first place, produced only by wage labour, which is, therefore, exploited. It would be useful and interesting to study the specificities of the exploitation of labour in today's world mining business. What is apparent is that poised against the wretched mining workers of the Third

World are not only the international bourgeoisie, represented by the large firms, but also their own national bourgeoisie that represent the firms. This important form of class struggle is the local counterpart of the global confrontation between, on the one hand, metropolitan mining operators, backed by their home governments' state apparatuses and, on the other, Third World landlord governments.

Another form of class struggle which can arise from mining, but which I have not analysed in the present study, may take place among factions of the local ruling classes for control of state power in minerals-exporting countries. Because minerals production in the Third World gives rise to large state revenues (the limited appropriation of rents notwithstanding), there are struggles among factions of the ruling class to control the state apparatus in order to preside over the spending of these large revenues. It would be useful to understand in whose factional class interests the state uses rent revenues in minerals-exporting countries, and why. What is immediately apparent is that although there are factional antagonisms among the ruling classes of Third World minerals-exporting countries, they are willing and able to cooperate (probably because of their various alliances with the international bourgeoisie) in order to exploit the mining workers of the Third World.

Notes

1. See Claude Ake, *Revolutionary Pressures in Africa* (Zed Press Ltd., London, 1978) pp. 17–18.

2. See Michael Tanzer, 'The State and the Oil Industry in Today's World: Some Lessons for Puerto Rico', *Monthly Review* 29, no. 10, March 1978, p. 2.

3. *Ibid.*

4. *Ibid.*

5. *Ibid.*

6. *Ibid.*, p. 4; my emphasis.

7. *Ibid.*, pp. 4–5; my emphasis.

8. *Ibid.*, pp. 5–6; my emphases.

9. *Ibid.*, p. 6.

Bibliography

Books

Ake, Claude. *Revolutionary Pressures in Africa* (Zed Press, London, 1978).

Amin, Samir. *The Law of Value and Historical Materialism* (Monthly Review Press, New York, 1978).

Banks, Ferdinand. *The World Copper Market* (Ballinger Publishing Co., Cambridge, Mass., 1974).

Baran, Paul A. *The Political Economy of Growth* (Monthly Review Press, New York, 1968).

Barber, William J. *A History of Economic Thought* (Frederick A. Praeger, New York, 1967).

Beckford, George L. *Persistent Poverty: Underdevelopment in Plantation Economies of the Third World* (Oxford University Press, New York, 1972).

Bose, Arun. *Marxian and Post-Marxian Political Economy* (Penguin Books Ltd., Harmondsworth, 1975).

Bostock, Mark, and Charles Harvey (eds.) *Economic Independence and Zambian Copper: A Case Study of Foreign Investment* (Praeger Publishers, New York, 1972).

Bowen, Robert, and Ananda Gunatilaka. *Copper: Its Geology and Economics* (John Wiley & Sons, New York, 1977).

Brewer, Anthony. *Marxist Theories of Imperialism: A Critical Survey* (Routledge and Kegan Paul, Ltd., London, 1980).

Brown, Martin S., and John Butler. *The Production, Marketing, and Consumption of Copper and Aluminium* (Praeger Publishers, New York, 1968).

Bye, Carl Rollinson. *Developments and Issues in the Theory of Rent* (Columbia University Press, New York, 1940).

Chevalier, Jean Marie. 'Theoretical Elements for an Introduction to Petroleum Economics', in A.P. Jacquemin and H.W. deJong (eds.) *Markets, Corporate Behavior and the State* (Martinus Nijhoff, The Hague, 1976).

Clarifield, Kenneth W., *et al*. *Eight Minerals Cartels: The New Challenge to Industrialized Nations* (McGraw-Hill, New York, 1975).

Connelly, Philip, and Robert Perlman. *The Politics of Scarcity: Resource Conflicts in International Relations* (Oxford University Press, New York, 1975).

Daniel, Philip. *Africanisation, Nationalisation, and Inequality* (Cambridge University Press, London, 1979).

Dean, Heather. 'Scarce Resources: The Dynamics of U.S. Imperialism', in K.T. Fann and Donald C. Hodges (eds.) *Readings in U.S. Imperialism* (P. Sargent

Publishers, Boston, 1971).

de Chungara, Domitila Barrios, and Moema Viezzer. *Let Me Speak! Testimony of Domitila, a Woman of the Bolivian Mines* (Monthly Review Press, New York, 1978).

Dobb, Maurice. *Theories of Value and Distribution Since Adam Smith: Ideology and Economic Theory* (Cambridge University Press, London, 1973).

Eaton, John. *Political Economy: A Marxist Textbook* (International Publishers, New York, 1966).

Emmanuel, Arghiri. *Unequal Exchange: A Study of the Imperialism of Trade* (Monthly Review Press, New York, 1972).

Engels, Frederick. *Anti-Dühring* (International Publishers, New York, 1976).

Engler, Robert. *The Politics of Oil: A Study of Private Power and Democratic Directions* (University of Chicago Press, Chicago, 1961).

—— *The Brotherhood of Oil: Energy Policy and the Public Interest* (University of Chicago Press, Chicago, 1977).

Everest Consulting Association and CRU Consultants, Inc. *The International Competitiveness of the U.S. Non-Ferrous Smelting Industry and the Clean Air Act*, 1982.

Faber, M.L.O., and J.G. Potter. *Towards Economic Independence: Papers on the Nationalisation of the Copper Industry in Zambia* (Cambridge University Press, Cambridge, 1971).

Faundez, Julio, and Sol Picciotto. *The Nationalization of Multinationals in Peripheral Economies* (Holms and Meir Publishers, New York, 1978).

Fortin, Carlos. 'The State, Multinational Corporations and Natural Resources in Latin America', in Jose J. Villamil (ed.) *Transnational Capitalism and National Development* (Humanities Press, Atlantic City, N.J., 1979).

—— 'Changing Roles of MNCs in the Evolving World Mineral Economy', in S. Sideri and S. Johns (eds.) *Mining for Development in the Third World: Multinational Corporations, State Enterprises and the International Economy* (Pergamon Press, New York, 1980).

Galeano, Eduardo. *Open Veins of Latin America: Five Centuries of the Pillage of a Continent* (Monthly Review Press, New York, 1973).

Garnaut, Ross, and Anthony Clunies Ross. 'A New Tax for Natural Resource Projects', in Michael Crommelin and Andrew R. Thompson (eds.) *Mineral Leasing as an Instrument of Public Policy* (University of British Columbia Press, Vancouver, 1974).

Gide, Charles, and Charles Rist, *A History of Economic Doctrines From the Time of the Physiocrats to the Present Day* (D.C. Heath and Co., Boston, 1948).

Gillis, Malcolm, and R. Beals. *Tax and Investment Policies for Hard Minerals: Public and Multinational Enterprises in Indonesia* (Ballinger Publishing Co., Cambridge, Mass., 1980).

Gillis, Malcolm, *et al. Taxation and Mining: Nonfuel Minerals in Bolivia and Other Countries* (Ballinger Publishing Co., Cambridge, Mass., 1978).

Girvan, Norman. *Copper in Chile: A Study in Conflict Between Corporate and National Economy* (University of West Indies, Kingston, 1972).

—— *Corporate Imperialism: Conflict and Expropriation* (M.E. Sharpe, Inc., New York, 1976).

Gluschke, Wolfgang, *et al. Copper: The Next Fifteen Years* (D. Reidel Publishing, Co., Boston, 1979).

Groennings, S.; Kelly, E.W.; and Leiserson (eds.) *The Study of Coalition Behavior*

(Holt, Rinehart and Winston, New York, 1970).

Hemmi, Kenzo, *et al. Trade in Primary Commodities: Conflict or Cooperation?* (The Brookings Institution, Washington, D.C., 1974).

Herfindahl, Orris Clemmens. *Copper Costs and Prices: 1870–1957* (The Johns Hopkins University Press, Baltimore, 1959).

—— *Resource Economics: Selected Works* (The Johns Hopkins University Press, Baltimore, 1974).

Hexner, Ervin. *International Cartels* (The University of North Carolina Press, Chapel Hill, 1946).

Hopkins, Terrence K., *et al. World-Systems Analysis: Theory and Methodology* (Sage Publications, Beverly Hills, 1982).

Howard, M.C., and J.E. King. *The Political Economy of Marx* (Longman Group, Ltd., London, 1975).

Hughes, Helen. *The Distribution of Gains From Foreign Direct Investment in Mineral Development* (The Asia Society, New York, n.d.).

Hunt, E.K., and J.G. Schwartz. *A Critique of Economic Theory* (Penguin Books, Baltimore, 1972).

Hveem, Helge. *The Political Economy of Third World Producer Association* (Universitetsjorlaget, Oslo, 1978).

Iwase, Niroko. 'Recycling and Substitution', in S. Sideri and S. Johns (eds.) *Mining for Development in the Third World* (Pergamon Press, New York, 1980).

Jalee, Pierre. *The Pillage of the Third World* (Monthly Review Press, New York, 1968).

—— *The Third World in World Economy* (Monthly Review Press, New York, 1969).

Johany, Ali D. *The Myth of the OPEC Cartel: The Role of Saudi Arabia* (John Wiley & Sons Ltd., New York, 1980).

Keiper, Joseph S., *et al. Theory and Measurement of Rent* (Chilton Co., Philadelphia, 1961).

Langdon, Steven. 'Multinational Corporations and the State in Africa', in Jose J. Villamil (ed.) *Transnational Capitalism and National Development* (Humanities Press, Atlantic City, N.J., 1979).

Lanning, Greg, and Marti Mueller. *Africa Undermined: Mining Companies and the Underdevelopment of Africa* (Penguin Books, Harmondsworth, 1979).

Leipziger, Danny M., and J.L. Mudge. *Seabed Mineral Resources and the Economic Interests of Developing Countries* (Ballinger Publishing Co., Cambridge, Mass., 1976).

Lenin, V.I. *The Agrarian Question and the "Critics of Marx"* (Progress Publishers, Moscow, 1976).

Magdoff, Harry. *The Age of Imperialism: The Economics of U.S. Foreign Policy* (Monthly Review Press, New York, 1969).

—— *Imperialism: From the Colonial Age to the Present* (Monthly Review Press, New York, 1978).

Marx, Karl. *Capital: A Critique of Political Economy* (3 Vols.) (International Publishers, New York, 1967).

—— *Theories of Surplus-Value* (3 Vols.) (Progress Publishers, Moscow, 1968).

—— *A Contribution to the Critique of Political Economy* (Progress Publishers, Moscow, 1970).

—— *Grundrisse: Foundations of the Critique of Political Economy* (Vintage Press, New York, 1973).

Massarrat, Mohssen. 'The Energy Crisis: The Struggle for the Redistribution of Surplus Profit From Oil', in Petter Nore and Terisa Turner (eds.) *Oil and Class Struggle* (Zed Press, London, 1980).

Meadows, Donella H., *et. al. The Limits to Growth: A Report for the Club of Rome's Project on the Predicament of Mankind* (Universe Books, New York, 1974).

Meek, Ronald L. *Studies in the Labor Theory of Value* (Monthly Review Press, New York, 1956).

Mezger, Dorothea. *Copper in the World Economy* (Monthly Review Press, New York, 1980).

Mikdashi, Zuhayr. *The Community of Oil Exporting Countries* (Cornell University Press, New York, 1972).

—— *The International Politics of Natural Resources* (Cornell University Press, Ithaca, 1976).

Mikesell, Raymond F. (ed.) *Foreign Investment in the Petroleum and Mineral Industries: Case Studies of Investor-Host Country Relations* (The Johns Hopkins University Press, Baltimore, 1971).

——*Nonfuel Minerals: U.S. Investment Policies Abroad* (Sage Publications, Beverly Hills, 1975).

—— *The World Copper Industry: Structure and Economic Analysis* (Johns Hopkins University Press, Baltimore, 1979).

Moran, Theodore H. *Multinational Corporations and the Politics of Dependence: Copper in Chile* (Princeton University Press, Princeton, N.J., 1974).

Murray, Robin. 'Underdevelopment, International Firms, and the International Division of Labour', in *Towards a New World Economy* (Rotterdam University Press, Rotterdam, 1972).

Nankani, Gobind. *Development Problems of Mineral Exporting Countries* (The World Bank, Washington, D.C., 1979).

Navin, Thomas R. *Copper Mining and Management* (University of Arizona Press, Tucson, 1978).

Nkrumah, Kwame. *Neo-Colonialism: The Last Stage of Imperialism* (International Publishers, New York, 1965).

Nore, Petter. 'Oil and State: A Study of Nationalization in the Oil Industry', in Petter Nore and Terisa Turner (eds.) *Oil and Class Struggle* (Zed Press, London, 1980).

Olson, Mancur. *The Logic of Collective Action* (Harvard University Press, Cambridge, Mass., 1965).

Oser, Jacob. *The Evolution of Economic Thought* (Harcourt Brace and World, Inc., New York, 1970).

Penrose, Edith. *The Large International Firm in Developing Countries: The International Petroleum Industry* (Greenwood Press Publishers, Westport, Conn., 1976).

Petras, James. *Critical Perspectives on Imperialism and Social Class in the Third World* (Monthly Review Press, New York, 1978).

Pirages, Dennis. *The New Context of International Relations: Global Ecopolitics* (Duxbury Press, North Scituate, Mass., 1978).

Prain, Ronald. *Copper: The Anatomy of an Industry* (Mining Journal Books, Ltd., London, 1975).

Radetzki, Marian. 'The Potential for Monopolistic Commodity Pricing by Developing Countries', in G.K. Helleiner (ed.) *A World Divided: The Less Developed Countries in the International Economy* (Cambridge University Press,

New York, 1976).

Radice, Hugo (ed.) *International Firms and Modern Imperialism* (Penguin Books, Inc., Baltimore, 1975).

Raw Materials and Foreign Policy (International Economic Studies Institute, Washington, D.C., 1976).

Ricardo, David. *The Principles of Political Economy and Taxation* (Everyman's Library, London, 1969).

Rifai, Taki. *The Pricing of Crude Oil* (Praeger Publishers, New York, 1975).

Rodney, Walter. *How Europe Underdeveloped Africa* (Tanzania Publishing House, Dar es Salaam, 1972).

Roemer, John. *Analytical Foundations of Marxian Economic Theory* (Cambridge University Press, New York, 1981).

Sampson, Anthony. *The Seven Sisters: The Great Oil Companies and the World They Shaped* (Bantam Books, New York, 1975).

Scott, Allen J. 'Land and Land-Rent: An Interpretative Review of the French Literature', in *Progress in Geography: International Review of Current Research* (St. Martins Press, New York, 1976).

Seidman, Ann (ed.) *Natural Resources and National Welfare: The Case of Copper* (Praeger Publishers, New York, 1975).

Skelton, Alex. 'Copper' in William Yandell Elliot *et al.* (eds.) *International Control in the Non-Ferrous Metals* (The Macmillan Company, New York, 1937).

Sklar, Richard. *Corporate Power in an African State* (University of California Press, Berkeley, 1975).

Smith, Adam. *The Wealth of Nations* (Ward, Lock & Co., London, n.d.).

Smith, David N. 'Information Sharing and Bargaining: Institutional Problems and Implications', in Gerald Garvey and Lou Ann Garvey (eds.) *International Resource Flows* (Lexington Books, New York, 1977).

Smith, David N., and Louis Wells. *Negotiating Third World Concession Agreements: Promises as Prologue* (Ballinger Press, Cambridge, Mass., 1975).

Sousa, Louis J. *The U.S. Copper Industry: Problems, Issues, and Outlook* (U.S. Bureau of Mines, Washington, D.C., 1981).

Spiegel, H.W. *The Growth of Economic Thought* (Prentice-Hall, Inc., New Jersey, 1971).

Sraffa, Piero, and Maurice H. Dobb. *The Works and Correspondence of David Ricardo* (10 Vols) (Cambridge University Press, Cambridge, 1962).

Stigler, George J. *The Organization of Industry* (Richard D. Irwin, Homewood, Ill., 1968).

Stocking, G.W., and M.W. Watkins. *Cartels or Competition* (Twentieth Century Fund, New York, 1948).

Stockpile Report to the Congress (GSA, Washington, D.C., 1975).

Stork, Joe. *Middle East Oil and the Energy Crisis* (Monthly Review Press, New York, 1975).

Sutulov, Alexander. *Minerals in World Affairs* (The University of Utah Printing Service, Salt Lake City, 1972).

Tanzer, Michael. *The Political Economy of International Oil and the Underdeveloped Countries* (Beacon Press, Boston, 1969).

———*The Energy Crisis: World Struggle for Power and Wealth* (Monthly Review Press, New York, 1974).

———*The Race for Resources: Continuing Struggles Over Minerals and Fuels* (Monthly Review Press, New York, 1980).

Tilton, John E. *The Future of Non-Fuel Minerals* (The Brookings Institution, Washington, D.C., 1977).

Turner, John Roscoe. *The Ricardian Rent Theory in Early American Economics* (New York University Press, New York, 1921).

Turner, Louis. *Oil Companies in the International System* (George Allen & Unwin Ltd., London, 1980).

Turner, Terisa. 'Nigeria: Imperialism, Oil Technology and the Comprador State', in Petter Nore and Terisa Turner (eds.) *Oil and Class Struggle* (Zed Press, London, 1980).

Vogely, William (ed.) *Economics of the Mineral Industries* (American Institute of Mining, Metallurgical and Petroleum Engineers, Inc., New York, 1976).

Wallerstein, Immanuel. *The Capitalist World-Economy* (Cambridge University Press, London, 1979).

Widstrand, Carl (ed.) *Multinational Firms in Africa* (Africana Publishing Co., New York, 1975).

Reports — Published

Intergovernmental Council of Copper Exporting Countries (CIPEC). *Annual Report* (CIPEC, Neuilly-sur-Seine, 1970, 1972, and 1974).
——*Modification of the CIPEC Agreement*, CIPEC's Conference of Ministers Document, CM/102.77 (CIPEC, Paris, June 22, 1977).
——*Statistical Bulletin* (CIPEC, Neuilly-sur-Seine), Various Issues.

Mikesell, Raymond F. 'International Collusive Action in World Markets for Nonfuel Materials: Market Structure and Methods of Marketing Control', a consultant paper prepared for the Bureau of Intelligence and Research INR X-1, U.S. Department of State, 25 July 1974.

Articles

Adelman, M.A. 'Is the Oil Shortage Real? Oil Companies as OPEC Tax Collectors', *Foreign Policy*, no. 9, Winter 1972–73.

Alleyne, D.H.N. 'The State Petroleum Enterprise and the Transfer of Technology', *Natural Resources Forum* 3, 1978.

'Anaconda Mulls World Class Smelter', *American Metal Market* 88, no. 233, 20 November 1980.

Asante, S. 'Stability of Contractual Relations in the Transnational Investment Process', *The International and Comparative Law Quarterly* 28, part 3, 1979.

Ball, Michael. 'Differential Rent and the Role of Landed Property', *International Journal of Urban and Regional Research* 1, no. 3, 1977.

Bergsten, C. Fred. 'The Threat from the Third World', *Foreign Policy* 14, Summer 1973.

Bierstecker, Thomas J. 'The Illusion of State Power: Transnational Corporations and the Neutralization of Host-Country Legislation', *Journal of Peace Research* 17, 1980.

Bobrow, David, and Robert Kudrle. 'Theory, Policy, and Resource Cartels: The Case of OPEC', *Journal of Conflict Resolution* 20, no. 1, March 1975.

Buchanan, D.H. 'The Historical Approach to Rent and Price Theory, *Economica* 9, June 1929.

Carlsson, Jerker. 'Gränges and the Undermining of Liberia: A Critique of a Joint Venture Arrangement', *Review of African Political Economy*, no. 23, January–April 1982.

Cohen, G.A. 'The Labor Theory of Value and the Concept of Exploitation', *Philosophy and Public Affairs* 8, no. 4, Summer 1978.

'Copper: In Constant Crisis', *Metals Week* 38, no. 9, 27 February 1967.

'Copper Industry Offers Recommendations for Revisions of the Clean Air Act', *Metals Week* 52, no. 11, 16 March 1981.

'Copper Price Controls: 1840–1965', *Copper Studies* 1, no. 2, 21 February 1967.

Cornell, Nina. 'Manganese Nodule Mining and Economic Rent', *Natural Resources Journal* 14, no. 4, October 1974.

Cotman, John Walton, 'South African Strategic Minerals and U.S. Foreign Policy, 1961–1968', *The Review of Black Political Economy* 8, no. 3, Spring 1978.

Curry, Robert L., Jr. and Donald Rothchild. 'On Economic Bargaining Between African Governments and Multi-National Companies', *The Journal of Modern African Studies* 12, no. 2, 1974.

Cutler, Antony. 'The Concept of Ground-Rent and Capitalism in Agriculture', *Critique of Anthropology*, nos. 4 and 5, Autumn, 1975.

de Brunhoff, Suzanne. 'Marx as an a-Ricardian: Value, Money, and Price at the Beginning of Capital', *Economy and Society* 2, 1973.

DiMaria, Eugene. 'CIPEC: A Measure of Maturity is Seen After 10 Years of Growing Pains', *American Metal Market*, 20 November 1978.

Drake, P.J. 'Natural Resources Versus Foreign Borrowing in Economic Development', *The Economic Journal* 82, no. 327, September 1972.

Eatwell, John. 'Controversies in the Theory of Surplus Value: Old and New', *Science and Society* 38, 1974.

Edel, Matthew. 'Marx's Theory of Rent: Urban Applications', *Kapitalistate*, nos. 4–5, 1976.

—— 'Rent Theory and Working Class Strategy: Marx, George, and the "Urban Crisis",' *Review of Radical Political Economy* 9, no. 4, 1977.

Emerson, Craig. 'Taxing Natural Resource Projects', *Natural Resources Forum* 4, no. 2, April 1980.

—— 'Mining Enclaves and Taxation', *World Development* 10, no. 7, July 1982.

Faber, M.L.O. 'Bougainville Renegotiated — An Analysis of the New Fiscal Terms', *Mining Magazine*, December 1974.

Fine, Ben. 'On Marx's Theory of Agricultural Rent', *Economy and Society* 8, 1979.

Fischer, Dietrich. Dermont Gately, and John F. Kyle. 'The Prospects for OPEC: A Critical Survey of Models of the World Oil Market', *Journal of Development Economics* 2, no. 4, December 1975.

Fisher, F.N. *et al.* 'An Econometric Model of the World Copper Industry', *Bell Journal of Economics and Management Science* 3, no. 2, Autumn 1972.

Fog, Bjarke. 'How Are Cartel Prices Determined?' *Journal of Industrial Economics*, November 1956.

'Four-Nation Conference Leaves Bad Taste', *Metals Week* 38, no. 24, June 12, 1967.

Fritzsche, Michael, and Albert Stockmayer. 'Mining Agreements in Developing Countries — Issues of Finance and Taxation', *Natural Resources Forum* 2, no. 3, April 1978.

Garnaut, Ross, and Anthony Clunies Ross. 'Uncertainty, Risk Aversion, and the Taxing of Natural Resource Projects;, *The Economic Journal* 85, no. 338, 1975.

——'The Neutrality of the Resource Rent Tax', *The Economic Record* 55, no. 150, September 1979.

——'Relationships Between Governments and Mining Investors', *Materials and Society* 5, no. 4, 1981.

Geddicks, Al. 'Raw Materials: The Achilles Heel of American Imperialism', *The Insurgent Sociologist* 7, no. 4, Fall 1977.

Girvan, Norman. 'Making the Rules of the Game: Company-Country Agreements in the Bauxite Industry', *Social and Economic Studies* 20, no. 4, 1971.

——'White Magic: The Caribbean and Modern Technology', *The Review of Black Political Economy* 8, 1977.

Gopalakrishnan, Chennat. 'Multinational Corporations, Nation States and Ocean Resource Management', *American Journal of Economics and Sociology* 38, no. 3, July 1979.

Groll, Shalom. 'The Active Role of "Use Value" in Marx's Economic Analysis', *History of Political Economy* 12, no. 3, 1980.

Hasab, F.A. 'The International Oil Price Mechanism', *Acta Oeconomica Academiae Scientiarum* 3, no. 1, 1968.

Hauser, Wolfgang. 'An International Fiscal Regime for Deep Seabed Mining: Comparisons to Land-Based Mining', *Harvard International Law Journal* 19, no. 3, Fall 1978.

Helliwell, John. 'Mineral Resources in the New International Economic Order', *Current History* 69, 1975.

Hexner, Ervin. 'International Cartels in the Postwar World', *Southern Economic Journal* 10, 1943.

Hodgson, Geoff. 'A Theory of Exploitation Without the Labor Theory of Value', *Science and Society* 44, no. 3, Fall 1980.

Hollander, Samuel. 'Ricardo and the Corn Laws: A Revision', *History of Political Economy* 9, 1971.

Hughes, Helen. 'Economic Rents, the Distribution of Gains From Mineral Exploitation, and Mineral Development Policy', *World Development* 3, nos. 11 & 12, 1975.

Hunt, E.K., and H. Sherman. 'Value, Alienation, and Distribution', *Science and Society* 36, 1972.

Hveem, Helge. 'Militarization of Nature: Conflict and Control over Strategic Resources and Some Implications for Peace Policies', *Journal of Peace Research* 16, no. 1, 1979.

Ilunkamba, Ilunga. 'Copper Technology and Dependence in Zaire: Towards the Demystification of the New White Magic', *Natural Resources Forum* 4, 1980.

Johansen, Leif. 'The Bargaining Society and the Inefficiency of Bargaining', *Kyklos* 32, no. 3, 1979.

Johnson, Charles J. 'Cartels in Minerals and Metal Supply', *Mining Congress Journal* 62, 1976.

——'Taking the Take But Not the Risk', *Materials and Society* 5, no. 4, 1981.

Jones, Linda Fairchild. 'Taxation of the Petroleum Industry in Indonesia: Issues and Objectives', *Law and Policy in International Business* 13, no. 4, 1981.

Krasner, Stephen. 'Oil is the Exception', *Foreign Policy*, no. 14, Spring 1974.

Laibman, David. 'Values and Prices of Production: The Political Economy of the Transformation Problem', *Science and Society* 37, 1973–1974.

——'Exploitation, Commodity Relations, and Capitalism: A Defense of the Labor Theory of Value Formation', *Science and Society* 44, 1980.

Lange, Oskar. 'Marxian Economics and Modern Economic Theory', *The Review of Economic Studies* 2, 1935.

McGeorge, Robert L. 'Approaches to State Taxation of the Mining Industry', *Natural Resources Journal* 10, no. 1, 1970.

McKelvey, V.E. 'Seabed Minerals and the Law of the Sea', *Science* 209, 25 July 1980.

Magdoff, Harry. 'The Limits of International Reform', *Monthly Review* 30, no. 1, May 1978.

Mead, Walter J. 'An Economic Analysis of Crude Oil Price Behavior in the 1970s', *The Journal of Energy and Development* 4, no. 2, Spring 1979.

Mezger, Dorothea. 'How the Mining Companies Undermine Liberation', *Review of African Political Economy*, no. 12, May–August 1978.

Mikdashi, Zuhayr. 'Collusion Could Work', *Foreign Policy*, no. 14, Spring 1974.
——'Cooperation Among Oil Exporting Countries with Special Reference to Arab Countries', *International Organization* 28, no. 1, Winter 1974.
——'The OPEC Process', *Daedalus* 104, no. 4, Fall 1975.

Mikesell, Raymond F. 'Options for Packaging Agreements to Meet Host Government and Foreign Investor Financial Goals', *Materials and Society* 5, no. 4, 1981.

Miller, S.M., Roy Bennett, and Cyril Alapatt. 'Does the U.S. Economy Require Imperialism?' *Social Policy* 1, no. 2, September–October 1970.

Mingst, Karen A. 'Cooperation or Illusion: An Examination of the Intergovernmental Council of Copper Exporting Countries', *International Organization* 30, no. 2, Spring 1976.

Moran, Theodore H. 'Multinational Corporations and Dependency: A Dialogue for Dependentistas and Non-Dependentistas', *International Organization* 32, no. 1, Winter 1978.

Murapa, Rukudzo. 'Nationalization of the Zambian Mining Industry', *The Review of Black Political Economy* 7, 1976.

Murray, Robin. 'Value and Theory of Rent: Part One', *Capital and Class* 3, 1977.
—— 'Value and Theory of Rent: Part Two', *Capital and Class* 4, 1978.

Ndulo, Muna. 'The Requirement of Domestic Participation in New Mining Ventures in Zambia', *African Social Research* 25, 1978.

Nuti, D.M. '"Vulgar Economy" in the Theory of Income Distribution', *Science and Society* 35, 1971.

Nwoke, Chibuzo N. 'World Mining Rent: An Extension of Marx's Theories', *Review* 8, no. 1, Summer 1984.

Oppenheim, V.H. 'Why Prices Go Up: The Past: We Pushed Them', *Foreign Policy*, no. 25, Winter 1976–1977.

Orchard, John E. 'The Rent of Mineral Lands', *Quarterly Journal of Economics* 36, 1922.

Ortiz, René G. '1982 Realities of the Oil Market: Can OPEC Retain Its Ability to Fix Oil Prices?' *Journal of Energy and Development* 7, no. 1, Autumn 1981.

Palmer, Keith F. 'Mineral Taxation Policies in Developing Countries: An Application of Resource Rent Tax', *I.M.F. Staff Papers* 27, no. 3, September 1980.

Panayotou, Theodore. 'OPEC as a Model for Copper Exporters: Potential Gains and Cartel Behavior', *The Developing Economies* 17, no. 2, June 1979.

Parra, Alirio A. 'The International Role and Commercial Policies of National Oil Companies', *OPEC Review* 6, no. 1, Spring 1982.

Patel, Surrendra J. 'The Technological Dependence of Developing Countries', *The Journal of Modern African Studies* 12, no. 1, 1974.

Penrose, Edith. 'Profit-Sharing Between Producing Countries and Oil Companies in the Middle East', *Economic Journal* 1, June 1959.

'Phelps Dodge to Modify Smelters', *Mining Journal* 196, no. 7592, 20 February 1981.

Pilling, Geoffrey. 'The Law of Value in Ricardo and Marx', *Economy and Society* 1, 1972.

Pindyk, Robert A. 'Gains to Producers for the Cartelization of Exhaustible Resources', *The Review of Economics and Statistics* 60, no. 2, May 1978.

Pindyk, Robert R. 'OPEC's Threat to the West', *Foreign Policy*, no. 30, Spring 1978.

Polanyi, George. 'The Taxation of Profits from Middle East Oil Production: Some Implications for Oil Prices and Taxation Policy', *The Economic Journal* 76, no. 304, December 1966.

Pollin, Robert. 'The Multinational Mineral Industry in Crisis', *Monthly Review* 31, no. 11, April 1980.

Radetzki, Marian. 'Metal Mineral Resource Exhaustion and the Threat to Material Progress: The Case of Copper', *World Development* 3, 1975.

—— 'Long-Term Copper Production Options of the Developing Countries', *Natural Resources Forum* 1, no. 1, 1977.

—— 'Market Structure and Bargaining Power: A Study of Three International Mineral Markets', *Resources Policy* 4, no. 2, June 1978.

Radmann, Wolf. 'Intergovernmental Cooperation: The Case of Foreign Investment in Zambia and Chile', *Pan-African Journal* 5, 1972.

—— 'CIPEC — The Copper Exporting Countries', *Inter-economics*, no. 8, August 1973.

—— 'The Nationalization of Zaire's Copper: From Union Minière to Gecamines', *Africa Today* 25, no. 4, October–December 1978.

Reid, Stan. 'The Politics of Resource Negotiation: The Transnational Corporation and the Jamaican Bauxite Levy', *Natural Resources Forum* 5, no. 2, April 1981.

Ricci, David M. 'Fabian Socialism: A Theory of Rent and Exploitation', *Journal of British Studies* 9, 1969.

Ridinger, D. 'Cost of Regulations to the Mining Industry', *Mining Congress Journal* 66, no. 2, February 1980.

Roberts, A.D. 'Notes Towards a Financial History of Copper Mining in Northern Rhodesia', *Canadian Journal of African Studies* 16, no. 2, 1982.

Roemer, Michael. 'Resource-Based Industrialization in the Developing Countries: A Survey', *Journal of Development Economics* 6, no. 2, June 1979.

Rosenbaum, H. Jon, and William Tyler. 'South–South Relations: The Economic and Political Context of Interactions Among Developing Countries', *International Organization* 29, no. 1, Winter 1975.

Rovig, A.D., and R. Doran. 'Copper: A Decade of Change and Its Meaning for the Future', *Mining Congress Journal* 66, no. 12, December 1980.

Rowthorn, Bob. 'Neoclassicism, Neo-Ricardianism, and Marxism', *New Left Review* 86, 1974.

Samuelson, Paul A. 'A Modern Treatment of the Ricardian Economy', *Quarterly Journal of Economics* 73, February and May 1959.

—— 'Understanding the Marxian Notion of Exploitation: A Summary of the So-Called Transformation Problem Between Marxian Values and Competitive Prices', *The Journal of Economic Literature* 9, 1971.

Seidman, Ann. 'Key Variables to Incorporate in a Model for Development', *African Studies Review* 17, 1974.

Sekina, Thomas T. 'The Necessity of the Law of Value', *Science and Society* 44, 1980.

Shaw, Timothy M., and Malcolm J. Grieve. 'The Political Economy of Resources: Africa's Future in the Global Environment', *Journal of Modern African Studies* 16, no. 1, March 1978.

Shivji, Issa G. 'Capitalism Unlimited: Public Corporations in Partnership with Multinational Corporations', *African Review* 3, no. 3, 1973.

Silver, Jim. 'Class Struggles in Ghana's Mining Industry', *Review of African Political Economy* 12, May–August 1978.

Singer, H.W. 'The Distribution of Gains Between Investing and Borrowing Countries', *Quarterly Journal of Economics* 40, 1950.

Smith, David N. 'New Eyes for Old: The Future, Present and Past in the Evolution of Mineral Agreements', *Materials and Society* 5, no. 4, 1981.

Smith, Tony. 'Changing Configurations of Power in North–South Relations Since 1945', *International Organization* 31, no. 1, Winter 1977.

Stigler, George J. 'The Ricardian Theory of Value and Distribution', *The Journal of Political Economy* 60, June 1952.

——'Ricardo and the 93% Labor Theory of Value', *The American Economic Review* 48, June 1958.

Sunkel, Osvaldo. 'Transnational Capitalism and National Disintegration in Latin America', *Social and Economic Studies* 2, March 1973.

Sweezy, Paul M. 'Corporations, the State and Imperialism', *Monthly Review* 30, November 1978.

Szymanski, Al. 'Capital Accumulation on a World Scale and the Necessity of Imperialism', *The Insurgent Sociologist* 7, no. 2, Spring 1977.

Takeuchi, Kenji. 'CIPEC and the Copper Export Earnings of Member Countries', *The Developing Economies* 10, no. 1, March 1972.

Tanzer, Michael. 'The State and the Oil Industry in Today's World', *Monthly Review* 29, no. 10, March 1978.

Taylor, H.C. 'The Differential Rent of Farm Land', *Quarterly Journal of Economics* 16, August 1903.

Tribe, Keith. 'Economic Property and the Theorisation of Ground Rent', *Economy and Society* 6, no. 1, February 1977.

Turner, Terisa. 'Two Refineries: A Comparative Study of Technology Transfer to the Nigerian Refinery Industry', *World Development* 5, no. 3, March 1977.

'Utah Copper and the $280 Million Investment in Clean Air', *Engineering and Mining Journal* 94, no.4, April 1979.

Vernon, Raymond. 'Longrun Trends in Concession Contracts', *Proceedings of the American Society of International Law*, April 1967.

——'Foreign Enterprises and Developing Nations in the Raw Materials Industries', *The American Economic Review* 60, May 1970.

Waelde, Thomas W. 'Lifting the Veil From Transnational Mineral Contracts: A Review of the Literature', *Natural Resources Forum* 1, 1977.

Walker, Richard A. 'Urban Ground Rent: Building a New Conceptual Theory', *Antipode* 6, no. 1, April 1974.

——'Contentious Issues in Marxian Value and Rent Theory: A Second and Longer Look', *Antipode* 7, no. 1, February 1975.

Wallerstein, Immanuel. 'Dependence in an Interdependent World: The Limited

Possibilities of Transformation Within the Capitalist World Economy', *African Studies Review* 17, no. 1, April 1974.

——'Class Formation in the Capitalist World Economy', *Politics and Society* 5, 1975.

Walters, Adelaide. 'The International Copper Cartel', *Southern Economic Journal* 11, no. 2, October 1944.

'Why CIPEC's No OPEC', *Forbes*, June 1977.

Zakariya, Hasan S. 'Sovereignty Over Natural Resources and the Search for a New International Economic Order', *Natural Resources Forum* 4, 1980.

——'Transfer of Petroleum Technology to Developing Countries', *OPEC Review* 6, no. 1, Spring 1982.

'Zambia Opens New Roads to Market', *Metals Week* 38, no. 19, 8 May 1967.

Zorn, Stephen A. 'New Developments in Third World Mining Agreements', *Natural Resources Forum* 1, 1977.

Newspapers

'Company Town Struggles to Survive Alone', *Washington Post*, 22 February 1981.

Crittendon, Ann. 'Phosphate: Taking a Leaf From Oil's Book', *New York Times*, 9 November 1975.

'Other Metals Are Making Inroads as the Copper Market Continues Unsettled', *New York Times*, 9 January 1967.

Simpson, J.C. 'Cleaning the Air: Anti-Pollution Costs Drive Copper Firms Into Debt, Make Them Take Over Targets', *Wall Street Journal*, 28 December 1975.

Unpublished Materials

d'Hainaut, Jean. 'A Brief Glimpse of CIPEC', CIPEC Document No. INFO/251/79, March 1979.

Eckbo, Paul Leo. 'OPEC and the Experience of Previous International Commodity Cartels', MIT Energy Laboratory Working Paper, No. 75-008WP, August 1975.

Ferraro, Vincent A. 'The Political Dynamics of International Resource Cartels: Case Studies of Petroleum and Copper', PhD dissertation, Massachusetts Institute of Technology, 1976.

Nwoke, Chibuzo N. 'The Political Economy of the State and the Limited Possibilities of Autonomous Development in the Periphery', paper presented at the fifth Fortnightly Gathering on Development (FGOD), Graduate School of International Studies, University of Denver, March 1980.

——'Economic Nationalism in the New International Division of Labor: Implications for Capital-Accumulation in Oil-Rich Nigeria', paper tabled at a conference organized by the Nigerian Political Science Association, Kano, April 1981.

——'The Evolution of Rent Theory in the History of Economic Thought', Graduate School of International Studies, University of Denver, 1982 (mimeographed).

Index

Allende, Salvador 60, 146-7, 149
aluminium as copper substitute 116, 123, 138-9
Alvarado, General J. V. 148
Amalgamated Copper Company (ACC) 115
American Producers' Association (APA) (copper) 115
Arab-Israeli War (October *1973*) 87, 89, 93
Australia 105, 108

Canada 105; copper production 119, 131; costs of production 42-3, 61, 173, 192
cartels, requirements for 89-92
Carter, Jimmy 154
Chile 60, 119; dispute with Kennecott 148-50, 159*n*; investment incentives 195; nationalization of copper industry 146-7; *see also* CIPEC; Third World
CIPEC (Conseil Intergouvernemental des Pays Exportateurs de Cuivre) (Chile, Peru, Zaire, Zambia): background data 142-3; copper promotion 153-4, 156; cost differential US/CIPEC production 165-81; dependence on MNCs 146-8, 155-6, 195; and environmental problems 179; extra-favourable investment provisions 190-9; formation 122-6; historical differences of members 87, 141, 144, 152; information-gathering activities 145, 155; labour costs 173-5; limited appropriation of differential rents 188-9; limited prospects for cartel 87, 129-44, 155; nationalization of foreign firms 122-4, 129, 145-8, 156; new membership provision 126, 154, 159-60*n*; and non-CIPEC producers 130-1, 134, 154; and ocean mining 140-1; operating costs, estimated 166-9; organizational framework 126-8; policy output 144-55; regulation of production

151-2; and secondary production 134, 136-9; share of world copper exports (Table) 135; share of world copper output (Table) 132-3; and stockpiling 139; *see also* Chile copper industry; copper MNCs; Peru; Third World; Zaire; Zambia
Club of Rome: *Limits to Growth* 89
coal 98-9
Copper Export Association (CEA) 116-17
Copper Exporters Inc (CEI) 117-18
copper industry: estimated world costs (Table) 168-9; history prior to CIPEC 112-22; ocean mining 61, 140-1; open-pit technique 42-3, 61; price instability 113, 118, 120, 150, 155, 157*n*; scrap recovery/secondary production 61, 104, 116, 120, 123, 130-9; substitute materials 61, 116, 123, 138-9; *see also* CIPEC; copper MNCs; United States
copper MNCs 122, 141; charges for management and technology 193-5; effective control of nationalized companies 146-8, 155-6, 164-5, 189; super profits 164-5, 167, 184-90, 199; *see also* MNCs (mining); United States
Copper Producers' Association (CPA) 115-16
Corn Laws 16-19, 22, 30, 38-9, 49-50*n*

Frei, Eduardo 124-5, 146-7

Indonesia 73, 84*n*
industrialized countries: fear of Third World cartels 89-90, 137-8; non-fuel minerals production 80, 104, 106-7; operating cost disadvantages 27-8; and super profits 99-102, 109; *see also* copper MNCs; MNCs (mining); United States

227